4⁰⁰

DISCARD

FEODOR DOSTOEVSKY

FEODOR DOSTOEVSKY

Alba Amoia

A Frederick Ungar Book
CONTINUUM • NEW YORK

1993

The Continuum Publishing Company
370 Lexington Avenue
New York, NY 10017

Printed in the United States of America

Library of Congress Cataloging-in-Publication Data

Amoia, Alba della Fazia.
    Feodor Dostoevsky / Alba Amoia.
        p.   cm. — (Literature and life. World writers)
    "A Frederick Ungar book."
    Includes bibliographical references and index.
    ISBN 0-8264-0563-0 (cloth : alk. paper)
    1. Dostoevsky, Feodor, 1821–1881. 2. Novelists, Russian–19th
century—Biography. I. Title. II. Series.
PG3328.A795   1993
891.73'3—dc20
    [B]   92-42648
                                                                  CIP

For Richard P. Stebbins,

vir bonus, dicendi peritus

Contents

Part 4: The Short Stories

Part 5: Theater, Memoirs, and Journalism

Part 6: The Zenith

Preface

The present volume briefly surveys the main facts of Feodor Dostoevsky's life and contributions to literature for students and others who seek a preliminary acquaintance with this complex genius. As an introductory synopsis, it seeks to offer some indication of the reasons for Dostoevsky's reputation as one of Russia's profoundest creative artists, a man who has himself inspired a biographical and critical literature of immense proportions.

Americans in search of wider knowledge are fortunate in having available the ongoing five-volume biographical study of Dostoevsky by Professor Joseph Frank, in course of publication by the Princeton University Press since 1976. The clarity, thoroughness, and readability of Professor Frank's presentation, the order he has introduced into the voluminous mass of Dostoevskian materials, his insight into times, persons, and events, and his interpretation of Dostoevsky as a product and one of the shapers of his age, make his work a model of scholarship and an ideal guide to further study.

This writer has been glad to follow Professor Frank's guidelines in the transliteration of Russian words and names and in sorting out the confusion of biographical, geographical, chronological, onomastic, and orthographical variations that characterize the available French, Italian, and English literature relating to Dostoevsky. I have also adopted his use of italicized titles for *all* Dostoevsky's publications, regardless of genre (long novels, short novels, novellas, short stories, and nonfictional works).

A brief appendix on Russian periodicals in Dostoevsky's time is intended to help the reader find his way among the titles and varied political tendencies of the reviews in which Dostoevsky's works originally appeared.

Short quotations from Dostoevsky's letters have generally been taken from the two available volumes of the five-volume *Complete Letters,* edited and translated by David Lowe and Ronald Meyer (vol. 1, Ann Arbor: Ardis Publishers, 1988) and by David Lowe (vol. 2, ibid., 1989), although I have preferred in some cases to use renditions of other translators. Brief quotations from Dostoevsky's works have been drawn from the various British and American translations listed in the bibliography.

Chronology

N.B. Dates are given according to the Julian calendar, which was retained in Russia until the 1917 Revolution and ran twelve days behind the Gregorian calendar during the nineteenth century.

1821   Feodor Mikhailovich Dostoevsky is born in Moscow on October 30, the second of seven children.

1831–37   Feodor and his older brother, Mikhail (b. 1820), together attend boarding schools in Moscow. Following the death of their mother in 1837, they are sent to a preparatory school in St. Petersburg.

1838   Feodor, but not Mikhail, is admitted to St. Petersburg's Academy of Military Engineers.

1839   Death of their father.

1843   Dostoevsky graduates from the Academy. Translates into Russian Honoré de Balzac's *Eugénie Grandet*.

1844   He translates George Sand's *La dernière Aldini* and works on *Poor Folk*, his own first novel.

1845   Friendship with the liberal Vissarion Grigorievich Belinsky, Russia's most influential critic.

1846   Publication of *Poor Folk*, *The Double*, and *Mr. Prokharchin*. Acquaintance with the utopian socialist M. V. Butashevich-Petrashevsky.

1847   Intensified contacts with the Petrashevsky group. Publication of *The Landlady*.

1848   Publication of several short stories, including *A Weak Heart*, *Polzunkov*, and *White Nights*.

1849   Publication of *Netochka Nezvanova*. Arrest and conviction for alleged political crimes.

1850–54 Penal labor in western Siberia.

1854–59 Compulsory military service in Semipalatinsk (southwest Siberia). Marriage to the widowed Marya Dmitrievna Isaeva in 1857. The couple are permitted to take up residence in European Russia in 1859, the year in which *Uncle's Dream* and *The Village of Stepanchikovo and Its Inhabitants* appear.

1860   Publication of the first part of *House of the Dead*.

1861   Mikhail and Feodor begin publication of *Time*, which publishes Dostoevsky's *The Insulted and Injured*.

1862   The second part of *House of the Dead* and *A Nasty Tale* are published in *Time*. Dostoevsky makes his first trip abroad, visiting several western European countries. Beginning of liaison with Apollinaria (Polina) Suslova.

1863   *Winter Notes on Summer Impressions* is published in *Time*.

1864   *Epoch*, successor to the banned magazine *Time*, publishes Dostoevsky's *Notes from Underground*. Death of Marya Dmitrievna, Feodor's wife, and of his brother Mikhail.

1865   *Epoch* ceases publication, ending Dostoevsky's five-year journalistic career. Polina Suslova declines his marriage proposal.

1866   *Crime and Punishment* and *The Gambler* are published.

1867   Dostoevsky is married to Anna Grigorievna Snitkina. The couple leave for western Europe, remaining abroad for over four years.

1868   Publication of *The Idiot*.

1870   Publication of *The Eternal Husband*.

1871–72 *The Devils* is published serially.

1873   Dostoevsky's *The Diary of a Writer* becomes a regular feature of the conservative weekly, *The Citizen*. Publication of *Bobok*.

1875   Publication of *A Raw Youth*.

1876   Dostoevsky becomes sole editor of a new monthly periodical entitled *The Diary of a Writer*, in which *A Gentle Creature* appears.

1877   Publication of *The Dream of a Ridiculous Man*.

1879–80 Publication of *The Brothers Karamazov*.

1881   Dostoevsky dies on January 28 at the age of fifty-nine.

Part 1
The Life

1

The Story of His Life

> You are close to me, because the *split personality* that exists in you is exactly the same as the one that exists in me, and which has existed in me throughout my life.... It brings great suffering but great pleasure as well.... If your intelligence were not developed... this split personality would not exist.[1]

Biographers seeking to unravel the complex personality of Russia's greatest novelist have not infrequently pointed to an interplay of masculine and feminine attributes as a key to the understanding of his life and writings. On the one hand, Dostoevsky comes across as a powerful Russian male writer — a personality with strong irrational drives, at times excessively vainglorious and egoistic, one who tended to see human relations in terms of a struggle for psychic domination. Yet at the same time he was clearly endowed in an unusual degree with those qualities of sympathy, tenderness, and compassion that our culture has traditionally associated with women. "Rarely did anybody understand the feminine soul and its sufferings as profoundly as Feodor understood and sensed them," his second wife is quoted as testifying.[2] Contacts with women, at every stage of his life, helped to define these qualities and to bring about the particular amalgam of male and female characteristics that distinguished the personality and work of the mature artist.

The opposition of masculine and feminine traits is already starkly evident in Dostoevsky's parents. His father, Mikhail Andreevich Dostoevsky, was a physician in the Mariinsky Hospital for the Poor in Moscow, where Feodor was born on October 30, 1821 (according to the Julian calendar; see Chronology). Dr. Dostoevsky's conscientious service in the hospital was recognized in an official acknowledgment of his status as a noble, so that despite the family's mediocre economic and social position, the names of his eldest sons could also be entered in the lists of hereditary nobility.

The elder Dostoevsky has alternately been portrayed as a faithful husband, responsible father, and believing Christian, and as a man of cruel, suspicious nature and uncontrollable temper. A similar duality and inner tension is apparent in his son Feodor, who may also have inherited from his father his reserved and somewhat saturnine disposition, his indifference to social manners, and a tendency to rhetorical exaggeration such as are found in these excerpts from his correspondence: "I will perish if I lose my angel; I'll either go mad or jump into the Irtish [River]" (*Letters*, I, 239); "If I can't place my novel [*Poor Folk*], then perhaps I'll throw myself into the Neva" (110); "If the business [the novel] is not a success, I may hang myself" (107); "I have a project: to become insane" (41).

Quite different influences emanated from Dostoevsky's mother, Marya Feodorovna, who had married the thirty-year-old physician in 1819 when she herself was nineteen years of age. Daughter of a Moscow merchant, Marya Feodorovna was considered unusually cultivated for a girl of her social station. She is said to have written unusually well and may have been endowed with some of the literary talent that distinguished her two older sons, Mikhail and Feodor.

More certain are the gifts of personality that made her a continuing presence in Feodor Dostoevsky's life and helped to establish his notion of marriage and the family as the natural framework of human felicity. Gentle and humble in manner, Marya Feodorovna was nonetheless engaging, cheerful, and intelligent. If she was warm and energetic as a mother, as a wife she was a docile, submissive manager of the household, one who viewed her role as that of a Christian servant of the family — a concept Dostoevsky clearly approved and invariably hoped to realize in his own matrimonial ventures. She was, moreover, the first woman whose illness and suffering evoked the pity and sympathy of her gifted son. All through Feodor's life his mother's voice would accompany him, blending with the image of Christ and the concept of "Mother Russia" at the emotional summit of his existence. Marya Feodorovna's creativity, accessibility, her generous shouldering of other people's burdens, and her availability as a confidante all became integrated into Feodor's individual being.

Seven children were born to the Dostoevsky couple before the mother expired at the early age of thirty-seven, worn out by repeated pregnancies and ravaged by tuberculosis. Mikhail, the eldest of the new generation, born in October 1820, was destined to be Feodor's closest friend, collaborator, and pecuniary support right up to the time of his death in 1864 at the age of forty-three. Throughout the greater part of this period — save for the four years of Feodor's imprisonment in Siberia — the two brothers' lives were closely intertwined, their literary tastes and political views coincided, and their personal development proceeded along parallel lines, although the more easygoing Mikhail lacked his junior's strength and genius.

Of Feodor's younger brothers and sisters, Varvara and Vera, born respectively in 1822 and 1829, would, with their respective husbands and children, play an important part in the writer's life. His brother Andrey, on the other hand, who was born in 1825, elicited no particular affection on Feodor's part, either in childhood or subsequently. "There's such a difference between fifteen and eleven that brothers are never real friends at those ages," he wrote in *The Brothers Karamazov* (267). Later, Andrey proved something of an encumbrance when the two were living together as students in St. Petersburg.

A still younger brother, Nikolay, born in 1831, managed to graduate from a civil engineering institute and showed promise as an architect, but suffered from poor health during most of his adult life. He has been described as an acute alcoholic who was regularly treated in a psychiatric hospital (cf. *Letters*, II, 133 n. 1), and had to be supported by his brothers and sisters. The youngest Dostoevsky child, Alexandra, born in 1835, was scarcely known to Feodor because of the difference in ages.

The imprint of his religious upbringing remained with Feodor throughout his life. No less important to the Dostoevsky home than the bubbling samovar — "the most essential thing in Russia," according to Feodor (*A Raw Youth*, 198) — was the *krasny ugol* or "beautiful corner" that served as a domestic church within the family dwelling. The icon of Christ, symbol of the meeting of heaven and earth, reflected the same union of masculine and feminine elements that some have discerned in Dostoevsky himself.

Although the Dostoevsky children were no doubt drawn to the mild and gentle brand of Christianity espoused by their mother, the family was organized on patriarchal lines and adhered to the strict code of morality laid down by Dr. Dostoevsky. The doctor's iron discipline prevailed in all household matters, but he is said to have refrained from inflicting the corporal punishments so prevalent at the time; indeed, the worst that is reported of him is his insistence that one of the boys prevent the flies from disturbing his summer slumbers.

Dr. Dostoevsky was also sufficiently enlightened to allot much of his meager salary to his children's education. He personally taught his sons Latin, demanding hard study and subordination and forcing them to remain standing during the lessons. Yet he sent his children to private schools in order to spare them the beatings habitually administered by public schoolmasters. Feodor's harshly resentful feelings toward his father in boyhood and youth were probably mitigated to an increasing degree by a desire to understand and sympathize. The only recorded instance of actual disobedience on his part was his habit of talking with the convalescents who strolled in the Mariinsky Hospital grounds.

The books and reviews that crammed the Dostoevskys' small apartment supplied the older boys with abundant food for the imagination. The family's basic reading, it is true, remained the Bible — the book that Dostoevsky would read and reread throughout his life, and of which he would write that it is the only book for all humanity, whether one has faith or not. Their father's readings from Nikolay Mikhailovich Karamzin's twelve-volume *History of the Russian State* (1816–29) instilled a reverence for the Russian autocracy, depicted in that work as the basis of national unity and independence, and a corresponding abhorrence of the supposedly decadent, moribund civilization of western Europe. Through their parents, the children also became acquainted with the sensational "Gothic" novels of Mrs. Ann Radcliffe, whose manipulation of the elements of mystery and suspense made an indelible impression on young Feodor's mind.

Poetry, both Russian and European, nurtured the sensibilities of the two older boys. Pushkin's works fertilized the deep moral and national values, the Slavic consciousness, which would sustain Feodor's creative universe. Mikhail Lermontov (1814–41), Russia's leading Romantic poet, who had helped direct Russian attention to the poetry and personality of Lord Byron, undoubtedly influenced Feodor through his novel, *A Hero of Our Time* (1840), in which the character of the "superfluous man" — a cynical person of superior accomplishments — recalls Pushkin's Evgeni Onegin.

Among older poets, Feodor was conscious of a special feeling for Schiller, writing to Mikhail in 1840 that he "memorized Schiller, quoted him, raved about him" and that the very name of Schiller had a sort of magic, dream-producing sound (*Letters*, I, 61). Up to the time of his encounter with the Russian revolutionaries of his own generation, it was Schiller's idealism that most permeated Feodor's thoughts. It was in Schiller that he found the notion of rectifying social injustice by a "sacred crime"; in Schiller, too, he discovered how the power of the individual must bend before divine justice.

Sir Walter Scott was another familiar presence in the Dostoevsky household. Feodor, by the time he was twelve, claimed to have

read all of the Scottish novelist's works. They may have helped
to establish his notion of the family as a bulwark of human society. He also devoured the early works of Nikolay Gogol, which
mingled fantasy and realism and, in one case, that of *The Terrible
Vengeance,* dealt with the universal theme of the conflict between
good and evil. Though he conceded genius only to Pushkin and
Schiller, Dostoevsky owed much to Gogol in his own spiritual and
artistic development. He was haunted by the memory of the Russian
storyteller even after the latter's death in 1852.

A decisive stage in Feodor Dostoevsky's intellectual and emotional development occurred in 1831–32 when his parents acquired
ownership of the village of Darovoe (known after 1930 as "Dostoevsky Kolkhoz") and the adjoining hamlet of Cheremoshnia, some
seventy-five or eighty miles southeast of Moscow. Dostoevsky's direct and almost mystical involvement with the Russian serfs, who
were bound to the soil and remained largely dependent on the whims
of the landowners until their emancipation in 1861 in the reign of
Tsar Alexander II, dates from the summers spent with the family
on their new property. Through his mother, a kindhearted estate
manager whose leniency and compassion for the serfs made a deep
impression upon him, he not only learned sympathy and pity for
the downtrodden but discovered similar qualities in the peasants
themselves.

Years later, during his confinement in a Siberian prison camp, he
would recall a peasant named Marey who had comforted him in
a moment of childish fright, smiling at him gently "like a mother"
and blessing him with the sign of the cross. "What delicate, almost
womanly tenderness, could fill the heart of a coarse, bestially igno-
rant Russian peasant serf," he wrote.[3] The incident may well have
nurtured his later conviction that the Russian serf, imbued with the
Christian spirit of love and self-sacrifice, was destined for equal part-
nership in a future harmonious unity between the educated classes
and the peasantry.

Autumn brought the family back to Moscow, where Mikhail
and Feodor, in addition to religious instruction and the paternal
Latin lessons, were now tutored in French by a certain Monsieur
Souchard, the proprietor of a preparatory day school whose Russian name, "Drachusov," had been arrived at by spelling Souchard
backward and adding the Slavic suffix -*ov.* This pedagogue eventually persuaded Dr. Dostoevsky to enroll his sons in the school, and
in January 1833 the two boys left their family for the first time.

Their sad experience in the Souchard-Drachusov institution is evoked in Dostoevsky's semiautobiographical novel, *A Raw Youth*. He plainly had little regard for the Souchard couple, describing the husband, under the name of Touchard, as "a man of crass ignorance" who beat his pupils, and the wife as "a very affected lady." In this and later school experiences, Dostoevsky was deeply distressed by occurrences that offended his compassionate instincts. Refusing to bait new pupils or join in brutal initiation rites, he would spring to the defense of the helpless and persecuted, comforting them with an almost feminine tenderness.

An even more dismaying prospect faced the Dostoevsky boys in 1834 when they were enrolled in L. I. Chermak's private boarding school, an outstanding Muscovite institution renowned for the excellence of its literature courses. But here they did find happiness in learning prose, poetry, and history under the guidance of an inspiring professor of Russian literature. Returning home on weekends and holidays, they spouted Pushkin's works for the benefit of the entire family. Pushkin's tragic death in consequence of a duel in January 1837 caused the Dostoevsky brothers immeasurable grief.

Four weeks later occurred the no less shattering loss of their own mother, Marya Feodorovna, who died on February 27, 1837, after a long decline. Her death was a turning point in the lives of all the Dostoevskys. Outwardly, at least, the readjustment was made easier by the fact that Mrs. Dostoevsky's older sister had married into a wealthy merchant family, the Kumanins, and was able to provide some financial assistance. Mikhail and Feodor were entered in a boarding school in St. Petersburg, and their preparations for departure were superintended by their aunt, Alexandra Feodorovna Kumanina. Later, the Kumanins would help pay Feodor's tuition at the Academy of Military Engineers, answer his urgent calls for financial aid, and see to the upbringing of the five younger Dostoevskys after their father's death.

Dr. Dostoevsky appears to have undergone a process of degeneration after the death of his wife. Prematurely old at forty-eight, he accompanied his sons to St. Petersburg and then, returning to Moscow, resigned his hospital post, pleading rheumatism and failing eyesight. Retiring to his estate, he occupied himself with his "favorite activity...harvesting the wheat" (*Letters*, I, 24); corresponded assiduously with his two elder boys; and fielded Feodor's frequent requests for money to buy tea, boots, books, stamps, pens, writing paper, and other sundries, including an "absolutely essential" subscription to the city's French library.

It has been asserted that the elder Dostoevsky was accompanied to

Darovoe by a former servant who became his mistress, and that he drank heavily, flogged his serfs, and became increasingly suspicious and irascible. Modern scholarship has cast doubt on the traditional belief that he was actually murdered by his own serfs;[4] but the circumstances of his death on June 8, 1839, less than two years after his bereavement, remain to be explained.

What is clear is that Dr. Dostoevsky had been unimpressed by his sons' passion for literature and distaste for science and mathematics, and had unilaterally decided that both boys should enter the relatively well-paid military engineering profession. It was for this reason that Mikhail and Feodor, now seventeen and sixteen respectively, were entered in the St. Petersburg boarding school of K. F. Kostamarov, which specialized in preparing young men for admission to the government-operated Academy of Military Engineers. Although Feodor would in due course fulfill the requirements for a career in military engineering, the impact on his sensitive mind of life in Russia's "northern capital" would far transcend the scope of any merely academic curriculum.

Founded as Russia's capital by Peter the Great in 1703, St. Petersburg exerted a powerful influence on both an intellectual and a mystical level. Intellectually, it stood as a symbol of enlightenment, progress, and affiliation with European culture — trends that Dostoevsky, as an adherent of the Slavophil camp, would later strongly oppose. Less easily resisted was the indefinable charm exerted by this "Venice of the North," with its innumerable canals and the "white nights" so characteristic of its northern latitude. Above all, the river Neva, in its dark mystery, literally took possession of Feodor's soul and became a haunting presence in many of his works.

The brothers' stay at the Kostamarov boarding school lasted less than a year, and on January 16, 1838, Feodor was admitted to the petty officer company of the Academy of Military Engineers, beginning a protracted course of study that would continue until August 1843 when he was twenty-two. Mikhail, on the other hand, was rejected by the Academy owing to the unsatisfactory condition of his lungs. He was enrolled instead in the Engineering Cadets and subsequently assigned to the Engineering Command in the Baltic seaport of Reval (Tallinn) in Estonia, a region originally colonized by Germans but ruled by Russia since 1710. Despite their physical separation, however, the brothers continued to maintain close contact.

The Academy of Military Engineers was located in St. Petersburg's massive Mikhailovsky Palace, where the half-mad Tsar Paul I, the

father of Alexander I and Nicholas I, had been assassinated in a court
conspiracy in 1801. Dostoevsky may have welcomed the change
from his small, cramped apartment, since he wrote in *Crime and
Punishment* that "low ceilings and cramped rooms crush the mind
and the spirit." In other respects, however, he found the atmosphere
of the academy bureaucratic, soulless, and brutal. The students, he
reported, slept on "heaps of straw covered with a sheet" (*Letters,*
I, 52).

The dullness of the prescribed courses on fortification and artillery
gave added zest to the reading that was his main extracurricular
activity. His choice of books continued to reflect a taste for the adventure, crime, and melodrama that featured the work of writers like
Mrs. Radcliffe, "Monk" Lewis, E. T. A. Hoffmann, and Eugène Sue.
Hoffmann, the German Romanticist whose demonic tales abound in
such gruesome figures as maniacs, specters, doppelgänger, or doubles, and automata, demonstrably exerted considerable influence
on Dostoevsky, whose second work, *The Double,* directly embodies
the Hoffmann-like concept of the divided man brought face-to-face
with himself.

Having managed by 1840 to complete the first three years of
the Academy's curriculum, Dostoevsky was permitted to leave the
Mikhailovsky dormitories and to share a tiny, dark, two-room
apartment with a fellow student, Adolph Ivanovich Totleben —
whose brother, Colonel Count Eduard Ivanovich Totleben, would
later achieve fame as the defender of Sevastopol in the Crimean War.
In the following year the two roommates were joined by Feodor's
young brother Andrey, who had come to St. Petersburg to study civil
engineering. But though he remained with them for a year, Andrey
was an unwelcome addition to the small household. "I have our
brother on my hands," Feodor lamented to Mikhail in Tallinn. "He
has such a strange and shallow character that everyone is repelled
by that; now that I've given him shelter, I greatly repent of my stupid
plan" (*Letters,* I, 73–74). A year later, however, when Andrey was
in funds and Feodor was in need, he was quick to beg financial aid
from this despised younger brother.

The pecuniary difficulties that accompanied Feodor through life
have been convincingly traced to the fact that up to the age of seventeen his parsimonious father allowed him no pocket money and
consequently no training or experience in financial management.
But where his father had been niggardly, Dostoevsky himself was
given to reckless generosity. At the same time, he suffered from
a chronic sense of humiliation and resentment toward the rich

relations with whom some of his family had become connected. His aunt, as already noted, had married into the Kumanin family before his mother's death. In addition, his seventeen-year-old sister Varvara was married on April 21, 1840, to Peter Andreevich Karepin, a wealthy widower who had become the custodian of Dr. Dostoevsky's estate and the legal guardian of his two older sons.

Income from his father's estate, received regularly if somewhat contemptuously from his new brother-in-law, supplemented Feodor's pay as an officer and enabled him to lead an active social life, attend the theater and concerts, and indulge in various other amusements, including card games in his apartment. Yet a congenital inability to manage his income or calculate his needs left him perpetually in debt. The vicious cycle of borrowing and spending was to plague him all his life and would help to fuel his later passion for gambling.

Granted a month's leave of absence in the summer of 1842, Feodor traveled by ship to Tallinn for a four-week visit to his older brother, who had recently married a young woman of German ancestry, Emilya Feodorovna von Ditmar. Although he enjoyed the time spent with Mikhail and his wife, Feodor found himself ill at ease in the "Teutonic" atmosphere of the Baltic city, and returned to St. Petersburg with a deep distaste for all things German that was to remain with him through life.

Only one year of study now remained to the twenty-one-year-old Feodor, who was promoted to the rank of second lieutenant and was graduated from the Engineering Academy on August 12, 1843, and assigned to active service in the drafting department of the St. Petersburg Engineering Command. This tedious desk assignment, which involved strict office hours, proved far from congenial to what Feodor called "the strong, ardent soul of one who cannot bear his banal daily schedule and calendar of life" (*Letters*, I, 48).

His living arrangements were equally unsatisfactory, for Mikhail, in an attempt to discipline his spendthrift brother, had arranged for him to share an apartment with a German physician, Dr. Igor Riesenkampf, in one of the poorer quarters of St. Petersburg. The experiment lasted only six months, from September 1843 to March 1844, for Feodor proved an impossible roommate. Dr. Riesenkampf's attempt to practice medicine in the shared apartment did give Feodor opportunities of "getting to know the proletariat of the capital better" and compassionately slipping them money, either from the doctor's professional fees or from his own pocket.[5] Just

as he had disregarded his father's injunction to avoid the convalescents in the Mariinsky Hospital grounds, he now ignored
Dr. Riesenkampf's exhortations to leave his patients alone.

By December of 1843, Feodor's dissipated life had all but exhausted his resources. So bad was his financial situation that he
recklessly renounced his claims on his parents' estate in exchange for
a small lump sum to be paid immediately by the reluctant Karepin,
whom he now calls "the swine...as stupid as an ox" (*Letters*, I, 98).
Correspondence with his brother is peppered with money images:
"[it] crawls like crayfish, all in different directions," or "melts away
like wax" (*Letters*, I, 107, 365).

In an attempt to augment his resources, Dostoevsky now plunged
into a free translation of Balzac's *Eugénie Grandet*, a condensed version of which appeared in June and July of 1844 in a St. Petersburg
journal bearing the grandiose title, *The Repertory of the Russian
Theater and the Pantheon of All European Theaters*. He also undertook to translate one of George Sand's so-called Venetian novels,
La dernière Aldini, only to discover that a Russian translation had
been published seven years earlier.

The appearance of his first published work emboldened Dostoevsky to resign the army commission he had so painfully earned. An
additional incentive was the threat of an assignment outside the
capital. "What would I do without Petersburg?" he asks Mikhail.
"What would I be fit for?" (*Letters*, I, 97). Discharged with the rank
of lieutenant on October 19, 1844, he could now devote himself
exclusively to the writing of his first novel.

His current roommate, the writer Dmitry Vasilievich Grigorovich,
was a more congenial companion than the unlamented Dr. Riesenkampf. He took a genuine interest in the progress of the book that
was to become *Poor Folk*, a "social" novel with significant psychological insights. After three drafts, Feodor could write to Mikhail
that he was "seriously pleased" and "excessively satisfied" with his
"austere and elegant work" — admitting, however, that it also had
"horrible deficiencies" (*Letters*, I, 106).

Grigorovich, to whom the entire work was read at a single sitting,
reacted with characteristic enthusiasm. Hugging the manuscript in
his arms, he hurried off to show it to Nikolay Alexeevich Nekrasov, the radical poet, journalist, and publisher. That personage, with
equal enthusiasm, took it to Vissarion Grigorievich Belinsky, the celebrated critic and champion of the new "Natural School" of socially
conscious literature. Belinsky at first was skeptical about Nekrasov's assertion that "a new Gogol is born to us." Nekrasov's "new

Gogols" sprouted like mushrooms, he sourly remarked. Belinsky did, however, agree to read the manuscript, which so impressed him that he actually sought out the author that very evening with a detailed analysis and critique of his work.

Dostoevsky long afterward remembered Belinsky's words with profound emotion. They marked a "solemn moment" in his life, a turning point from which there could be no going back, a source of strength and courage that would remain with him through the bitter years of Siberian exile. "Because you are an artist," Belinsky had said, "truth is revealed to you; you have the gift of perceiving the truth; cherish your gift; remain true to it, and you will be a great writer!" (*The Diary of a Writer,* January 1877). In his admitted "boundless vanity," Dostoevsky basked in this flattering attention even while he was melodramatically threatening to hang himself if *Poor Folk* turned out a failure.

Contact with Belinsky and his progressive circle intensified over the next couple of years. But though the critic's humanitarian, utopian socialist ideas were thoroughly congenial to the struggling young writer, Dostoevsky was dismayed by the older man's aggressive atheism and vigorously anticlerical stance. Feodor himself would always remain a devout believer in Christ, the ideal figure of his childhood faith, and could not permanently identify himself with a group whose religious ideas were diametrically opposed to his own.[6]

It was at a gathering of the Belinsky circle in November 1845 that Dostoevsky first made the acquaintance of Ivan Sergeevich Turgenev (1818–83), a man three years his senior who was destined to be one of Russia's outstanding novelists and dramatists. Although the two became friends for a brief period, their temperaments were fundamentally unsuited to one another. The cultured, rather skeptical Turgenev was disturbed by what he took to be the younger man's arrogance, and the literary rift between them gradually widened to an open breach.

Despite his somewhat uncouth manners, Dostoevsky had become something of a literary lion by the time *Poor Folk* appeared in the *Petersburg Miscellany* — an almanac edited by the progressive Nikolay Alexeevich Nekrasov — for January 15, 1846. Among the refined literary salons in which the young man was now received was that of Ivan Ivanovich Panaev, who would be associated with Nekrasov in editing *The Contemporary,* an increasingly radical left-wing journal, until its suppression in 1866. In the Panaev circle, Feodor wrote his brother, he was spending his time "merrily" and

falling in love with his hostess: "Yesterday I was at Panaev's for
the first time, and I seem to have fallen in love with his wife. She's
intelligent and attractive, in addition kind and wonderfully direct"
(*Letters,* I, 118).

This Avdotya Yakovlevna Panaeva, known also as "the beautiful
Eudoxia," was herself a writer of novels and eventually became the
mistress of Nekrasov, her husband's collaborator. In her memoirs
she described the quarrelsome manner in which Dostoevsky reacted
to the ridicule and deliberate provocations he encountered in society.
She herself, though genuinely sorry when his so-called friends turned
to baiting him, was unable to restore his psychic balance when it
had been disturbed. Feodor, after nourishing a respectful passion
for several months, wrote Mikhail that he had been truly in love
with Panaeva, but that it was passing quickly.

Women of a different class shared the young writer's attention.
The "Minushkas, Klarushkas, Mariannas and so on have grown
impossibly attractive but cost a terrible lot of money," he complains
to his brother. "... My debts are at their former point" (*Letters,* I,
119). His contacts with demimondaines and prostitutes meant more
than sexual release; such women also represented an important stage
in his spiritual progress and understanding. Disregarding the negative judgments of society, he sought to enter into their personal
struggles, to comprehend the complexities of their psychology, acknowledging their capacity for Christian love, in order to encompass
them, too, in his mystical devotion to the Russian motherland.

Dostoevsky had been misled by the enthusiasm his first novel initially aroused in St. Petersburg society. When *Poor Folk* made its
public appearance in January 1846, the reviewers harshly criticized
its lack of form and faulty language and composition. Nor were
they more favorably impressed by a second work of fiction, the
short novel entitled *The Double; or, The Adventures of Mr. Golyadkin,* which appeared a fortnight later in *Notes of the Fatherland,* the
leading progressive journal of the time. Dostoevsky had entertained
high hopes for this second novel, writing his brother that it was ten
times better than *Poor Folk.* After its poor reception, however, he
declared that Golyadkin, his central figure, had become "repulsive"
to him. "One doesn't want to read it," was his final pronouncement.

The social euphoria that accompanied Feodor's literary debut had
by this time given place to an atmosphere of critical backbiting.
While Turgenev and Nekrasov were polishing an anti-Dostoevskian
epigram, Belinsky still found lukewarm words of praise for *The
Double,* mixing them, however, with a dose of negative poison in-

tolerable to his sensitive former protégé. Belinsky's icy comments on subsequent Dostoevsky stories elicited from Feodor the not unjustified charge that the older man's literary notions were constantly changing. At bottom, Belinsky's didactic, socialistic, and realistic conceptions of literature were sharply at variance with Dostoevsky's more romantic and idealistic approach. By early 1847 the two men had broken completely, although Dostoevsky paid homage to the critic's memory on learning of his death from tuberculosis in the following year.

For Feodor this was a period of discouragement and nagging financial worry. Trapped in a cycle of chronic indebtedness, he had become completely dependent economically on the editor of *Notes of the Fatherland*, Andrey Alexandrovich Kraevsky. That socially conscious periodical published in October 1846 a new story, *Mr. Prokharchin*, which Feodor had written during the preceding summer and which featured the stock figure of a miser who dies in his squalid quarters on a mattress filled with money. The piece, he reported, was "terribly disfigured" by the censorship even before publication. They "crossed things out all over the place," he complained to Mikhail. "All the life has disappeared. Only the skeleton...is left. I'm renouncing my story" (*Letters*, I, 133).

This fiasco did not, however, prevent the twenty-five-year-old writer from plunging into the composition of a new story, *The Landlady*, a haunting novel of the supernatural that would occupy him for nearly a year before its publication in *Notes of the Fatherland* in October–December 1847. In the meantime, an inconsequential story, *A Novel in Nine Letters*, was dashed off in a single night and published in the January 1847 issue of the new *The Contemporary*. Other short stories, including *A Weak Heart, Polzunkov,* and *White Nights*, followed, most of them again published in *Notes of the Fatherland*.

In spite of hard work and good resolutions, Dostoevsky was constantly in debt. "I'm fighting with my petty creditors like Laocoön with the snakes," he will write to Kraevsky, while to his brother he laments, "When will I get out of debt? It's a bad thing to work as a day laborer. You'll destroy everything, including talent and youth and hope, grow disgusted with your work, and in the end become a pen pusher, not a writer" (*Letters*, I, 170, 144).

He was confident, however, that his next major work would restore his critical standing and ensure his financial recovery. This was the novel *Netochka Nezvanova*, which he had been mulling over for a year and whose first two parts appeared in *Notes of the Father-*

land in January and February 1849. The third part, in which he focused on the conflict between egoism and love and experimented with other themes prominent in his later novels, was delayed until May and then appeared without the author's name. For Dostoevsky, by a cataclysmic stroke of fate, had meanwhile been arrested and imprisoned on suspicion of revolutionary activity, an action that would remove him from the literary scene for an entire decade.

As early as the spring of 1846, Dostoevsky had become acquainted with the radical conversationalist and socialist thinker Mikhail Vasilievich Butashevich-Petrashevsky, a follower of the French social philosopher F. M. C. Fourier and the center of a reading and discussion group in St. Petersburg that came to be known as the Petrashevsky circle. By the spring of 1849, the Tsarist government, alarmed among other things by the outbreak of revolutionary violence in several western European countries, had determined to put an end to this group's activities.

Dostoevsky, who had been voicing increasingly radical opinions on such subjects as freedom of the press, the abolition of serfdom, and reform of the judiciary, had become a marked man. On April 23, 1849, he was arrested, together with thirty-three other members of the Petrashevsky circle and a satellite group,[7] on charges of participation in activity aimed at the overthrow of the state.

Also arrested some days later was Feodor's brother Mikhail, who had by this time retired from government service, settled in St. Petersburg with his wife and three children, and joined the Petrashevsky circle, possibly at Feodor's instigation. Though Mikhail was released shortly afterward, Feodor was imprisoned in the dreaded Peter and Paul Fortress, an immense and gloomy building where some of the Decembrist rebels of 1825[8] had been imprisoned until their execution or banishment to Siberia. After appearing before an investigating commission on May 6, Dostoevsky continued in solitary confinement pending completion of the investigation.

Although his health suffered in prison, Feodor kept up his courage and found unsuspected reserves of inner strength. Despite his anxiety, he not only succeeded in thinking out three short stories and two novellas but actually wrote the long short story entitled *A Tale of Childhood,* an amazingly delicate account of the emotions and exploits of an eleven-year-old knight-errant and the stirring of his erotic passion for a married lady. Presumably it reflects something of Dostoevsky's own reaction to representatives of the other sex. It was published anonymously in *Notes of the Fatherland* in 1857 under the title, *A Little Hero.*

The Commission of Inquiry, completing its work on September 17, 1849, reported its conclusion that twenty-eight of those held in custody were guilty of criminal actions. Trial by a mixed military-civil court began on September 30, and, on November 16, fifteen of the accused, including Dostoevsky, were sentenced to execution by firing squad — "for participation in criminal designs...and an attempt along with others to disseminate works against the government" (*Letters,* I, 431–32). In addition to being sentenced to death, Dostoevsky was shorn of his civil rights and property.

Three days later, Tsar Nicholas I commuted this draconian sentence to four years' hard labor, to be followed by service in the ranks as a common soldier for an unspecified period. Dostoevsky and his fellow prisoners, however, were given no notice of this action but, in accordance with the provisions of applicable law, were permitted to believe right up to the end that the sentence of execution would be carried out on schedule. Two passages in *The Idiot,* both dealing with the psychic ordeal of the criminal awaiting execution, give us an idea of what Dostoevsky must have gone through during the terrible minutes of waiting in the frigid temperature of St. Petersburg's Semyonovsky Square at 9 A.M. on December 22, 1849. On the tsar's instruction, all preparations for the ghastly ceremony were completed before the prisoners were told that their lives were to be spared.

The reprieved men were then returned to the Peter and Paul Fortress, from where, two days later — on Christmas Eve — Dostoevsky and his companions set out in fetters for the two-thousand-mile journey to Tobolsk in western Siberia. Only once did he shed tears, when he found himself at "the border of Europe, Siberia ahead, and an enigmatic fate in it, all the past behind" (*Letters,* I, 185).

Two incidents during the stopover at Tobolsk illuminate hidden depths in Dostoevsky's personality. A fellow convict, on the verge of committing suicide, was by his own account dissuaded by the "sympathetic, gentle voice of Dostoevsky, his tenderness and delicacy of feeling, even some of his capricious sallies, *quite like a woman.*"[9]

If, in this case, Dostoevsky's "feminine" qualities helped a comrade to survive a personal crisis, Dostoevsky himself was helped by the wives of three of the Decembrists who had followed their husbands into Siberian exile. These "sublime sufferers," in Dostoevsky's phrase, exhibited an exalted sense of morality and an ardent spirit of solidarity. Intensely religious and instinctively charitable, they endured cold and risk to help the newly arrived convicts at Tobolsk.

One of them, Madame Natalya Dimitrievna Fonvizina, gave Dostoevsky a copy of the New Testament, the only book allowed in the forced labor camp. Kept under his pillow throughout the four years of his confinement, it undoubtedly played some role in what has been called his "conversion" or the "regeneration of his convictions."[10] From the transit prison at Tobolsk, Dostoevsky was sent on to the prison camp at Omsk, five hundred miles farther up the Irtish River, arriving on January 23, 1850. Here he was to live, among common thieves and murderers, for the four-year period described in his own *House of the Dead* — a period that ended with grim precision at the end of January 1854.

During his years of penal servitude, Dostoevsky was fitted with leg irons and employed in manual labor under the auspices of the engineering department. As an educated member of the nobility, he found himself exposed to the hatred and contempt not only of the prison guards but equally of the common criminals whose fate he shared. It would be difficult to exaggerate the wretchedness of an existence marked by harrowing hardships and illnesses. Among them was a series of epileptic seizures, a malady to which he had been subject since as long ago as July 1847.[11] Yet Dostoevsky not only survived the experience but drew from it the inspiration for his entire subsequent life.

A letter addressed to his brother Mikhail on his release from prison camp, dated January 30–February 22, 1854 (*Letters*, I, 183–93), leaves one almost incredulous at the man's sheer courage, resiliency, optimism, and will to survive. He simply refused to be destroyed by pressures that would have lastingly upset a weaker person's psychic and mental stability. In his own words, he allowed himself to become only "temporarily useless" (*Letters*, II, 94). Invoking the Christian symbolism of the Resurrection, he wrote of his four years in prison as a time when he was "buried alive and locked up in a coffin.... I imagined release from prison as a bright awakening and resurrection into a new life" (*Letters*, I, 201). "I remember that it was only a passionate desire for resurrection, for renewal, for a new life that strengthened my will to wait and hope" (*House of the Dead*, 339).

The renewal that Dostoevsky experienced during his prison years profoundly affected both his personal religious outlook and his attitude toward his fellow creatures. Rejecting the facile, reformist social theories that had led to his arrest, he not only accepted his punishment but came to see the common people of Russia as the embodiment of the suffering Christ, the way to union with God and

Jesus. His new profession of faith, after his release from prison, was addressed to Madame Fonvizina, whose Bible he had read and reread until he became convinced of the impossibility of living without God. "I'll tell you of myself," he wrote,

that I have been a child of the age, a child of disbelief and doubt up until now and will be even (I know this) to the grave.... And yet God sometimes sends me moments at which I'm absolutely at peace; at those moments I love and find that I am loved by others, and at such moments I composed for myself a credo in which everything is clear and holy for me. That credo is very simple:... to believe that there is nothing more beautiful, more profound, more attractive, more wise, more courageous and more perfect than Christ... (*Letters*, I, 194–95).

The archetypal figure of Jesus had become for Dostoevsky a symbol of compassion and forgiveness, the response to his inner need to understand, embrace, and extend a comprehensive sympathy to sinful humanity. His rough associates of the Siberian prison, unpromising as they appeared on the surface, would also become an essential element in this process. They too were among the "insulted and injured," and he humbled himself before them even as he studied them with the same intense curiosity he had brought to the study of human types at the Mariinsky Hospital, in Dr. Riesenkampf's waiting room, and among the members of the Petrashevsky circle.

Dostoevsky's intellectual life continued active even amid numbing influences of prison routine. "I can't tell you how much torment I endured in prison because of not being able to write," he noted after his release. "But all the same, inner work was in full swing.... I created there in my head, my long definitive novel" (*Letters*, I, 233). He was cruelly starved for reading matter. "Books are my life, my future!" he later wrote Mikhail, requesting money and a formidable list of volumes that included Kant's *Critique of Pure Reason* and "especially" Hegel's *History of Philosophy:*

Send me European historians, economists, the Church fathers, as far as possible all the ancients (Herodotus, Thucydides, Tacitus, Pliny, Flavius, Plutarch and Diodorus and so on. They've all been translated into French.) Finally, the [works of Carl Gustav] Carus and a German dictionary.... Also send me Pisarev's physics and a work on physiology. (*Letters*, I, 190–91, 197–98).

In conformity with the terms of his sentence, Dostoevsky on his release from prison was assigned to the remote garrison town of

Semipalatinsk, four hundred miles farther up the Irtish River in
Kazakhstan — a desolate region where the "Khirghiz steppe begins [and]...there is absolutely no vegetation...not a single tree"
(Letters, I, 197). To a modern reader, the desolation of the scene is
suggested by the fact that the first Soviet atomic bomb was tested
near Semipalatinsk in 1953. Here the former tsarist officer and
writer was enrolled as a private in the 7th Line Battalion of the
Siberian Army Corps.

He had lost no time in initiating steps to regain his rights as a
Russian citizen, secure a transfer to the civil service or a promotion to commissioned rank, and obtain permission to publish as
a means of reestablishing himself on the literary scene. "But," he
wrote to Mikhail, "until then, please feed me. Without money, I'll
be crushed" — a refrain that will be heard throughout the life of
this devoted brother whose pocket Feodor drew upon as though it
were his own (Letters, I, 190–91).

The thirty-three-year-old ex-convict found another friend and
benefactor in Baron Alexander Wrangel, the new prosecuting
magistrate for criminal affairs in the district. Kind, humane, respon-
sive, and cultured, this twenty-one-year-old St. Petersburg official
brought money and letters from Dostoevsky's family and would be
of great assistance both then and later. As late as 1865, Wrangel,
then Secretary at the Russian Embassy in Copenhagen, would extend renewed financial help and protection to Dostoevsky, who, as
usual, was deeply in debt at the time.

Now, in remote Kazakhstan, the two men shared a dacha or villa
outside of Semipalatinsk, in a natural setting ideally suited to further Feodor's spiritual recuperation. In Wrangel he discerned some
of the feminine qualities with which he himself has been credited:
"[he] has a very weak character that is impressionable in a feminine
way...; what infuriates and enrages someone else saddens him —
the sign of a superior heart" (Letters, I, 224). Dostoevsky at this
period seemed also to prefer women writers: "I don't like Ostrovsky, I haven't read Pisemsky at all, Druzhinin [minor writer and
chief critic for The Contemporary] nauseates me, Yevgenia Tur [a
woman writer specializing in historical tales and novels] drove me to
ecstasy. I also like Krestovsky [pseudonym of another contemporary
woman writer]" (Letters, I, 192).

Feminine influence of a more immediate kind was found in the
person of Marya Dmitrievna Isaeva, the well-read, cultivated, but
unappreciated wife of a customs official named Alexander Ivanovich Isaev. This individual Dostoevsky described as "carefree as a

gypsy, vain, proud"; while his wife, in contrast, was a "God-sent" acquaintance whose pity and sympathy had "resurrected [Feodor's] soul." For Dostoevsky, the illicit romance with Marya was a new step toward self-realization. It was his passion for her that goaded him to return to public life as a writer. She filled the desperate hours of waiting for replies to his petitions. She inspired him to improve his lowly status as a soldier. Wrangel, a close observer of Dostoevsky's devotion both to Marya and to Christ, recalls in his memoirs his friend's buoyancy whenever he returned home after a visit to Marya — "in a sort of ecstasy, enraptured beyond words."[12]

Dostoevsky's raptures were short-lived, however, for Marya's husband had resigned his position in Semipalatinsk and found new employment in the distant town of Kuznetsk in Tomsk province. The prospect of separation changed Dostoevsky's bliss to torment, and for a second time one is made privy to his weeping. As Marya and her husband drove away in their carriage, Wrangel recalls, Dostoevsky "stood as if rooted to the spot, silent, his head lowered, tears coursing down his cheeks."[13] In subsequent letters to Marya, Feodor wrote that without her he felt as desolate as in 1849 when his arrest and imprisonment had torn him away from everything he held dear.

But this phase, too, proved extraordinarily brief, for Isaev died from natural causes on August 4, 1855, leaving Marya a widow and enabling Dostoevsky to ask for her hand, although a full eighteen months were to elapse before she accepted his proposal. The marriage was approved by the military authorities on February 1, and took place at Kuznetsk on February 6, 1857. For the time being, the couple were obliged to reside in Semipalatinsk while Dostoevsky pursued his efforts to effect a literary comeback.

The marriage proved less blissful than Dostoevsky, with his strong promatrimonial philosophy, had perhaps anticipated. Marya Dmitrievna, who like Dostoevsky's own mother suffered from tuberculosis, had accepted him at least in part because of practical considerations, especially the need to provide for her son Paul. Still, the two did complement one another in a relationship marked by love as well as unfaithfulness, harmony as well as discord. If Dostoevsky may be credited with certain feminine characteristics, he perceived in Marya Dmitrievna, among other qualities, a masculine "knightliness": "I felt pity for her, and then she completely came back to me...truly noble (a knight in female clothing), she has the heart of a knight."[14]

The good impression wrought by Dostoevsky's faithful military service, the flattering tone of his petitions to the government, and his repeated expressions of patriotism and loyalty had been greatly reinforced by the death of Tsar Nicholas I and the accession to the throne of his more liberal son, Alexander II, on February 18, 1855. The increasingly propitious political climate, combined with his own poor health, determined him to request, early in 1858, a medical discharge from the army and permission to reside in Moscow.

Formal consent to his resignation from the service was finally granted on March 18, 1859, when he was pensioned with the rank of second lieutenant and at the same time placed under permanent police surveillance, as he himself was perfectly aware. "Ever since my return from exile," he wrote Mikhail seven years later, "I have been under surveillance and still am" (*Letters*, II, 192).

At first denied permission to live in Moscow or St. Petersburg, the Dostoevsky couple left Semipalatinsk in the summer of 1859 for the provincial city of Tver — "the most hateful city on earth," in Dostoevsky's opinion (*Letters*, I, 370). Later that year, the ban on residence in Petersburg was lifted, and Feodor Dostoevsky was able to return in mid-December, with his wife, to the capital from which he had been absent for a full ten years.

Dostoevsky had not been idle during those months of waiting. In addition to polishing and repolishing *House of the Dead,* as his fictionalized memoir of prison life was to be called, he had been pondering a new novel that would appear in 1861 as *The Insulted and Injured.* In addition, he had written and published two rather substantial "bagatelles," as he called them, a comic story called *Uncle's Dream,* published in the March 1859 issue of a new left-wing magazine, the *Russian Word,* and a long tale, *The Village of Stepanchikovo and Its Inhabitants* (also called *The Friend of the Family*), which appeared in *Notes of the Fatherland* in November and December 1859.

Neither story aroused much critical interest. Turgenev was now in the ascendant, and the mood of the moment was more attuned to works of high social and cultural import than to comic accounts of life on a country estate. Dostoevsky, who claimed to have poured his "soul, flesh and blood" into *The Village of Stepanchikovo,* admitted one of its shortcomings: "There's very little tenderness in the novel (that is, little of the passionate element...)." But these minor works at least marked his return to the printed page after a decade's absence.

As in the 1840s, brother Mikhail was assigned an essential role in planning for Dostoevsky's subsistence during the 1860s, an undertaking complicated by the fact that both brothers were now married men. While Feodor and Marya Dmitrievna waited in Semipalatinsk, the brothers had laid plans to start their own political and literary periodical, with Mikhail as titular director — since Feodor, as an ex-convict, could not legally assume the editorship. With the St. Petersburg Censorship Committee's authorization, the first number of *Time,* as the new monthly periodical was called, appeared in January 1861.

Even while preparations for *Time* were being completed, Dostoevsky's literary reputation had received another lift from the publication of the first four chapters of his *House of the Dead,* which had appeared in the weekly the *Russian World* — not to be confused with the *Russian Word* — beginning in September 1860. The reading public was thus in some measure already prepared for the new novel, *The Insulted and Injured,* which was carried in the first seven issues of *Time* in January–July 1861. Seeking a middle position between the radicalism of such periodicals as *Notes of the Fatherland* and the conservative stance of journals like the *Russian Messenger, Time* also reprinted the earlier chapters of *House of the Dead* in April 1861, and published the remaining chapters beginning in September 1861 and concluding in December 1862.

This was a period when all Russia was absorbed by the social and economic changes attendant upon the emancipation of the serfs, an epochal initiative that was formally proclaimed by Tsar Alexander II on February 19, 1861. More private cares affected the Dostoevsky household, where the initial rapport between Feodor and his wife Marya Dmitrievna had largely disintegrated by the time of their arrival in St. Petersburg. Their very first months in the capital had been complicated by another in the series of feminine relationships through which Dostoevsky perpetually sought to realize his own ideal and find the road to personal integration.

Alexandra Shubert (née Kulikova, 1826–1909), a cultivated and talented actress who had made her stage debut in the capital as far back as 1843, attracted Dostoevsky's notice both by her stage presence and by a social poise that was the more remarkable because, as the daughter of serf parents, she could also be regarded as a symbol of the Russian soil and of the "mother Russia" from whom the writer drew his own strength. To Alexandra he confided something of his conjugal distress as well as his literary ambitions. She represented, in a sense, a "way station" on the road to his tempestuous liaison, two years later, with the militant young writer, Apollinaria Suslova.

By the middle of 1862, the initial success of *Time* and the favorable

reception of his own writings had persuaded the forty-one-year-old
Dostoevsky that despite considerable unpaid debts, the time had
come to realize his long-standing dream of a trip abroad. "To Italy,
to Italy!" he had written an acquaintance in 1861. "But instead of
Italy I landed in Semipalatinsk, and before that in the Dead House"
(*Letters*, II, 27). He was by this time quite detached from Marya,
and though he regretted leaving the hardworking Mikhail behind,
he departed on June 7, 1862, for a summer in Europe — one that
proved as remarkable for the number of cities he was able to visit on
an empty pocket as for his markedly critical reactions to the foreign
peoples he encountered.

During his brief stay in London, Dostoevsky met twice with the
exiled radical and socialist writer, Alexander Herzen, and it is said
that he also made the acquaintance of Mikhail Bakunin, the celebrated revolutionary anarchist, who, like himself, had been confined
to a penal settlement in Siberia but had escaped and made his way
to London via Japan and the United States.

The Crystal Palace Exhibition then in progress in the British capital would become for Dostoevsky a metaphor for all he detested in
the materialistic civilization of the West as seen, for instance, by his
future "underground man"; while the hustle and bustle of the London streets would find echoes in such late works as *The Gambler*
and *The Dream of a Ridiculous Man.* "Everything [in London] is so
huge and abrupt in its individuality," he would write, and, an ecol-
ogist before the time, he bitterly complained against "that polluted
Thames; that air saturated with coal dust."[15]

Returning to St. Petersburg in September 1862, Dostoevsky crystallized his reactions to the European experience in *Winter Notes
on Summer Impressions,* published in *Time* in February and March
1863. (A short story, alternately entitled *A Nasty Tale* and *An Unpleasant Predicament,* appeared in the same periodical in December
1862.) *Time,* by then, had also begun to publish the fictional contributions of the fiery young feminist named Apollinaria (Polina)
Suslova, with whom Dostoevsky was about to begin an amorous
liaison that would dominate his emotional life over the next three
years.

Polina, like Alexandra Shubert, was the daughter of an emanci-
pated serf and thus responded to Dostoevsky's need for identification
with the Russian soil. She has been described as chaotic, contradictory, cruel, and severe, but also as ardent, generous, and passionate.
Although she undoubtedly played with Dostoevsky's emotions and
may have deliberately sought to inflict pain upon the man who be-

came her first lover, she was met on his side with immeasurable kindness, sensitivity, and almost preternatural patience. Even her rejection of his proposal of marriage after his wife's death did not destroy their relationship, nor did their correspondence cease until after Dostoevsky's remarriage in 1867. In his farewell letter he still addresses this archetypal figure of the devouring mistress as "eternal friend."

Quite early in their association, Polina left her lover in St. Petersburg and traveled alone to Paris, where she promptly became enamored of a Spanish medical student. Dostoevsky, meanwhile, had been left to support his brother in an acute crisis that had arisen in May 1863 with the official banning of *Time* in consequence of a misunderstanding of its position on the Polish question.

Leaving Mikhail to petition the authorities for permission to resume publication, Feodor borrowed money for another trip abroad, ostensibly to obtain medical treatment but in reality to join Polina in Paris. After trying his luck at the roulette tables in Germany, he reached the French capital in mid-August and was obliged to hear the tale of Polina's misadventures with her Spanish lover, who had already deserted her. Relegated to the role of paternal counselor and platonic friend, Dostoevsky remained for a time at Polina's side in Paris, then set out with her "as brother and sister" for Baden-Baden — where he had several meetings with Turgenev and lost heavily at roulette — and thence for Italy.

Rome and Naples "impressed [him] strongly," and from the Eternal City he wrote: "Could [Rome] really be described in letters?...Yesterday morning I looked at St. Peter's. A strong impression...with a shiver down the spine. Today I looked at the *Forum* and all its ruins. Then the *Coliseum!* Well what can I tell you" (*Letters,* II, 72). After a whirlwind tour of the peninsula, they separated in Berlin in October, Polina returning to Paris and Feodor to St. Petersburg.

Although the future of *Time* was still unsettled, permission was shortly forthcoming to start a new monthly review, *Epoch,* the first issue of which appeared in March 1864. Sarcastically dubbed "The Petticoat" by the satirist Shchedrin (Mikhail Evgrafovich Saltykov), the new periodical featured in its first issue a prose poem by Turgenev, entitled "Phantoms," which Dostoevsky had urgently solicited but in which he privately found "a good deal of rubbish" and later caricatured in *The Devils.* Also published in the inaugural issue was the first part of Dostoevsky's *Notes from Underground,* the concluding portion of which would appear in the June number.

The cynical, satirical *Notes from Underground,* Dostoevsky's next
novel, reflects his deepening disillusionment and bitterness as he kept
vigil at the bedside of his dying wife, Marya Dmitrievna, who succumbed to pulmonary tuberculosis on April 15, 1864, less than a
decade after their first acquaintance. A much heavier blow than the
loss of his semi-estranged wife was the death on July 10, 1864,
of his brother Mikhail, his friend and companion through life,
his most reliable support in time of need, and the partner of his
literary enterprises. Exhausted by overwork and financial worry,
overwhelmed by the adversities of the previous year, the calm and
equable Mikhail had been further tormented by the outbreak of a
venomous feud between his new magazine, *Epoch,* and *The Contemporary,* which had emerged as the organ of the radical left-wing
group surrounding Nekrasov and the novelist Nikolay Gavrilovich
Chernyshevsky.

Feodor had always dominated the more passive Mikhail, and had
often accused him of laziness and apathy; but the death of his favorite brother filled him with loneliness and despair. "Ahead are a
cold, lonely old age and my falling sickness," he wrote. "For the
sort of brother that he was I would give up both my head and my
health." His life, he felt, was now "broken in two," and he saw
"nothing left to live for" (*Letters,* II, 127, 152). Still another crushing blow was the death on September 22, 1864, of the poet and
critic Apollon Grigoryev, a friend, collaborator, and valued ally who
had only lately welcomed *Notes from Underground* as a sign that
Dostoevsky's literary talent was finding the right channel.

At forty-three years of age, Dostoevsky with his deeply scarred
personality had arrived at a critical turning point, the threshold of a
new stage in his development as a person and an artist. Saddled with
the responsibility for two families — his own and Mikhail's — and
for his younger brother Nikolay as well, he embarked upon a heroic
struggle to keep the magazine afloat, negotiating with authors and
censors, correcting articles for publication, reading proofs, searching
for funds, and suffering continuously because he could find no time
to publish his own work.

His love life, meanwhile, was in as much disarray as ever. Matrimony he now considered essential to his personal salvation, and it
would seem that he made proposals of marriage to no fewer than
four women before his acceptance by a fifth in 1867. Polina being still abroad, he first fell in love with the twenty-year-old Anna
Vasilievna Korvin-Krukovskaya (1843–87), a beautiful young girl
from an excellent family whom he met in March 1865, not quite a

year after Marya Dmitrievna's death. Known as "Russalka" (Lorelei) because of her long hair and smiling green eyes, Anna was a talented writer and had contributed two stories to *Epoch*,[16] just as Polina had contributed to *Time*.

Witty, bold, original, and intellectually curious, Anna may nevertheless have been somewhat overwhelmed by this man of more than twice her age. Dostoevsky proposed in April 1865 but was rejected. He "seems to be enveloping me all the time, to be absorbing me into himself," she writes; "in his presence I am never my own self."[17] Their ideas, too, were diametrically opposed. Anna, after a period of mysticism, had become a convinced nihilist, while Dostoevsky continued to cherish his conservative convictions. She later married a French revolutionary, Victor Jaclard, and personally took part in the Paris Commune of 1871 before returning to Russia with her husband.

Anna's rejection coincided with the failure of *Epoch*, the Dostoevsky brothers' second review, which ceased publishing for financial reasons after the first two issues of 1865. The first installment of Dostoevsky's unfinished story, *The Crocodile*, appeared in the very last issue. After transferring subscribers to another periodical, the writer once again sought relief from personal problems in a trip abroad. Desperately short of funds and besieged by creditors, he signed on July 2, 1865, an extortionate contract with an unscrupulous publisher, Feodor Timofevich Stellovsky, in which he authorized the publication of a three-volume collection of his own works and also obligated himself to submit a new novel by November 1, 1866.

With Stellovsky's funds in hand, Dostoevsky took the train to Berlin. After five years of intense journalistic work, he was beginning a new era toward which, he wrote, he was advancing with "feline vitality." In most of its features, however, the new era seemed depressingly like the old, with more tempestuous encounters with Polina and more gambling sprees in Wiesbaden. Putting aside his commitment to Stellovsky, he worked on the "story" that later became *Crime and Punishment*, exhausting himself in futile attempts to obtain an advance payment from one of the Russian reviews. Several publications, including Nekrasov's hostile *The Contemporary*, declined the offer, but the rights were finally sold to the ultraconservative *Russian Messenger*, the organ of Mikhail Nikiforovich Katkov, the well-known Russian Orthodox and Pan-Slav nationalist. With the proceeds, Dostoevsky was able to spend ten days in Copenhagen as guest of his old friend from Semipalatinsk, Baron Wrangel.

Returning to St. Petersburg by sea, the novelist continued work on *Crime and Punishment*, weaving into it a separate story, *The Drunkards*, which had previously been rejected by *Notes of the Fatherland*. A final break with Polina, who had also returned to Russia, occurred that winter, and the resultant emotional stress left its mark upon the pages of what was to be one of the world's best-known novels. As its author struggled to keep ahead of the printers, *Crime and Punishment* actually began appearing serially in Katkov's *Russian Messenger* in January 1866 and was completed in December of the same year.

Work on the novel had advanced sufficiently by mid-1866 to permit a prolonged visit to Dostoevsky's sister Vera and her family in their dacha at Lyublino outside Moscow, where he could enjoy the natural setting of lake and forest and the cheerful relaxations of country life. Vera, some eight years his junior, had been married for more than two decades to Dr. Alexander Pavlovich Ivanov, and the family was perhaps the most congenial of all Dostoevsky's relatives with the exception of his brother Mikhail.

For his niece, Sofia Alexandrovna Ivanova, he conceived a particular affection. She became the repository of his confessions — a person who, he felt, completed his own personality by supplying an element he himself lacked. The deep sympathy that developed between the two would make Sofia Ivanova one of his favorite correspondents, one with whom he could share details of his artistic creation and to whom he later dedicated his novel *The Idiot*.

Dostoevsky's summer with the Ivanovs seems also to have witnessed two further matrimonial proposals by this distracted author who looked upon a solid marriage as the key to personal salvation. One of them was to a friend of the Ivanova girls, Marya Sergeevna-Pisareva, whom he describes in one of his letters as "an amazing jester"; the other, to the same girls' aunt by marriage, Elena Pavlovna Ivanova, whose husband was extremely ill at the time and not expected to live. Although a marriage to Elena seems actually to have been agreed upon in principle (cf. *Letters*, II, 217–18, 222), her husband remained alive until 1869, by which time Dostoevsky had long since remarried.

While at Lyublino, Dostoevsky was belatedly planning the outlines of *The Gambler,* the novel he was committed to turn over to publisher Stellovsky by the beginning of November. Into it went much of his unhappy experience with Polina as well as the passion that drove him repeatedly to the gaming tables. Returning to St. Petersburg in September and realizing that little more than six weeks remained before the deadline, he followed the suggestion of a friend that he try to gain time by engaging a stenographer. With the help of a nineteen-year-old amanuensis named Anna Grigorievna Snitkina, who copied out the entire manuscript, he managed to fulfill his commitment and, in the process, found the life's companion he had so long been seeking.

As the daughter of an affluent, well-ordered family, Anna Snitkina was herself well educated, self-possessed, and self-reliant, with a firm character and a good sense of humor. Unlike Dostoevsky's earlier loves, she was deeply religious and politically conservative, although she ardently supported the growing movement for women's emancipation. Despite differences in age and character, the two collaborators grew rapidly closer, and on November 8, 1866, barely a month after their first meeting, Dostoevsky asked for Anna's hand in marriage. They were wedded on February 15, 1867, in St. Petersburg's Trinity Izmaylov Cathedral.

The crises of Dostoevsky's existence, both practical and emotional, were now behind him. With his marriage to Anna Grigorievna, he had reached safe harbor; he could now devote himself to realizing his ideals of matrimony and family life, even as he continued to conceive and execute those works of literature that stand among the masterpieces of our civilization.

The first four years of the Dostoevsky couple's married life, from 1867 to 1871, were spent in western Europe, and it was there that their first two children were born, though only one of them survived. The couple proceeded first to Dresden, where Dostoevsky lost himself in admiration of the religious paintings of the High Renaissance and Baroque periods, and thence to Baden-Baden, where he incurred the usual gambling losses and quarreled violently with Turgenev in reaction to the latter's exaltation of western European over Russian culture.

Dostoevsky's own conservative and nationalistic views could only be strengthened by news that there had been an assassination attempt, the first of many, against the "Tsar Liberator," Alexander II, while on a state visit to Paris on May 25, 1867. At Geneva, a few weeks later, the novelist seemed pleased to have seen Garibaldi, the Italian patriot, but was horrified at the "wretchedness" uttered by such revolutionaries as Bakunin and others who were "deciding the fate of humanity" at a so-called Peace Congress.

The Dostoevskys remained in Geneva — "the foulest spot in all of Switzerland" he would write — throughout the winter of 1867–68. He worked on *The Idiot*, struggling to clarify the personality of his central character, Prince Myshkin — the "representation of a perfect man" — and to give the clearest possible expression to his detestation of Russian liberalism.

The Idiot, like Crime and Punishment, was published serially in the Russian Messenger, beginning in January and continuing until December 1868. On February 22 of the same year, a girl was born to the Dostoevskys and was given the name of Sofia after the writer's favorite niece. She lived but three months, and at the end of May the bereaved parents moved to Vevey farther up Lake Geneva. There they continued through the summer in spite of Dostoevsky's denunciation of the place as "a dirty hole" without the shadow of an art gallery, museum, or Russian newspaper.

The travelers left for Italy in September 1868 and, in November, arrived in Florence to begin an eight months' sojourn that would prove the happiest and most peaceful of Dostoevsky's voluntary "second exile." Here the author expanded his design of a "huge novel," to be entitled Atheism, which would illustrate the temper of the young people of his time. He also began writing the short novel, The Eternal Husband, a study of jealousy and masochism in which he returned to one of the main themes of The Idiot, the impossibility of solving the "eternal" problems of human relationships since these are rooted in psychological factors resistant to reason. It was published in the Russian Messenger in January and February of 1870.

Leaving Florence in July 1869, the couple traveled northward via Bologna, Venice, Trieste, Vienna, and Prague to Dresden, where they were to remain for nearly two years and where their daughter Lyubov was born on September 14, 1869. Here Dostoevsky continued work on the great novel that, he wrote his niece Sofia Ivanova, would be "as large as [Tolstoy's] War and Peace," would take five years to complete, and would be both his last work and the culmination of his career. Although the writer did not live to complete this grandiose effort, the title of which had meanwhile been changed to The Life of a Great Sinner, it served as a storehouse of material for his last three novels, The Devils, A Raw Youth, and The Brothers Karamazov.

The writing of The Devils (also called The Possessed) was prompted by the historical incident known as the Nechaev affair, in which a Russian revolutionary student who failed to obey orders was murdered by his comrades in an underground group headed by Sergey G. Nechaev. Learning of the episode early in the Dostoevskys' stay in Dresden, the novelist undertook the writing of what was originally an "anti-Nihilist" pamphlet (entitled "The Devils") but presently grew into a substantial novel. The first portion of this new work was sent to the *Russian Messenger* in October 1870 and published early in 1871. Completed after the author's return to Russia in July of the same year, the remainder of the novel appeared in the course of 1872, and the entire work was published in three volumes in January 1873. It aroused political passion on all sides and, predictably, was harshly denounced by the Left, but sold three thousand copies to a receptive public.

The Franco-Prussian War of 1870, the collapse of France's Second Empire, and the popular rising known as the Paris Commune all occurred while the Dostoevskys were living in Dresden. Of more private but nonetheless great significance was the novelist's complete and permanent renunciation of gambling after sustaining new and heavy losses at Wiesbaden in April 1871. Desperately homesick and loathing all Europe, Dostoevsky finally obtained the necessary travel funds from his publisher and left for St. Petersburg with his wife and infant daughter at the beginning of July 1871.

Back in the Russian capital but lacking either lodgings or furniture, the Dostoevskys had to engage the most modest of furnished rooms, and it was there that their first son, Feodor, was born on July 16, 1871, barely a week after their return. Thanks to the success of Dostoevsky's writings and to Anna's good management, their financial situation gradually improved from this time on. By the following year, they were able to spend the summer at Staraya Russa, a spa in Novgorod province that became their regular vacation home and where they purchased a house in 1877.

The ongoing publication of *The Devils* had left the literary world in no doubt of Dostoevsky's conservative credentials, and it was in the conservative and reactionary circles of the capital that he was most warmly welcomed. Among his new acquaintances was Prince Meshchersky, who had launched the conservative weekly, *The Citizen*, in 1871 and now invited Dostoevsky to become its new editor. Appearing under Dostoevsky's editorship from January 1873 onward, *The Citizen* published several of his short stories, including the black comic *Bobok*, while its supplement, entitled *The Diary of a Writer*, gave him a personal forum for reactionary comment on current affairs. This latter feature was, however, discontinued at the end of 1873, partly because of differences with Prince Meshchersky — who, among other things, approved the surveillance of students by the secret police — and partly because Dostoevsky wished to concentrate on work of a more permanent character.

Further testimony to Dostoevsky's belated acceptance by the dominant elements of nineteenth-century Russia was the commissioning of his formal portrait at the request of P. M. Tretyakov, the merchant and art patron whose name survives in Moscow's famed Tretyakov Gallery. The artist Vasily Perov was entrusted with this work, which to Anna seemed to capture her husband's expression at the moment of full creativity. The author of *The Double*, who had a wart on his right cheek, offered a personal opinion in *Bobok:* "I think that artist painted me not for the sake of literature, but for the sake of the two symmetrical warts on my forehead" (166).

Although his domestic and professional situation had by this time vastly improved, Dostoevsky's health still gave cause for concern. Since his last European sojourn he had been troubled by the emphysema that would ultimately cause his death, and on the suggestion of his physician he spent several weeks in the summer of 1874 at the German spa of Ems while the family remained at Staraya Russa. This pattern would be repeated in most of the summers from 1874 to 1880.

Both at Ems and at Staraya Russa, he worked intensively on the writing of *A Raw Youth,* which was published serially in *Notes of the Fatherland* during 1875. After another thermal cure at Ems that summer, he returned to Staraya Russa for the birth of Aleksey, the Dostoevskys' second son and last child, who died less than three years later. It was also during that summer that the Russian government finally decided to discontinue the police surveillance to which the writer had been subjected ever since his resignation from the army in 1859.

The Diary of a Writer, Dostoevsky's personal organ, which had appeared during 1873 as a supplement to *The Citizen,* was revived at the beginning of 1876 as an independent monthly publication, with Dostoevsky as editor and Anna as administrator and proofreader. Its reappearance coincided with a further heightening of Pan-Slavic sentiment in connection with the new crisis in the Balkans and the Near East that preceded the Russo-Turkish War of 1877–78. At the same time, Dostoevsky was provided a platform from which to voice his growing dismay at the aggressiveness of the Russian revolutionary movement, which by then had sponsored several unsuccessful attempts on the life of Tsar Alexander II.

Two "fantastic tales," as Dostoevsky called them, were also published in *The Diary of a Writer* at this period. In November 1876 appeared *A Gentle Creature,* another elaboration on the theme of *The Idiot* and *The Eternal Husband.* April 1877 brought *The Dream of a Ridiculous Man,* a work of "space fiction" about an uncorrupted society, situated on another planet, which is contaminated and ravaged by the evil introduced by a man from earth.

Dostoevsky surrendered his highly successful editorship of *The Diary of a Writer* after December 1877 in order to devote himself to the writing of *The Brothers Karamazov,* the second in the series of novels that were to have composed *The Life of a Great Sinner.* The first eight books of this supreme masterpiece, which has been called, "after *King Lear,* the greatest work ever written to illustrate the moral horrors that ensue when family bonds disintegrate,"[18] appeared in the *Russian Messenger* during 1879, and the last four books and the epilogue in 1880.

Nervous tension and exhaustion were the consequences of Dostoevsky's grief over the death of his son, his own failing health, and his unstinting application to the writing of his novel. Yet in spite of the hoarseness and asthma that accompanied his increasingly severe emphysema, he was able during 1879 to give a number of successful public readings from *The Brothers Karamazov.* While the family sojourned as usual at Staraya Russa, he proceeded to Ems for the customary cure, but his illness this time resisted treatment. His peevish, fretful mood at the time seemed to reflect the political agitation and unrest that were still gaining ground in Russia in these last years before the assassination of the reigning tsar.

In May of 1880, Dostoevsky traveled to Moscow to take part in a series of ceremonies, meetings, and banquets in connection with the inauguration of an important statue of Pushkin. The climax of the occasion — and, in a sense, of Dostoevsky's entire career — was the impassioned address in which the now venerated novelist reaffirmed his belief in Russia's mission of reconciling "European contradictions" and uniting the nations of Europe under her aegis. Here, for once, both Slavophils and Westerners could share in the general exaltation, as representatives of both camps — including even the estranged Turgenev — thronged to embrace the speaker.

Such a triumph could only encourage the elaboration of new literary projects. At fifty-nine years of age, the writer still had much to say to the world. With *The Brothers Karamazov* approaching completion, he planned a sequel that would further illuminate the subject of human dignity and the role of Russian Orthodoxy in guiding Russians to moral and spiritual principles. He also planned a fresh revival of *The Diary of a Writer,* and actually delivered the manuscript of a first issue to the printer on January 25, 1881 — his final literary contribution to the world.

Next day, there occurred a violent quarrel with his sister Vera over a matter of inheritance rights. Rupture of a lung artery brought on a series of hemorrhages and led directly to his death on the evening of January 28, 1881. Thus was attained the goal toward which the writer had struggled throughout his life, against debilitating illness, crushing debts, and misfortunes of a singular poignancy — the "one goal" he had identified in an early letter: "to be free" (*Letters*, I, 55).

A large crowd followed his cortege to St. Petersburg's monastery of St. Alexander Nevsky, one of the four highest ranking monasteries of the Russian Orthodox Church. There he was buried with solemn funerary honors in the institution's Tichvin cemetery on February 1, 1881. It was just a month later that Tsar Alexander II, Dostoevsky's beloved emperor, himself met death at the hands of the revolutionary movement whose aims and methods Dostoevsky had done his utmost to combat.

On hearing of Dostoevsky's death, Lev Tolstoy wrote: "I never saw the man, and never had any direct relations with him, yet suddenly when he died I understood that he was the nearest and dearest and most necessary of men to me. Everything that he did was of the kind that the more he did of it the better I felt it was for men. All at once I read that he is dead, and a prop has fallen from me."[19]

Anna Grigorievna, Dostoevsky's young widow, survived him for thirty-seven years, living for the most part quite comfortably on royalties from her husband's works. Following the Bolshevik Revolution of 1917, however, she died in poverty in the Crimea in 1918 at the age of seventy-two. It was there, too, that Polina Suslova, who had played such a role in the writer's tempestuous middle period, succumbed at the even later age of seventy-eight.

Part 2
The Novels

2

Crime and Punishment (1866)

Probably the most widely known of Dostoevsky's greater novels, *Crime and Punishment* claims priority of notice by reason of its special appeal to our contemporary society as well as its universal qualities. One critic, writing early in the twentieth century, offered this appraisal of the novel's enduring value:

> For the deepest essence of tragedy, though it avoid the final catastrophe — for the evocation, that is to say, of the profoundest feelings of pity and of terror which can purge the reader's heart — there is, I believe, no work of literary fiction that can take its place by the side of Dostoevsky's *Crime and Punishment.* ... Who shall describe the multitude of wonderful, heart-searching passages in which [it] abounds? In this book the piteous, the terrible, the human and the sublime seem gathered into a vast compendium.[1]

To readers of our own generation, *Crime and Punishment* offers insight into some of the sources of the antisocial behavior patterns so characteristic of certain predominantly youthful segments of contemporary society. Interwoven with his guiding theme of redemption through suffering, Dostoevsky's reflections on the psychology of crime, punishment, and repentance are as relevant to today's conditions as to those of the 1860s. In its rebellion against established social structures like the family, school, and church, the alienated youth of today unconsciously replicates the attitudes and behavior of such earlier young people as Rodion Raskolnikov, the central figure of *Crime and Punishment,* whose attempt to prove his superiority to established social norms would culminate in the commission of a grisly murder that he would spend the rest of his life in expiating.

Dostoevsky's own situation, in material terms at least, was not dissimilar to that of Raskolnikov at the period in the mid-1860s when the novelist was beginning the composition of *Crime and Punishment.* Like Raskolnikov, cramped "in a square yard of space" and "up to the neck in debt to his landlady [whom he was] afraid of meeting," Dostoevsky was then living in a cheap hotel in Wiesbaden, Germany, deeply in debt and consequently at the mercy of the proprietor and his staff.

Writing in September 1865 to Mikhail Katkov in the hope that his novel could be published in the latter's *Russian Messenger*, the starved and humiliated author described his work as "a psychological study of a crime...a novel of contemporary life" (*Letters* II, 174.) His synopsis of the book, as he conceived it at that time, still serves as a useful summary of the action:

A young man, a former student of Petersburg University who is very hard up, becomes obsessed with the "half-baked" ideas that are in the air just now because of his general mental instability. He decides to do something that would save him immediately from his desperate position. He makes up his mind to kill an old woman moneylender. The old woman is stupid, greedy, deaf and ill; she charges exorbitant interest on her loans; she is bad-tempered and she is ruining the life of her younger sister whom she keeps as a drudge. She is absolutely worthless, there seems to be no justification for her existence, etc. All these considerations completely unhinge the mind of the young man. He decides to kill her, rob her of her money, so as to be able to help his mother, who lives in the provinces, and save his sister, who is employed as governess in the house of a landowner who is trying to seduce her, as well as finish his own studies at the university. Then he plans to go abroad, and spend the rest of his life as an honest citizen doing "his duty towards humanity" without swerving from the path of honor and righteousness. This, he is convinced, will atone for his crime, if indeed one can call a crime this murder of a stupid and wicked old woman who serves no useful purpose in life and who, besides, would most probably not live for more than a few months anyhow.

In spite of the fact that such crimes are as a rule committed in a very clumsy fashion, the murderer usually leaving all sorts of clues behind him since he relies too much on chance which almost invariably lets him down, the young man succeeds in committing the murder quickly and successfully.

Almost a month passes between the crime and the final catastrophe. He is never under suspicion, nor indeed can there be any suspicion against him. But it is here that the whole psychological process of the crime unfolds itself. The murderer is suddenly confronted by insoluble problems, and hitherto undreamed of feelings begin to torment him. Divine truth and justice and the law are triumphant in the end, and the young man finishes by giving himself up against his own will. He feels compelled to go back to the society of men in spite of the danger of spending the rest of his life in a prison in Siberia. The feeling of separation and dissociation from humanity which he experiences at once after he has committed the crime, is something he cannot bear. The laws of justice and truth, of human justice, gain the upper hand. The murderer himself decides to accept his punishment in order to expiate his crime.

... My novel, besides, contains the hint that the punishment laid down by the law frightens the criminal much less than our legislators think, partly because he himself feels the desire to be punished. I have seen it happening myself with uneducated people, but I should like to show it in the case of a highly educated modern young man.... Our papers are full of stories which show the general feeling of instability which leads young men to commit terrible crimes.... I am quite sure that the subject of my novel is justified ... by the events that are happening in life today. (*Letters* II, 174–75, but translation as it appears in David Magarshack's introduction to *Crime and Punishment*, 12–13.)

Who, then, is this poor St. Petersburg law-school dropout, who suffers from "general mental instability," is addicted to "half-baked ideas," and to whom Dostoevsky gave the unforgettable name of Rodion Romanovich Raskolnikov? (The surname derives from the Russian word *raskol'nik*, signifying a dissident or schismatic.) The author describes him as "quite an extraordinarily handsome young man, with beautiful dark eyes, dark brown hair, over medium height, slim, and well-built." Usually, however, he seems to be sunk in "a sort of deep reverie" or "a kind of coma"; he is given to "indulging in soliloquies"; and if he appears "confused and weak," it is because for days he has had "hardly anything to eat."

Raskolnikov has chosen to set himself apart and be a stranger in his own society. He is a loner and a rebel trapped inside himself. Involved lucubrations and convoluted reasoning have convinced him that he must "cut himself off from everyone and everything." The "half-baked ideas" to which he has fallen a prey grow out of the pseudo-scientific rationalism and revolutionary nihilism of Raskolnikov's generation, described in such books as Turgenev's *Fathers and Sons* and Chernyshevsky's *What Is To Be Done?*, and to which Dostoevsky imputed much of the blame for the violent crimes occasionally committed by educated young people.

To escape from his social and economic limitations and attain a position in which he can exercise the talent he is sure he possesses, Raskolnikov conceives and carries out what has been called a "philosophical crime," the hatchet murder of a "useless, even harmful" old woman who lends money at usurious rates — and whom Raskolnikov has privately condemned to death on what he considers unanswerable intellectual grounds. In addition, he impulsively commits a second murder of a purely expedient character, using his hatchet to split the skull of the woman's half-witted sister when she inadvertently enters the room where her sister has just been murdered. In the wake of this all too vividly described murder, Raskolnikov himself is seized with feelings of "horror and disgust" — a leitmotiv of the novel. For the time being, however, he neither repents nor considers himself a criminal.

As the implications of the deed unfold in his conscience over the following weeks, Raskolnikov at first attempts to justify his action as a "rational" crime, committed in "an act of boldness" by an "exceptional man." "One must have the courage to dare"; "I wanted to become a Napoleon"; "I wanted to find out whether... I am some trembling vermin or whether I have the *right*" — these are some of the well-known descriptions of his attitude, uttered by himself in the course of his later confession.

Much of the novel is taken up with a process of self-analysis in the course of which Raskolnikov, this nineteenth-century "superman," gradually reveals the nature of his own motivations. Some of these he had already put forward in a published article in which he had stressed a supposed distinction between "ordinary" and "exceptional" human beings. A member of the latter group, Raskolnikov contends, has "a right... to permit conscience to step over certain obstacles... if it is absolutely necessary for the fulfillment of his ideas on which... the welfare of all mankind may depend." Such figures as Lycurgus, Solon, Mahomet, and Napoleon, according to Raskolnikov, had been superior benefactors, lawgivers, and arbiters of mankind; and each of them had shed rivers of blood promulgating new laws for a new world order. He, too, Raskolnikov indicated, had determined to commit an act of hubris or moral presumption in order to take his place among humanity's proud exceptions.

Raskolnikov is highly knowledgeable, well-read, and intelligent, as well as courageous; but his almost insane vanity is incompatible with normal social behavior. Ragged, unshaven, and tousled, he is uncommunicative and solitary and wears a fixed expression of haughtiness and arrogant mockery. Mankind fills him with existential nausea — "a sort of infinite, almost physical feeling of disgust with everything he came across — malevolent, obstinate, virulent. He hated the people he met in the street, he hated their faces, the way they walked, the way they moved. If any man had addressed him now, he would have spat on him or perhaps even bitten him" (II, 2).

And yet despite his strange silence — a silence that, in Bernard Shaw's words, is "the most perfect expression of scorn" — Raskolnikov considers himself an idealist who is concerned about the betterment of "all suffering humanity." Deep within his hardened heart he cherishes his family; indeed, one of the original motivations for his crime was the desire to help his mother and sister in their personal predicament. In some ways one is reminded of Dostoevsky himself, who at times preferred to be cruel rather than put his real feelings into words. "I have such a vile, repulsive character," he once wrote Mikhail, "sometimes when my heart is swimming in love you can't get a tender word from me" (*Letters*, I, 150).

Raskolnikov's heart and mind, indeed, seem almost to operate in separate, watertight compartments. His one friend, the warm-hearted Razumikhin — a character most certainly modeled on Mikhail Dostoevsky — observes that Raskolnikov, hiding his real feelings, sometimes becomes cold and inhumanly callous "just as if there were two people of diametrically opposed characters living in him, each taking charge of him in turn" (III, 2). Seeking "the moral solution" for the crime he is about to commit, Dostoevsky tells the reader, Raskolnikov "could no longer find any conscious objections to his plans *in his mind*. But *at heart* he never really took himself seriously, and he went on ... fumbling for some valid objections ... *as though someone were compelling and pushing him to do it*" (I, 6, italics added).

This innate duality defeats Raskolnikov's attempts to rationalize his actions after the murders have been committed. He vacillates between supreme vanity and humble submissiveness, and only later will his conscience enter into the analysis of the sorrow he has brought upon himself. "Whoever has a conscience will no doubt suffer, if he realizes his mistake," he reflects. "That's his punishment — on top of penal servitude. ... Let him suffer, if he is sorry for his victim. Suffering and pain are always necessary for men of great sensibility and deep feeling. Really great men, it seems to me, must feel great sorrow on earth." Accused of having turned his face from God, Raskolnikov will readily concede that it was Satan who had tempted him and goaded him into committing the crime: "It was the devil who killed the old hag, not I" (V, 4).

Such traits help to explain why Raskolnikov has been called a "pure" assassin, a seeming contradiction in terms. Rather than a manifestation of innate wickedness, his gratuitous crime seems to be the momentary error of a puppet who has fallen into the hands of Satan. Since he is capable of accepting punishment from within rather than from without, he is not the hardened, unrepentant criminal but rather the sorrowful deviate, sensitive to the voice of conscience, who will freely choose to expiate his crime.

Back in his "cupboard" after committing the two hatchet murders, Raskolnikov feels increasingly confused and shaken as incipient inner torment takes possession of him. "What...is my punishment already beginning?" he wonders as he feverishly attempts to remove the traces of blood from his clothing. The terror that takes hold of his soul plunges him into that "sickness" that Kierkegaard had described in 1845 as "the natural state of the Christian." It is only after a long illness, marked by fever and delirium, that a haggard and pale Raskolnikov finally resolves to try to undo his crime, "because *he did not want to go on living like that.*"

The two options open to him seem to underscore his vacillation between arrogant pride and humble resignation. He can take his own life — a solution he rejects after having witnessed with indifference a woman's attempted suicide by drowning — or he can surrender to the police in an act of final desperation.

One may wonder how far Dostoevsky intended Raskolnikov's two victims to reflect the assassin's own duality. Alyona Ivanovna, the usurer and primary victim, is a loathsome female miser who maltreats her half-crazed sister. She is "a very small, wizened old woman of about sixty, with sharp malevolent eyes, a small sharp nose, and a bare head. Her unattractive, colorless hair...was smothered in oil. Some sort of flannel rag was wound about her long, thin, neck, which looked like a hen's leg" (I, 1). Raskolnikov knows that Alyona Ivanovna hides her fortune in a securities box whose key is always on her person; he knows, too, that her money is being accumulated for the (to him) senseless purpose of endowing memorial masses for the repose of her own soul. Alyona Ivanovna may be seen as a symbol of the crass venality Raskolnikov so hates that he has no qualms about killing her in the most brutal manner.

The usurer's half-sister, Lisaveta, is another matter. Her presence, it has been noted, seems to hover over the novel even after her death, as though the memory of her personality and tragic fate could never be erased from Raskolnikov's mind. Lisaveta was "a tall, ungainly, shy, and meek woman of almost thirty-five, almost an idiot, who was held in complete subjection by her sister, working for her day and night, bullied and even beaten by her" (I, 5). Although notorious for sexual promiscuity, Lisaveta is good, generous in her poverty, and possessed of a gentle, childlike innocence. Her almost passive stance under Raskolnikov's onslaught — as though she sensed rather than saw the murderer — suggests the blindfolded Fortune against which Raskolnikov turns his rage. When, later in the novel, Lisaveta's name is inadvertently mentioned, Raskolnikov kneels, perhaps in deference to the unpredictable power personified by Fortune.

If Raskolnikov's nature is dual and his emotions are ambivalent, the associates with whom he interacts on a plane of at least nominal equality — his mother and sister, his friend Razumikhin, the prostitute Sonia, and the investigator Porfiry Petrovich — are consistent, integrated personalities. Raskolnikov may be the author of his own punishment, but these are the vessels of his redemption and the mirrors of his soul.

A deep love-hate relationship binds the young man to his mother, Pulcheria, and his sister, Dunya, who have come to St. Petersburg at a crisis of their own affairs. His brooding on their miserable plight had already assumed the "terrifying and unfamiliar guise" of the murder that was taking shape in his mind. So strong and so contradictory are his emotions when he unexpectedly finds them waiting for him in his room, a few days after the crime, that he stands frozen on the spot, face-to-face, as it were, with his own conscience. Prevented from embracing them by a sudden, unbearable awareness of the horror he has perpetrated, Raskolnikov staggers toward them but falls to the floor in a dead faint. When he regains consciousness, his mother glimpses "poignant suffering" and "something unbending and almost insane" in her son's expression (III, 1).

Where Raskolnikov is feverish and agitated, his mother — who, he fears, may either go blind from knitting shawls and weeping, or simply waste away from lack of food — is calm and serene. She looks much younger than her forty-three years — "which," says Dostoevsky, "is almost always the case with women who keep their serenity of mind, the freshness of their impressions, and a pure and sincere warmth of heart to their old age." "We may add in parentheses," Dostoevsky continues, in a curious bit of cosmetic advice to the middle-aged woman, "that to possess all this is the only way a woman can preserve her beauty even in old age" (III, 1).

His sister Dunya, graceful and somewhat haughty in outlook and manner, has just escaped the clutches of the lascivious landowner Svidrigaylov, in whose household she had served as governess. Though anxious to protect his sister from Svidrigaylov's advances, Raskolnikov balks at surrendering her to a wealthy parvenu named Peter Luzhin, a particularly cruel and treacherous representative of bourgeois venality, to whom she has become engaged. "Love yourself before everyone else, for everything in the world is based on self-interest" is Luzhin's philosophy (II, 5).

Dunya's altruistic motive in accepting Luzhin's marriage proposal had been the hope of obtaining funds for her brother's law-school studies and getting him future work in Luzhin's legal office. But while such a marriage would offer escape from the unwelcome attentions of Svidrigaylov, it would clearly place Dunya in an equally unhappy situation. It was her personal helplessness that had first excited Luzhin's interest; he dreamed of her as a submissive wife who would regard him as her savior and look up to him, obey and admire him, humbly and reverently acknowledge him as her lord and master. Such a beautiful and virtuous wife, he had believed, would help immeasurably in furthering his own ambitions.

Raskolnikov, with an instinctive understanding of a woman's feelings, understood perfectly that for Dunya a loveless marriage to such a personage would be no less degrading than outright prostitution — that Dunya, in fact, would "rather live on bread and water than sell her own soul" (I, 4). Refusing to accept his sister's intended sacrifice, Raskolnikov deliberately insults Luzhin, provoking a rupture of the engagement and incidentally paving the way for Dunya's eventual marriage to his friend Razumikhin.

On later visits with his mother and sister, they gently try to engage Raskolnikov in conversation, but he realizes that he "would not ever be able to talk to anyone about anything" (III, 3). On the verge of falling into a deep sleep, in which he will relive the murder and all his subconscious torments, the semidelirious Raskolnikov struggles to confess and at the same time to hide his crime. "Mother, sister — how I loved them! Why do I hate them now?" he asks (III, 6). In a moving farewell scene on the day of his decision to surrender to the police, Raskolnikov kisses his mother's feet and asks for her unqualified love and her prayers.

Throughout the novel, the two women seem to embody Dostoevsky's credo that God is the only source of redemption and that through willingness to face personal suffering, humans may draw close to God. Raskolnikov both loves and hates his family — loving them because they suffer, yet hating them because he is still not prepared to accept suffering himself.

Also consistent through and through, albeit unpolished, is Razumikhin, Raskolnikov's former fellow student and Dunya's admirer and future husband. (His name derives from *razum,* the Russian word for reason.) This frank, cheerful, good-natured, and honest fellow, who "could make himself at home even on a roof," offers a refreshing change from Dunya's other followers. "Razumikhin possessed the gift of revealing his true character all at once, whatever mood he might be in, so that people soon realized who they were dealing with," Dostoevsky writes of this engaging youth.

Razumikhin dreams of establishing a publishing firm in which he and Raskolnikov will be partners — "a business of translating, publishing, and learning all at once" in which he will concern himself with "the business side of the whole thing" — another hint that this faithful friend is modeled on Mikhail Dostoevsky, who had similar qualities of amiability and obligingness. As an epitome of reason and good sense, Razumikhin serves as Dostoevsky's spokesman and commentator on the contemporary state of knowledge and progress: "What are we today?" he sensibly exclaims. "So far as science, general development, thoughts, inventions, ideals, aims, desires, liberalism, intelligence, experience ... [are] concerned, we are all ... still in the preparatory class at school. We've acquired a taste for depending on someone else's brains" (III, 1).

Razumikhin is also Dostoevsky's ideal model of friendship. In a charming and touching scene, we find him nursing the delirious Raskolnikov, putting his arm around him "as clumsily as a bear" and feeding him mouthfuls of soup, first blowing on it to make sure his sick friend does not burn his mouth. But it is in the more serious matter of Raskolnikov's guilt that his friend's unerring sense of pity and affection, as well as his sensitive intuition, are most clearly revealed.

Without the utterance of a single word, Razumikhin is able to interpret the burning, piercing facial expression with which Raskolnikov communicates the ghastly truth of the crime. From that moment, Razumikhin knows that he must assume a decisive role in the affairs of the Raskolnikov family. It will be he who intervenes when Dunya, toward the end of the novel, is again assailed by the lecherous Svidrigaylov and when Raskolnikov himself is exiled to Siberia, leaving his helpless mother and sister behind.

Arkady Ivanovich Svidrigaylov, Dunya's persecutor and one of Dostoevsky's most problematical characters, seems to have somewhat baffled even his creator, who, as though unable fully to grasp his essence, repeatedly used approximative adverbs in describing his features. Smartly dressed, handsome, but "somewhat repulsive" in aspect, Svidrigaylov had "a peculiar kind of face, which looked like a mask: white, with red cheeks, with bright red lips, a light, flaxen beard, and still very thick, fair hair. His eyes were, somehow, a little too blue, and their expression was, somehow, too heavy and motionless" (VI, 3).

Still erotically obsessed with Dunya even after her dismissal from his household by his jealous wife, Svidrigaylov theatrically reappears, in the fourth part of the novel, on the threshold of Raskolnikov's room — a fitting conclusion to the nightmare in which Raskolnikov has just been reenacting his murderous deed. Explaining that he has come to seek the young man's help in a matter concerning his sister, the visitor plunges into a lengthy autobiography from which he emerges as, in his own words, "an idle and immoral man," utterly indifferent to evil. He lives in the depths of a pathological boredom, relieved only by the visitations of persons whose death he has caused. He has strange notions about human psychology ("from time to time women find it very pleasant indeed to be humiliated"), and even stranger ones about the mysteries of life, death, and eternity: "What if... you suddenly find just a little room there, something like a village bathhouse, grimy, and spiders in every corner, and that's all eternity is" (IV, 1).

Like Raskolnikov, Svidrigaylov neither repents of his misdeeds — he has indirectly caused the death of his wife and a servant — nor does he consider himself a criminal. Before undertaking "a certain journey" he has planned, he has called on Raskolnikov in order to make some "preliminary arrangements," including an offer to Dunya of ten thousand rubles to atone for the embarrassment and worry he has caused her and to enable her to break with Luzhin, her objectionable fiancé.

His gesture seems to suggest that though immoral and somewhat mad, Svidrigaylov is no more devoid of altruistic sentiments than is Raskolnikov himself, with whom he claims to have much in common. Svidrigaylov, however, is quite unlike Raskolnikov in his unashamed sexual obsessions. To the younger man, he is nothing but "a low, depraved sensualist... a dirty villain and voluptuous *roué* and a scoundrel" (VI, 5). Having learned of Raskolnikov's guilt by eavesdropping on a private conversation, Svidrigaylov reveals his true colors in an unsuccessful attempt to use the secret as a means of pressure on Dunya — who, however, summons all her resolution and successfully resists his advances.

The last night of Svidrigaylov's existence, unfolding in macabre hallucinations and reminiscences of past misdeeds, is passed in a grimy hotel where the landowner shares his miserable bedsheets with a scampering mouse — the animal that has been seen as a reflection of Dostoevsky's obsession with the voluptuousness of evil and the morbid enjoyment of viscid horror. Svidrigaylov's tragic career is ended by the bullet he puts through his head under a high watchtower near the river Neva — the point of embarkation for the "certain journey" he has been planning.

Raskolnikov, in contrast, is more consistent in his invocation of those abstract principles that, he sincerely believes, will lead to the betterment of humankind; but he is waylaid by Satan, who tempts him into the folly of a double murder. Unlike Svidrigaylov, he will reject suicide and find the courage to confess his crime, accept his punishment, and live out his tragic destiny despite what he at first sees as its "absurdity."

Another of the puzzling "preliminary arrangements" made by Svidrigaylov was a guarantee of moral and financial support for the poverty-stricken Marmeladov family, another of the constituent elements of this rich and multilayered novel. Marmeladov, the chronic drunkard of another work of fiction Dostoevsky incorporated into *Crime and Punishment,* had been killed — or perhaps had willfully sought escape — in a street accident in which he had been trampled under horses' hoofs; and Svidrigaylov, before his suicide, not only placed substantial funds in trust for the small Marmeladov orphans but also made provision for rescuing Sonia, the older daughter, from the quagmire of prostitution.

A retired titular counselor long since reduced to penury and alcoholism, Marmeladov had experienced every feeling of degradation in his unequal struggle to preserve his human dignity. Invariably he wore an old tuxedo with only one button, just to "be correct." It was this humiliated individual whom Raskolnikov had encountered in a tavern just after a preliminary visit to the scene of his intended crime. He had found himself unwillingly drawn toward the drunkard, who leaned his elbows on the dirty table, his head in his hands, an anguished look on his face. "It's not joy I thirst for, but sorrow and tears," he had told his reluctant listener.

Confessing all his failures and his sense of guilt, Marmeladov is the first to enunciate an idea that runs through the novel like a leitmotiv: "Poverty is not a crime." "Drunkenness isn't a virtue either," he continues, "but chronic destitution is a crime. When you're poor, you're still able to preserve the innate nobility of your feelings, but when you're destitute you never can. For being destitute a man is not even driven out with a stick, but is swept out with a broom from the society of decent people in the most humiliating way possible.... [W]hen I'm down and out I'm ready to be the first to humiliate myself. Hence the pub!" (I, 2).

A drunkard out of despair, Marmeladov takes voluptuous pleasure in being beaten and humiliated by his wife, Katerina Ivanovna, an "educated woman of high character," who, through misery and illness, has also been reduced to a situation of utter despair. The mother of three small children, she can await nothing but madness and a hideous death from tuberculosis. Roaming the streets of St. Petersburg with her costumed children, forcing them to perform and sing in the hope of earning a few coins, Katerina Ivanovna succumbs to a pitiless fate and leaves her orphans at the mercy of the hostile city.

The poverty of the Marmeladovs, it has been noted, contrasts with that of Raskolnikov by reason of their powerlessness as compared with the latter's relative powerfulness. Whereas the Marmeladov family has been thrust inexorably into drunkenness and prostitution, Raskolnikov can at least enjoy his freedom and detachment from the society he detests. Yet even Raskolnikov must yield to the overpowering aura of love and affection radiated by the younger Marmeladovs. The ten-year-old Polya, crying softly over the loss of her father, nestles in Raskolnikov's arms, hugging and kissing him hungrily in what becomes a first turning point in the life of the bloodstained criminal. Pressing his unshaven face close to Polya's, he pleads, "Darling Polya...please say a prayer for me, too, sometimes — 'and thy servant Rodion' — and nothing more" (II, 7).

But it is eighteen-year-old Sonia, Marmeladov's attractive, blond, blue-eyed daughter by a previous marriage, who will ultimately bring about Raskolnikov's redemption and salvation. Even before the story opens, Sonia has been goaded by her distraught stepmother to go on the streets to try to earn money for the starving family. And, since their landlady would not tolerate the presence of "a certified woman of the streets," Sonia had been forced to find damp and smoky quarters of her own — a scantily furnished room "rather like a shed" — where her father visited her only to filch money to support his own vice.

Sonia has submitted to her life of sin and shame, passively accepting the terrible consequences her father's drunkenness has settled on the family. Although as a prostitute she is in league with "sinners," she is instinctively guided by an innate generosity and selflessness; she nurtures "*insatiable* compassion" even for the unsympathetic stepmother who has set her on the path of destruction. As a pattern of resignation, love, and forgiveness, Sonia makes no personal claims; love, brotherhood, and human solidarity are instinctive in her. Simple and innocent, she is perhaps the supreme representative of Dostoevsky's "meek" or "gentle" creatures who symbolize all of suffering humanity.[2]

The absence of any reference to Sonia in Dostoevsky's 1865 letter to Katkov suggests that the figure of the redeeming prostitute did not appear significantly in the first version of *Crime and Punishment*. In the extant version, however, Sonia's role is crucial to the explication and ultimate resolution of Raskolnikov's inner turmoil. More than the members of his own family, more than any representative of law and justice, it is Sonia who will redeem Raskolnikov's life, deepen his self-knowledge, and lead the way along the path of repentance. "It was to her, Sonia, that he had gone with his first confession; when he was in need of the companionship of a human being, it was in her that he found the human being; and she would be with him wherever he might be" (VI, 8).

Why did Dostoevsky choose a prostitute as the sole person to whom Raskolnikov can speak freely, to whom he can relate, and with whom he can interact to the exclusion of all others? His choice, reminiscent in some ways of the earlier *Notes from Underground* (see chapter 11), may perhaps find an explanation in what has been hinted at concerning the author's own life. Familiarity with the world of prostitution had represented an important stage in Dostoevsky's spiritual progress and understanding. His contacts with the prostitutes of the Russian capital had changed and enriched his human psychology, impelling him to reflect on suffering, sin, and social misery. To him, they represented important milestones along the path to self-knowledge and ultimate reconciliation with God and humanity. Undeterred by social taboos, Dostoevsky enjoyed his "natural" experiences with prostitutes, who helped him in gaining access to a community of persons well versed in faith and charity. His bitter and tragic "underground man," in contrast, illustrates the inability of an overweening egotist to respond to the genuine love offered him by a woman of that class.

The fateful mystery that culminated in Sonia's decision to go on the street inspires Raskolnikov not only with respect for her personal dignity but also, perhaps at an unconscious level, with curiosity about the parallel mystery culminating in his own decision to commit murder. He sees both himself and Sonia as outcasts, in spite of valuable human qualities, from among those whom society deems worthy of consideration.

The scene in which Sonia puts Raskolnikov's true feelings to their first test is generally accounted the pivotal episode of *Crime and Punishment* (IV, 4). When Raskolnikov visits her a few days af-

ter the still unconfessed murder, she bemoans the dire events that
have befallen her family; and Raskolnikov gibes at her, grinning
callously and painting a black picture of her future and that of her
sister Polya in the "nasty, stinking sty" of prostitution. Confronted
by Sonia's calm assurance that God is their recourse, the visitor attempts to bring her to doubt the existence of a God who allows
so many abominations on earth. Sonia, unable to counter his well-
turned arguments, bursts into tears as her tormentor laughs in cruel
triumph. But then, moved by the girl's infinite sorrow, his lips trembling convulsively, Raskolnikov bows down and kisses her foot in
a Christ-like gesture so out of keeping with his usual behavior that
Sonia recoils as from a madman. And, indeed, Raskolnikov at that
moment looks like a madman, caught in an insane struggle between
the promptings of his mind and heart on the one hand and the devil
seeking his soul on the other.

To Sonia's admonition that he must not bow before a dishonorable
creature and a "great, great sinner," Raskolnikov replies, "I did not
bow down to you. I bowed down to all suffering humanity." "It is
quite true that you are a great sinner," he says.

And do you know why...? Because you have betrayed and ruined yourself
for nothing.... It is horrible that you should live in this filth which you hate
and at the same time know yourself...that you are not helping anyone
by it and that you are not saving anyone from anything.... How can such
shame and such disgrace live in you side by side with your other quite different and holy feelings? Would it not have been a thousand times more just and
more sensible to throw yourself into the river and finish it all at one blow?

In reality, Raskolnikov knows that Sonia's pure soul lacks the arrogant pride that is needed for a person to take his own life; he knows,
too, that he himself had refused that option. In questioning her will
to live, Raskolnikov seems to be trying to probe his own heart and
his own will to survive.

Noticing a copy of the New Testament — a gift, Sonia tells him,
from the murdered Lisaveta — Raskolnikov asks her to find "the
place about the raising of Lazarus." Here, it has been observed, is
spun an intricate web uniting the murdered victim (Lisaveta), the
murderer (analogous to the dead Lazarus), and his resuscitator (Sonia), as all three join in what amounts to a "behold the Lord"
happening. Sonia reads aloud the eleventh chapter of St. John's
Gospel, slowly and distinctly, the value and power of her voice
and body uniting to act out the supernatural event. Raskolnikov

is struck with amazement at her exaltation and joyous anticipation of the miracle.

In these pages, Dostoevsky brings out the innate skill of the unschooled, uneducated, and unsophisticated Sonia in arousing the sensitivity of the educated man to the wonders of speech. The *Word* as Logos — a divine gift to humans — is frequently stressed throughout the novel: the illusion of *words* versus reality; the *new word* as synonymous with a new order; the *word* as revelatory of true inner feelings, etc. Mediated through Sonia's evangelical spirit, the Gospel — the expressed mind and will of God — turns Raskolnikov toward Christ. Ultimately, he too will be resuscitated, like Lazarus, and reintegrated into the Russian national community through the miracle of the *word*. Such is the essence of this crucial scene, in a dingy room bathed in a poetic atmosphere where "the murderer and the harlot . . . met so strangely over the reading of the eternal book."

Revealing to Sonia that he has now broken definitively with his family, Raskolnikov attempts to link himself to the young girl: "I have only you now. . . . Let's go together. . . . We're both damned. . . . All I know is that we must go the same way. . . . We've one goal before us!" Yet he remains ambiguous, underlining on the one hand his Christlike attitudes ("We have to break with what must be broken with once and for all . . . and we have to take the suffering upon ourselves"), while on the other he is still obsessed with "freedom and power — power above all. Power over all the trembling vermin and over all the anthill. That's our goal."

Thoroughly dazed by his strange words, Sonia is even more confounded and horrified when Raskolnikov tells her that if he returns on the morrow, he will reveal the name of Lisaveta's murderer. And he does return, with the double purpose of tormenting her afresh and of asking her forgiveness for his cruelty. A prey to constant ambivalence and extreme emotion, Raskolnikov at one moment is overcome by a sensation of bitter hatred for Sonia; yet, in looking intently at her anxious expression, he finally realizes that "there was love in that look"; whereupon "his hatred vanished like a phantom. It was not hatred at all: he had mistaken one feeling for another. It merely meant that *the* moment had come."

As the two confront each other face-to-face, just as Razumikhin had learned of his friend's guilt without a single word being spoken, Sonia now divines that Raskolnikov, the man she loves, is himself the murderer of the usurer and her sister. "Her feeling of horror suddenly communicated itself to him; exactly the same expression of terror appeared on his face; he, too, stared at her in the same way" (V, 4). The two sinners are one person reflected in a single image.

Embracing and kissing him, sobbing hysterically, Sonia understands that Raskolnikov is truly the unhappiest man in the world. She drops to her knees before this suffering man who has hopelessly lost his battle for separation from others. "A feeling he had not known for a long time overwhelmed him entirely, and at once softened his heart. He did not resist it: tears started in his eyes and hung on his eyelashes" (V, 4). He begs her not to leave him; she pledges to remain forever at his side — even to follow him to prison in Siberia.

But now Sonia seeks to probe the reasons for the suffering man's crime. His varied explanations, ranging from a banal need for money to an altruistic desire to help his hungry mother, culminate in what he describes as a misguided attempt at self-validation: "I wanted to *dare* and — and I committed a murder. I only wanted to dare, Sonia, that was my only motive!...I wanted to murder, Sonia, to murder without casuistry, to murder for my own satisfaction, for myself alone....I had to find out...whether I was a louse like the rest or a man."

In gloomy exaltation, Raskolnikov tries to analyze the growing bitterness and spleen that had led him to set himself apart, skulking "like a spider" in his low-ceilinged hovel. Instead of studying, he confesses, he had sold his books; instead of seeking employment, he had preferred to lie on his couch and think about "the people" — fools who never change — and nurture his own need to commit an act of daring. "He who is firm and strong in mind and spirit will be [the] master [of the people]," he tells Sonia. "He who dares much is right....He who dismisses with contempt what men regard as sacred becomes their lawgiver, and he who dares more than anyone is more right than anyone." How sadly does Sonia realize that "this gloomy expression of faith was Raskolnikov's religion and his law" (V, 4).

At the end of his long tirade, his face hideously contorted with despair, Raskolnikov turns to Sonia to seek an answer. What should he do now? Her eyes flashing fire, Sonia proclaims the Christian message. He must immediately go to stand at the crossroads, prostrate himself, kiss the earth he has defiled, and bow down to all four corners of the world, saying to all men aloud, "I am a murderer!" This is the only way, Sonia maintains, that he can relieve his soul. "Then God will send you life again....Accept suffering and be redeemed by it — that's what you must do."

Sonia nourishes a genuine belief in God's goodness; she believes that humans have an urgent need to confess, ask pardon of others, put themselves in a position of inferiority. Raskolnikov, for the second time, is struck with amazement at Sonia's exaltation and the power of her *words*. It is as though Christ had whispered his secret to her, investing her with authority to demand Raskolnikov's self-denunciation. Sonia seems in league with Christ himself, the source of her convictions and her fortitude.

After the all-important confession scene, Raskolnikov wanders aimlessly through the streets, possessed by a feeling of dreary desolation and discerning only a dismal future — "a sort of 'eternity on a square yard of space' " (V, 5). The reader glimpses Raskolnikov's existential anguish in the oppressive feeling of "an idiotic and purely physical malady, caused by a sunset." Returning to his "cupboard," he receives a visit from Porfiry Petrovich, the fat, round little police investigator, small of stature but of great astuteness, with whom he deliberately enters into a game of thrust and parry, flirting with danger in a cat-and-mouse duel that will unfold through chapter after chapter.

Porfiry, like Svidrigaylov, is a figure hard to define. As representative of law and justice, he seems a genuine believer in God and appears truly concerned about Raskolnikov, who, however, regards his examiner with "disgust and undisguised hatred." Dostoevsky seems not without sympathy for his personified rubber ball, "rolling in different directions and rebounding all at once from every wall and corner." Allowing Porfiry to describe himself as "a figure that arouses nothing but comic ideas in people. A buffoon" (V, 5), the novelist does not lack respect for the "profound psychological methods" by which the investigator keeps his suspect in a "state of continual terror and suspense" until he eventually turns himself in.

"You see," Porfiry explains,

he [the criminal] won't run away from me because there's no place to run to. He won't run away from me *psychologically*...even if he had some place to run to, because of a law of nature. Ever watched a moth before a lighted candle? Well, he, too, will be circling round and round me like a moth round a candle. He'll get sick of his freedom. He'll start brooding. He'll get himself so thoroughly entangled that he won't be able to get out. He'll worry himself to death. And what's more...he'll keep on describing circles around me, smaller and smaller circles, till — bang! he'll fly straight into my mouth and I'll swallow him! (IV, 5)

Porfiry understands how to play upon Raskolnikov's most sensitive trait, his obsession with the "exceptional" man. Shrewdly referring back to Raskolnikov's published article, the investigator undertakes to demonstrate the weakness of "the man who is an *exceptional* case." "[He will] tell his lie wonderfully well, most cunningly, in fact," Porfiry says,

so that it would seem that he had scored a real triumph and could henceforth enjoy the fruits of his wit — but, bang! off he goes in a faint at the most interesting and most inappropriate moment.... He'll turn pale ... as though in mere play; but, unfortunately, he'll turn pale *too naturally* ... and again he arouses suspicion.... Comes [to] himself and starts demanding why he has not been arrested long ago.... Human nature is a mirror, sir. A mirror, clear and smooth. Look into it and marvel.... But why have you gone so pale, my dear fellow?

Overcome with emotion and involuntarily following Porfiry's own script, Raskolnikov protests:

Porfiry Petrovich, I ... I can see very clearly ... that you really suspect me of the murder of that old woman and her sister Lisaveta.... If you think that you have a legal right to charge me with the murder, then charge me with it. If you want to arrest me, then arrest me. But I shall not permit you to laugh in my face and torment me.

Some writers have seen a good deal of Dostoevsky himself in Porfiry's subtle psychologizing, especially in his judgment of Raskolnikov's crime and of his moral need for atonement. But there is an alternative view that holds that Porfiry's devious inquisitorial methods make a travesty of real justice — that, in fact, the villainous Porfiry sadistically abuses his power, indecently enjoys Raskolnikov's agony and, incidentally, drives to *his* breaking point a young workman who, after having been wrongly accused of the same crime, makes a false confession out of mere terror.[3]

But where Porfiry's tactics and methods fail, Sonia's succeed. For it is only after making his confession to the prostitute and doing his public penance, to the jeers of the passersby, that Raskolnikov will surrender himself to the investigator. Porfiry will maintain to the end that the criminal *"can't do without us"* (VI, 2); but this is true only in the sense that Raskolnikov, like a Prometheus or a Sisyphus seeking punishment from the gods, cannot "do without" the expiation of his crime. The epilogue to *Crime and Punishment* offers a glimpse of the eagle gnawing at the vitals of this Prometheus, of the stone this Sisyphus must incessantly roll to the summit, until his tragic plight is ultimately resolved through the sovereign power of love. Like much else in Dostoevsky's literary output, this epilogue has been the subject of diametrically opposed evaluations. Some see it as a mere appendage, lacking congruity with the rest of the novel and hastily written to satisfy an editorial requirement. Others consider it the very key to the author's intentions and the culmination of the novel's entire movement.[4] In its pages, based in large part on Dostoevsky's own prison experience, the novelist accompanies Raskolnikov toward the recognition and avowal of his guilt, foreshadowing the spiritual change occurring in his mind and heart under the influence of Sonia's calm, courageous love.

In the opening paragraph of the epilogue, the reader's eye is guided from the vast to the particular. "Siberia" telescopes into "the banks of a broad, deserted river," where "there stands a town"; in the town, "there is a fortress"; in the fortress, a prison, and in the prison, Rodion Romanovich Raskolnikov. There, Raskolnikov falls "ill from wounded pride." The true source of his illness, it appears, is his inability to understand why he should be a helpless plaything of the gods, why all his efforts to escape the situation should have been in vain. "What he was ashamed of was that he, Raskolnikov, should have perished so utterly, so hopelessly, and so stupidly because of some blind decision of fate, and that he should have to humble himself and admit to the *absurdity* of that sort of decision."

Contemplating the desolate steppe in this mood of frustration, Raskolnikov notes the approach of a thin, pale, shabbily dressed figure who turns out to be an evanescent, almost unreal Sonia. She has followed him to Siberia, and though her physical strength is being sapped by hardship, she seems to possess unlimited spiritual resources and all the fortitude that is needed to give Raskolnikov the courage to face his tragedy. Sonia releases the man she loves from his morbid oppression; she lightens his burden by making her own heavier; she dispels his frightening nightmares by appearing at his side, overflowing with gentleness and love.

Raskolnikov's long-awaited redemption, the final integration of his heart, mind, and soul, takes place during Sonia's visit. When the guard's back is turned, Raskolnikov lowers his eyes, throws himself at Sonia's feet, and weeps as he embraces her knees. Sonia understands that the moment she has waited for has finally arrived. Tears well in the eyes of the criminal and of the harlot. Pale and thin, with ravaged faces, they turn together toward "the dawn of a new future, of a full resurrection to a new life.... It was love that brought them back to life: the heart of one held inexhaustible sources of life for the heart of the other." Having accomplished his pilgrimage in the company of Sonia, "the sinner," Raskolnikov is restored to a better, higher, more worthy state and has earned the right to return to the human fold. Love, the miracle of reciprocal love, allows him to be reborn.

3

Poor Folk (1846)

Years before *Crime and Punishment* was written, Dostoevsky's sympathy for the weak and oppressed had found expression in the three lesser novels that preceded its composition. As their titles imply, *Poor Folk*, *Netochka Nezvanova* (roughly translatable as Nameless Nobody, 1849), and *The Insulted and Injured* (1861) all revolve largely around the themes of poverty, humiliation, and social ills.

"I have a most brilliant future before me!" the twenty-five-year-old Dostoevsky wrote his brother Mikhail of the enthusiastic welcome accorded by St. Petersburg society to his first major work, the sentimental tragicomedy entitled *Poor Folk*. In a series of letters supposedly exchanged between a pedantic, down-at-heels government clerk and a young girl half his age, *Poor Folk* records the course of an unhappy love affair and illustrates the oppressive conditions and social inequities prevailing in the reign of the autocratic Tsar Nicholas I.

Makar Alekseyevich Devushkin, the homely and timid petty clerk who has worked for almost thirty years as a copyist of official documents, still trembles in the presence of his superiors. Imperfectly educated, humiliated by poverty, ridiculed by his fellow workers, he has withdrawn from society and set himself to cultivate a meaningful inner life in complete solitude. Until recently, he had lived in a place of "absolute stillness [where] if a fly took wing it could plainly be heard buzzing." Now, however, he has moved to a tenement building in St. Petersburg's slums, where "all is turmoil and shouting and clatter." One of his letters describes the building in its sordid detail:

The scullery . . . is greasy, dirty, and odoriferous, while the stairs are in rags, and the walls so covered with filth that the hand sticks fast wherever it touches them. Also, on each landing, there is a medley of boxes, chairs, and dilapidated wardrobes; while the windows have had most of their panes shattered, and everywhere stand washtubs filled with dirt, litter, eggshells, and fish-bladders. The smell is abominable. . . . Each of [the rooms] seems to contain something which gives forth a rank, sickly-sweet odor... but a couple of minutes will suffice to dissipate it, for the reason that *everything* here smells... and one grows accustomed to the rankness.... Every morning, when fish or beef is being cooked, and washing and scrubbing are in progress, the house is filled with steam.

But "one can grow used to anything," Devushkin concludes in a typical attempt at self-deception reinforced by the approach of spring (April 12).

Why has Devushkin chosen to live in this smelly, noisy tenement? Because the window of his adored young lady, Varvara Alexievna Dobroselova, is located just across the courtyard, where he can see her whenever she passes. Through Varvara — whose feelings for him are merely those of gratitude and affection — Devushkin has experienced an emotional rebirth.

For until you came into my life I had been a lonely man — I had been, as it were, asleep rather than alive. In former days my rascally colleagues used to tell me that I was unfit even to be seen; in fact they so disliked me that at length I began to dislike myself, for, being frequently told that I was stupid, I began to believe that I really was so. But the instant that *you* came into my life, you lightened both my heart and my soul" (August 21).

The enamored copyist has devised a "clever plan" for exchanging messages across the courtyard, without effort or outlay on Varvara's part. By raising or lowering her curtain, she can indicate that her thoughts are with him, signal that she is well and happy, or tell him it is time for him to go to bed. Why is this discreet mode of communication needed? Because Devushkin fears "gossip and scandal," and it is too light to slip across the courtyard unobserved during Petersburg's cursed "white nights." Despite Varvara's repeated invitations, his excessive timidity restrains him from visiting her. Only when she falls seriously ill can he momentarily overcome his caution, ministering to her assiduously until he realizes that "people [are] beginning to notice things."

Although Devushkin cuts a ridiculous figure as a lover, he does possess both a poetic soul and a strong sense of human dignity. His letters reveal deep feeling and exquisite delicacy. Dominated by pity and affection for the sickly, submissive, pure-minded Varvara, he considers it a duty as well as a pleasure to lighten her toilsome existence. Untiringly he invents ways of pleasing her, sending her little gifts of potted geraniums, sweets, and grapes that he can ill afford. She in turn expresses her concern over his weak eyes, observing that his candle burns until midnight as he pores over his work and the books they exchange. Both are tender and affectionate creatures, captives of their poverty but solicitous for each other and well endowed with the good qualities Dostoevsky believes to exist potentially in every human being.

From the girlhood diary that Varvara sends her friend to beguile his lonely hours, Devushkin learns that after a happy childhood in the provinces, her family had been forced to move to St. Petersburg, where they had encountered "nothing but rain, bitter autumn frosts, dull skies, ugliness, and crowds of strangers who looked hostile, discontented, and disposed to take offense" (June 1). After her father's death, the fifteen-year-old Varvara and her mother had moved into the home of one Anna Feodorovna, a distant relative who had turned out to be a vicious procuress and had maneuvered the innocent Varvara into becoming the mistress of a wealthy landowner, Bykov.

In Anna Feodorovna's home there had resided also a poor, consumptive student, named Petrovsky, who was actually an illegitimate offspring of this same Bykov. That personage, without the boy's being aware of their relationship, had paid for his studies and secured him a place as tutor to Anna Feodorovna's niece in exchange for his board and lodging. Petrovsky, however, imagined his father to be an unkempt, amorphous, strange-looking old man, Zakhar Petrovich by name, whose frequent visits caused him acute embarrassment. The ailing student could feel no filial respect for this pitiful drunkard and buffoon who tried so hard to preserve his dignity and shower affection on his "son."

Young Petrovsky dies, and in one of the novel's most moving scenes, the old man runs after the hearse that is bearing him to the cemetery through a heavy downpour. Books protrude from all his pockets as he strains to keep up with the hearse, drawn by trotting horses. The books are volumes he has salvaged from Petrovsky's collection, and include a complete edition of Pushkin's works that he and Varvara had offered the dying young man as a birthday present.

Varvara, of course, had been in love with the younger Petrovsky, and it is his death and that of her own mother that have driven her from Anna Feodorovna's home to the lodging where she now ekes out a straitened existence by taking in embroidery work. And here, Devushkin's "acts of charity" toward the forlorn girl have presently reduced him to such poverty that he can see no outlet and, in despair, takes to drink. Varvara understands that she must somehow cease to be a burden to him, but she too is ill and Devushkin is soon faced with the horror of having to try to borrow money for her immediate needs.

In another comic yet heartbreaking scene, the wet, bedraggled borrower humbly approaches the moneylender's residence. A dog attacks him, and he upsets some milk jugs being filled by an old woman. Eventually, he is escorted into the usurer's waiting room, which he finds embellished with severe-looking military portraits. "I had better come again tomorrow," Devushkin reasons, "for the weather may then be better, and I shall not have upset the milk, and these generals will not be looking at me so fiercely" (August 15).

The pathetic copyist is further tormented by the mockery of his fellow lodgers over a florid billet-doux addressed to Varvara that had inadvertently dropped from his pocket. "O beloved, what laughter there arose at the recital!" he writes her. "How those scoundrels mocked at and derided you and myself!" Unable to gain the respect of others, he laments his inability to protect the young girl either socially or economically. He feels that he himself is rated lower than the mat on which his fellow workers wipe their boots.

Varvara, the voice of reason, sensibly reproves him: "You are not only driving me to distraction but also ruining yourself with this eternal solicitude for your reputation. You are a man of honor, nobility of character, and self-respect...; yet at any moment you are ready to die with shame!" Exhorting him to give up his alcoholic "debauchery," she begs him to "be your better self once more — the self which can still remain firm in the face of misfortune. Poverty is no crime." Stronger, more determined than he, she urges him to visit her and bring "sincere repentance and trust in God" (August 14) — two of the leitmotivs that will be further developed in *Crime and Punishment*.

Not doubting the sagacity of Varvara's words, Devushkin nevertheless remains perplexed about the supposed justice of the social order. "Why should I mind the soles of my feet coming through my boots?" he asks rhetorically. "The sole of one's foot is a mere bagatelle — it will never be anything but just a base, dirty sole.... Yet why...should I be insulted and despised because of them?" And how is it, he asks Varvara, "that *you* are so unfortunate? How is it that *you* are so much worse off than other people? In my eyes you are kindhearted, beautiful and clever; why, then, has such an evil fate fallen to your lot? How comes it that you are left desolate — you, so good a human being! while to others happiness comes without an invitation at all?...why should that raven, Fate, croak out upon the fortunes of one person while she is yet in her mother's womb, while another person it permits to go forth in happiness from the home which has reared her?"

Like Raskolnikov, though in a much humbler tone and with no thought of personally attacking the problem of an unjust social order, Devushkin ruminates upon the way fate denies to some the very means of survival. Comparing himself to the organ grinder — an "honorable pauper" who suffers hunger even though he works all day according to his capabilities — Devushkin feebly protests that "more could be asked of no one, nor ought I to be adjudged to do more" (September 5).

The emphasis of the novel now shifts from the theme of poverty as such to focus on one of its more sinister consequences, the loss of individual independence and personal integrity. With the approach of St. Petersburg's dull, damp, and dark September, Devushkin's mind is increasingly troubled. His thoughts recur to his childhood in the beauty and mystery of the countryside. The more vividly the past stands out before him, the dimmer and darker seems the present. Increasingly fearful of death, he twice refers to the existence of a "double" in his life. "I have been afraid to be left by myself," he writes, "for I keep fancying there is someone else in the room, and that someone is speaking to me." Summoned by a superior about an error in his work, he confesses that, "I was greatly ashamed of my appearance (a glance into the mirror ... had frightened me with the reflection of myself that it presented) ... I had always been accustomed to comport myself as though no such person as I existed" (September 9).

It is in this already precarious state of mind that Devushkin receives the shattering news of Varvara's impending marriage to her former patron, the crude and wealthy Bykov, who has now formally sought her hand and invited her to share his wealth and hunt hares with him on his estate in the steppes. Varvara knows that Bykov's only purpose is to obtain a legal heir in order to disinherit a worthless nephew; yet she sees no reasonable alternative to accepting his humiliating proposal. Her poor health, her present helplessness, and the possibility of reestablishing her social position leave her no choice, she explains to Devushkin. Insisting that her decision will ease her friend's lot as well, she assures him that the marriage plans are irrevocable.

"I should have come to the church tomorrow, but, alas! shall be prevented from doing so by the pain in my loins," Devushkin writes on September 29, the day before the ceremony. The reader can imagine the tears welling in the poor clerk's eyes as he writes his

first and last lie: "You must be of good cheer, my darling. *I am so,
and shall always be so long as you are happy.*" He himself will move
into Varvara's old room, he tells her. "Yesterday I inspected your
empty room in detail, and inspected your embroidery-frame, with
the work still hanging on it ... and saw that you had used one of my
letters for a spool upon which to wind your thread"—cruel proof,
it would seem, that Devushkin is no longer a significant presence
in Varvara's life.

To material want is now added, for Devushkin, the moral distress
that will culminate in loss of heart and self-respect and a relapse into
chronic alcoholism. The two epistolary lovers must part forever; Devushkin's dream of winning Varvara is ended; he is left crushed and
lonely in the drab underground existence that is the lot of St. Petersburg's poor. Her last letter, in which she bids her "only friend"
farewell, is filled with expressions of gratitude: "You alone have
loved me.... But now you must forget me.... How lonely you will
be!... kind, inestimable, but solitary, friend of mine."

His reply, the final letter in the book, is full of romantic declama-
tion: "Would that they had torn my heart out of my breast rather
than have you taken away from me!... It must be that you are being
abducted against your will ... it must be that—that you *love* me ... I
will go with you; I will run behind your carriage if you will not take
me—yes, I will run, and run so long as the power is in me, and until
my breath shall have failed.... When you are gone ... I shall die—
for certain I shall die, for my heart cannot bear this misery. I love
you as I love the light of God; I love you as my own daughter; to
you I have devoted my love in its entirety; only for you have I lived
at all." The reader may note a parallel between Devushkin's words
in 1846 and Dostoevsky's own behavior as Marya Dmitrievna and
her husband drove away from Semipalatinsk some nine years later.

Devushkin's tormented mind is now invaded by wish-fulfilling
fantasy: "The floods will stop your carriage. No sooner will it have
passed the city barriers than it will break down.... For what is he to
you, this Monsieur [Bykov]? Why has he suddenly become so dear
to your heart? Is it because he can buy you gewgaws? ... One should
consider human life rather than mere finery." Poor Devushkin's frenzied love can be expressed only in writing, and only through words
can he muster all his inner resources: "I am writing merely for the
sake of writing, and to put as much as possible into this last letter
of mine.... Ah, dearest, my pet, my own darling!" (September 30).

Its obvious sentimentalism aside, the special merit of *Poor Folk*
lies in the way in which Dostoevsky can combine a simple but mov-

ing story with a devastating critique of the heartless, indifferent society amid which he himself had come to maturity. Devushkin may be an insignificant, low-ranking clerk, but he has a depth of soul that finds expression in tender and self-sacrificing love. Through him, Dostoevsky offers insights into the torments of the humiliated "man of peaceable disposition, like all men of small stature." Although Devushkin scarcely expects his voice to be heard, he raises it in protest against the indifference of the rich and powerful to the misery that plagues him and Varvara and fills him with indignation.

Might Varvara have saved Devushkin from his sorry fate by rejecting Bykov, whose short temper, ill humor, and possessive spirit manifested themselves even before the wedding? Her behavior has been interpreted in opposite ways. Some view her as a submissive, sexually oppressed female, a persecuted heroine forced into prostitution by family circumstances, a victim of the sinister procuress who sold her to the wealthy libertine. To this sickly orphan, whose very life is at the mercy of her creditors, marriage to Bykov offered not only a reasonable solution to her own plight but also a means of alleviating the burden placed on Devushkin's shoulders.

Others, however, have taxed Varvara with "shabby egotism" or "cold despotism"; and it must be acknowledged that she is far more pragmatic and less sentimental than her elderly admirer. When she expresses a desire for a bouquet of roses, or sends him running errands for her trousseau of "frills and fripperies," she may be manifesting mere thoughtless insensibility; but it may also be because she knows that the fulfillment of her wishes brings him immeasurable joy. "I have throughout known how well you love me," she acknowledges. "A single smile of mine, a single stroke from my pen, has been able to make you happy" (September 30).

Inordinately preoccupied as he is with his appearance and reputation, Devushkin's poverty seems only to heighten his need for self-esteem and his thirst for dignity as a man. He knows he needs boots — which cost more than he can afford — to protect himself against the malicious tongues of his fellow-workers: "Boots... are necessary to maintain one's dignity and good name.... If one has holes in one's boots, both are lost." Worn-out boots and loose buttons are recurring symbolic images in the novel. "My boots are wearing through and have lost every button," he laments; "one blushes when one can see one's naked toes projecting through one's boots, and one's buttons hanging by a single thread!" (August 1). But despite his poverty, Devushkin's infinite compassion and generosity anticipate a well-known phrase in Dostoevsky's later novel,

The Insulted and Injured: "One learns that the most downtrodden, humblest man is a man, too, and a brother."

To the protagonist of *Poor Folk*, it is a truism that "once a man has lost his self-respect... he falls headlong, and cannot choose but to do so." By the time of *The Insulted and Injured,* however, fifteen years have passed and Dostoevsky has come to feel that the process of degeneration is not necessarily ineluctable but can be a matter of free choice. In a curious evocation of the earlier novel, the shady but sympathetic Masloboev in *The Insulted and Injured* says of *Poor Folk:* "When I read [it], I almost became a respectable man....I was almost becoming one, but I thought better of it, and preferred to remain a disreputable man."

4

Netochka Nezvanova (1849)

Netochka Nezvanova, Dostoevsky's second and unfinished novel, was originally conceived as a work of great scope in a form its author described as "a confession, like *Golyadkin* [*The Double*]" (*Letters,* I, 150). Work on this grandiose production was begun as early as 1846 but was repeatedly interrupted and in the end remained unfinished owing to the author's arrest, trial, and exile to Siberia. It did, however, mark an important forward step in Dostoevsky's literary career at the very time when his worldly prospects were being blasted by the government's antirevolutionary crackdown. In contrast to *Poor Folk,* Dostoevsky this time gave life to a heroine who was no longer a paradigm of humility and submissiveness but a strong-willed young lady who refused to yield to adverse fortune.

The first part of Netochka's fragmentary "confession" relates, in the simplest of autobiographical language, the story of a child who is born of humble parents and passes her early childhood in an abject poverty not unlike that of the Marmeladovs in *Crime and Punishment.* Originally intended as the prologue to a major novel in six parts, this introductory section sounds a number of themes that will later appear and reappear in Dostoevsky's mature works. It also sets the pattern for a series of triangular relationships that will provide a framework for the development of Netochka's own personality.

Netochka's opening sentences delineate the first of the triangles of which she has a clear recollection: "I cannot remember my father. He died when I was two years old. My mother remarried, but it was a marriage that brought her great suffering. . . . My stepfather was a musician."

This stepfather, Yefimov by name, was a "dreamer" who suffered from delusions of grandeur, behaved irresponsibly toward his wife and stepchild, and squandered whatever coins he could come by on spirituous liquors. Self-satisfied, vain, and complacent, he answered his wife's reproaches with the haughty assertion that he was an "artist"; that his art could not be expected to flourish in a stuffy room shared with a starving family; that marriage in fact was the death of talent. Netochka, supposing Yefimov to be her real father, was carried away by his fantasies of a better life of ease and glory that would be brought about by his artistic talent — but only after her mother's death. Dazzled by these bright prospects, Netochka found herself wishing her mother already in the grave.

Yefimov's origins help to explain his unreliable, vainglorious character. The son of a poor musician on the estate of a wealthy landowner, he had inherited from a disreputable Italian orchestra conductor a black tailcoat and a violin, and, at twenty-two, had set out, penniless, on a vagabond existence. After numerous wanderings, "already thirty and tired and weary," he had come to rest in a St. Petersburg garret where he made friends with another violinist, a German named B. who had little talent but hoped to make his mark in the musical world by dint of methodical perseverance and practice.

Yefimov, for his part, continued to nourish his dreams of a brilliant musical future with spasmodic fits of instrumental rapture but without sustained effort. A basic theme of these first chapters, it has been noted, is the distinction between talent and technique, both of which are essential to the true artist although they are here divided between the lazy and negligent Yefimov, supposedly endowed with exceptional natural talent, and his friend B., who has little natural talent but enormous will to perfect his art.[1]

Yefimov's flamboyant musical style, so the reader is told, was his way of giving expression to an unconscious despair at the thought of his wasted talent. His obsession with his self-imputed genius found expression in the most egoistic and inhuman behavior, but apathy, grief, and boredom gradually took possession of him. His bouts of enthusiasm became rarer. Depressed and gloomy, he neglected his violin, took to drink, and even broke off relations with B., who went on to find an influential patron and a good position in the opera orchestra.

As a crowning act of irresponsibility, the starving Yefimov rushed headlong into marriage with Netochka's widowed mother, who, at that time, possessed a thousand rubles as well as her two-year-old daughter. Herself no less a "dreamer" than her new husband, she married him for love but subsequently became increasingly hot-tempered, irritable, and shrewish in face of the realities of their situation. Whatever Yefimov managed to earn he spent in eating and drinking with his cronies, at the same time blaming his misanthropic and badgering wife for all his unhappiness.

In defiance of all the evidence, Yefimov continued to believe himself the finest violinist in St. Petersburg, attributing his lack of success merely to persecution by an evil fortune. Persuading himself that the burial of his spouse would signify his own resurrection — "when mother dies I shall be born again" — he put away his violin and vowed never to play it again until the eagerly awaited day when his talent would blossom afresh.

Netochka, in her recollections, recalls a violent argument between her parents in the course of which she herself rushed to protect her father. Later, in her mother's absence, he had kissed her and stroked her hair, put her on his knee, and let her nestle close to him. From the moment of that paternal caress, the child felt that she herself had begun to live, as though suddenly awakened to consciousness after a deep sleep. Henceforth she felt a strange, boundless love for her supposed father — not a childlike but, rather, a compassionate, motherly feeling. If her own mother was too stern with Yefimov and with her, must she not cling to her father as a fellow sufferer?

During the period that Netochka actually calls "the happiest time of [her] life," Yefimov taught her the alphabet. After their lessons, he would narrate a fairy tale while she sat spellbound, her mind drifting dangerously as she gave free rein to her fancy. Unable to distinguish between fact and fiction, she would conjure up the wildest, most impossible phantasms. Her father, too, would appear as a character in her daydreams, contributing immeasurably to the progressive deformation of her childish psyche.

Something in the nature of an Electra complex was apparently developing in the child. "This strange devotion," she writes, "developed into quite a romance." Torn between duty to her mother and love for her father, she is caught up in a bewildering play of sin, guilt, and responsibility in which she reaches the point of supporting her father's vice with money given her by her mother to buy food. Her father had promised her rewards of sweets if only she would steal her mother's money "of her own free will." Reconciled to her father's terrible demands, she finds her only hope in the expectation of her mother's early death, to be followed by an escape with her father to a splendid existence that is symbolized, for her, by "the house with the red curtains" across the street. This luxurious dwelling, where sumptuous carriages discharge lavishly dressed ladies, becomes an emblem of regal magnificence and fairy-tale en-

chantment in which she is certain that she too will participate as
soon as her father becomes a great violinist.

But Yefimov's desperate effort to sustain his faith in his own talent
is doomed to catastrophic failure. A single performance by a truly
great violinist suffices to crush his deluded view of himself and complete his utter frustration. Sitting beside the body of his wife (who has
coincidentally died), he mechanically performs his last, despairing
gestures. He covers the corpse with the family's old clothing, takes
out the long-silent violin, and begins to play in Netochka's presence. The child is thoroughly traumatized by the scraping sounds
that seem to embody her father's own wailings: "I heard groans,
the cries of a human voice. Complete despair flowed forth in these
chords and when, at the end, there resounded the last awful note, in
which was expressed all that is terrible in a cry, the agony of torture
and the misery of hopelessness, I could bear it no longer."

After this macabre performance, the half-mad Yefimov brutally
thrusts some coins into the girl's bodice, uncovers his wife's body,
points a trembling finger and, characteristically, disavows all responsibility for her death: "*Do you hear? It wasn't me, I'm not guilty
of this.*" He takes Netochka roughly by the hand and leads her
into the snowy streets. For a moment, the infatuated child expects
the realization of her dazzling visions of "a better life." But reality
promptly obtrudes itself as the crazed Yefimov takes to his heels and
heartlessly deserts the shocked child. Discovered in a state of raving
madness, he dies shortly afterward, his illusions shattered and with
nothing to hope for but the disgraceful death that is the natural
sequel to his misspent life.

Rescued by a kindly passerby, the orphaned Netochka is now
transported into a new triangular relationship of a very different
character, complete with a new set of surrogate parents as well as
a young girl companion of her own age. The wealthy Prince X., a
man of superior moral and human qualities — the type, in fact, of
Dostoevsky's "perfectly good man" — has found the destitute child
lying on the sidewalk before his mansion and has determined upon
the risky experiment of introducing her as a member of his own
family.

His wife, Princess X., hypocritical, cold, and cruel, has no sympathy for this project, although she is not above using the "little
orphan" as a conversation piece in her salon. The conversation
there, of course, is conducted in French, of which the impressionable Netochka understands nothing except that she is being forced
to play the role of the despised social outcast and contrasted with

the "great Princess" in a scene that is sharply focused on the injustice of class and educational barriers. Most of Netochka's time in the great St. Petersburg mansion is spent in seeking a place to hide, a corner where she can give free rein to her remembrance of things past while suppressing all recollection of the final, ghastly episodes of her former life.

Netochka's starved need for love finds expression in a complicated erotic relationship with the young daughter of the household, Katya, to whom she is irresistibly attracted but who at first does not by any means reciprocate her affection. Spoiled, headstrong, and willful, petted by the entire household, Katya nevertheless possesses good instincts and generosity. "The greatest influence over her was her father, whom she adored. Her mother loved her to distraction, but was terribly strict with her." Katya's upbringing, "a strange combination of pampering and ruthless severity," parallels Netochka's former situation vis-à-vis her own parents, albeit on a completely different social level.

Each day more enraptured by the glamorous Katya, Netochka dreams of her as though they were a couple in love. In her childish insecurity, she is cruelly taken aback by her idol's sudden, sharp manifestations of individual temperament. Dostoevsky outdoes himself in painting the differences between the two girls, minutely analyzing their temperaments, characters, and physical attributes, and expertly bringing out the contrast between Katya's playful exuberance and Netochka's gloomily pensive disposition.

The psychological fencing between the two girls — one seemingly born for happiness, the other for misery — culminates in a harrowing encounter with a fierce bulldog, Sir John Falstaff by name, whose own psychology is also skillfully probed by the novelist. Katya displays her prowess in dealing with the monster as though she were a knight battling for a lady's love. (A similar scene, this time with a boy and a mettlesome horse, occurs in the story of *A Little Hero,* discussed below.) Symptoms of the sentimental crisis now brewing in Katya's little heart prompt her alarmed mother to send for the medical doctors; but Netochka, more perceptive, realizes that it is not a question of "children's illnesses" or of "Katya's age," but that the moment has come when Katya will at length swallow her own infernal pride and requite Netochka's deathless devotion.

The two girls will in fact indulge their passionate love for one another during the brief time until Katya and her parents are called away from St. Petersburg by family exigencies. But with this cruel separation, Netochka Nezvanova's newly awakened life lapses into physical and mental lethargy. "Only when I was sixteen did I wake up again," she tells us.

Her new awakening, at an age when she is able to reflect on the experiences that have formed her character and shaped her past life, occurs after a stay of some years in the home of another wealthy Petersburg couple. Alexandra Mikhailovna, her hostess and de facto guardian, is a daughter of Princess X. by her first husband and is thus Katya's half sister, though quite unlike the latter in situation and temperament. Netochka will recount her experience in this, the third of her triangular relationships, in the more sophisticated style appropriate to a perceptive young adult.

Quiet, gentle, and loving, Alexandra Mikhailovna is tormented by some secret sorrow that casts a shadow over her beautiful features and is causing her slowly to waste away, nervously and even physically. As though painting her portrait on canvas, Dostoevsky delineates her face and character with unparalleled artistry. His portrait of her husband, Peter Alexandrovich — a portrait that actually hangs in that worthy's study — is likewise traced in a painterly fashion that brings out all the ambivalence and secret evil in the personality of this well-to-do, respectable, and sadistic official.

The relationship between the maternal Alexandra Mikhailovna and the adolescent Netochka Nezvanova develops into one of deep affection and mutual respect. Unburdening herself of her inner conflicts, the orphan finds release in revealing her past to her guardian and teacher. "After such 'lessons' I felt as lighthearted and happy as if there had been no misfortune in my life," she writes. Dostoevsky brings affectionate skill to the description of the young girl's growing-up process, articulating her new impressions, interests, and unconscious impulses as well as her thirst for creative activity and excitement.

Netochka becomes impatient at having to read only permitted books, and is soon indulging her curiosity about the volumes that are kept under lock and key in the library. Her reading offsets the flatness of reality, and this new magic gives rise to stunning and fantastic panoramas. A new consciousness and a new state of mind begin to illuminate Netochka Nezvanova's past life and to deepen her understanding of herself and of humankind.

Alexandra Mikhailovna's self-complacent, self-assured husband makes a distinctly negative impression on the child, who feels chronically ill at ease when the three of them are together. She realizes that there is a secret between husband and wife, one that he seems to be using against her despite his apparent solicitude for her comfort and welfare and her apparent affection for him. Dostoevsky minutely examines the psychology of the submissive wife whose affectionate demonstrations fail to conceal an inward distress; who feels awkward with her husband yet is unable to live without him.

Netochka, observing the couple's strange behavior, resents the husband's supercilious, condescending behavior and is baffled by the mystery that seems to underlie their charade. The tormented Alexandra suffers crises of depression, prostration, and hysterics; her health grows steadily worse. Unable to confront her inner torments — to externalize them in a way that would bring psychological release — she will ultimately be indebted to young Netochka for her escape from the horror that holds her in thrall.

Browsing in the library and opening at random a novel by Sir Walter Scott, Netochka is surprised to see a sheet of yellowed paper fall from the volume. A farewell letter of terrible finality, it abruptly reveals the secret that has been gnawing at Alexandra Mikhailovna's heart. It was a platonic friendship for a man of inferior social standing, Netochka learns, that had caused scandal in Alexandra's social circle and forced him into permanent exile from his beloved's presence. The condemnation of this innocent relationship by her peers had been the force that had driven Alexandra Mikhailovna to withdraw into solitude.

Even now, her husband will not allow her to forget what he regards as her "sin." Dostoevsky vividly tells the reader how the man habitually prepares to visit his wife by standing before a mirror and changing his expression and personality from smiling relaxation to a tyrannical bitter snarl, a gloomy eye, and a creased forehead. Thus he dons the mask that is designed to keep his wife's guilt alive and poison her life.

Netochka's reading of the purloined letter precipitates a change in her own personality. When Peter Alexandrovich surprises her in the library, she attempts to protect Alexandra Mikhailovna by pretending that the letter is her own. In the tempestuous scene that follows, the triangle disintegrates. Netochka Nezvanova defends the suffering wife against her oppressor; but Alexandra Mikhailovna, in her sick and tormented mind, has come to suspect her husband of being sexually attracted to Netochka. Now morally transformed, Netochka relentlessly accuses Peter Alexandrovich of merciless vanity, jealous egocentricity, and cruel injustice toward his wife. She angrily bids him farewell — and here, unfortunately, ends the surviving portion of Dostoevsky's unfinished novel.

What exists of *Netochka Nezvanova* is a classic record of a young

girl's moral and emotional maturation. Netochka's memory moves
from the confusion of childhood to the consciousness of adolescence and thence to the courageous resolution of young adulthood.
Her childish hatred of her mother and subsequent guilt feelings are
overcome in her adolescence, when she achieves the self-surrender
needed to win over the headstrong, socially superior and capricious
Katya. In her defiance of the loathsome Peter Alexandrovich and
her identification with his victim, she is transformed from a humble
ward into an important protagonist who refuses to be crushed by
superior forces.

The disintegration of Netochka Nezvanova's successive triangular relationships is thus matched by the gradual integration of her
own personality and the resolution of her own inner conflicts. In
the first triangle, the confused child is caught between two battling
parents. Netochka's mother, though not without redeeming qualities, offers a flat and sordid reality that the child prefers to obliterate
from her mind — whereas her father holds forth glittering illusions
that she nurtures to the point of incipient incest. Only later in life
does Netochka begin to wonder how she could have developed such
strong hate feelings for her suffering and hardworking mother. Only
when she has come to understand her own injustice and cruelty do
pangs of conscience and self-reproach begin to torment her. Only
then does she recall her own strong urge to hug her mother, cling
to her and weep with her — an urge she had stubbornly refused to
gratify while there was still time.

Clearly her inner self, during that dark, strange period of her
childhood, had actually been seeking her mother's love, even while
her outer self was refusing it and setting up an unbearable tension in
her little heart. Torn between love for her father and a need for love
for and from her mother, "I felt that I could not help secretly loving
her," she writes. "I have noticed that many children are abnormally
unfeeling and if they do love one person it tends to be to the exclusion
of others. And that is how it was with me." " ...I had to choose
between them," she adds. "I had to side with one or the other and
I took the side of the half-crazy man because he seemed so pitiful,
so humiliated, and because he roused my fantasy."

But here a Dostoevskian twist brings the reader a surprise; for Netochka now admits that she "most probably" preferred the father
"because I was less afraid of him and indeed had less respect for him
than for my mother. In a way he was nearer my own level. I gradually felt I was rising above him, that I could dominate him a little
and that he needed me." This young child, the reader realizes, was

already calculating enough to understand the human power game, and prepared to use her own advantage! She was already shrewd enough to sense that maternal severity was to be respected and that her mother's existence was not the only obstacle that blocked the way to her father's self-realization as an artist. Netochka Nezvanova was actually making use of her stepfather, exploiting his need for her, and unconsciously enjoying his subjugation.

In the second of her triangular relationships, in Prince X.'s household, we encounter a parallel psychological study in the analysis of the spoiled, mercurial Katya. Her apparent disdain of Netochka, her hot reactions of disappointment, indignation, or shame when punished for naughtiness, are part of a profound analysis of the little princess's pride and egocentrism. Aware that sadism and masochism are but two sides of an identical impulse, Dostoevsky traces with sovereign mastery the unfolding love-hate dialectic between the two little girls. While Katya's torture of Netochka can actually be read as a manifestation of love for her, Netochka herself experiences strange delight at being tortured by the little girl whom she adores.[2]

Katya, in the earlier stages of their acquaintance, behaves with the utmost cruelty. She seems to feel nothing but dislike, hatred, even a will to persecute the adoring Netochka. She mercilessly wields her power over the poor orphan and enjoys the latter's emotional insecurity exactly as her mother, Princess X., does in the adults' salon. But Katya, a model for later Dostoevsky protagonists who will struggle against pride and egoism in order to surrender to love and self-sacrifice, eventually overcomes the feelings of superiority and conceit that have kept her from reciprocating Netochka's love.

Katya, of course, is able to make the adjustment with no real difficulty, since she has been born for happiness and raised in the lap of luxury. It is Netochka Nezvanova, the nameless nobody, who must pass through a real *via crucis* in order to transcend her inferior social status, overcoming mockery, derision, and humiliation before she can obtain the splendid requital of her love.

Netochka's third triangular relationship opens her mind to the love of knowledge and the cultivation of her talents. Alexandra Mikhailovna, her benefactress, not only encourages the development of her mind but even contemplates enrolling her in the Conservatory, since it appears that she has a fine singing voice. The reader is led to believe that she will become an accomplished vocalist — if only because she remembers that B., the German violinist, himself achieved success through will and perseverance.

It is thanks to this expansion of her own ego that Netochka is able to handle the extremes of tension that permeate the atmosphere of her foster residence, even to stand up to the socially superior though morally inferior Peter Alexandrovich. Seeing clearly into the latter's dark soul, she can understand, though she condemns, his desire to keep his wife submissive by exploiting her sick imagination and guilt feelings. Dostoevsky here offers a stunning picture of the lowly, courageous orphan who manages by sheer force of character to deflate the self-satisfaction and respectability of a high civil servant.

A reading of *Netochka Nezvanova* should make it clear that Dostoevsky, still well under thirty years of age on the eve of his Siberian exile, had already mastered the tools of psychological analysis he would employ so brilliantly in later and more mature works.

5

The Insulted and Injured (1861)

The violinist Yefimov, Dostoevsky had written in *Netochka Nezvanova,* was "one of those people who are very fond of seeing
themselves among the insulted and injured" and even find "secret
comfort" in such a status. That segment of humanity which the
writer designated as the "insulted and injured" would provide the
title for his next novel, the first among his major post-Siberian works
and one in which at least four of the characters seem positively to
enjoy exacerbating their own misery through willful blindness, sheer
stubbornness, foolish pride, or sterile wrath. More than mere victims
of social injustice, some at least among the "insulted and injured"
seem also to be the prey of powerful egoistic forces that prevent
them from manifesting their feelings of compassion and love.

The Insulted and Injured is generally considered the weakest of
Dostoevsky's full-length novels, though some of its passages do certainly capture the authenticity that characterizes his greater works.
The book encountered a mixed reception on the part of the critics,
yet its melodrama and bathos did not destroy its mass appeal but
gave a definite lift to Dostoevsky's reputation after his prolonged
absence from the literary scene.

"I am writing a novel based on Petersburg life similar to *Poor
Folk* (but the idea is better than *Poor Folk*)," Dostoevsky had written *(Letters,* I, 321, in Frank's translation). In tones reminiscent of
Charles Dickens, he described the story as "one of those gloomy
and distressing dramas which are so often played out unseen, almost mysterious, under the heavy sky of Petersburg, in the dark
secret corners of the vast town, in the midst of the giddy ferment of
life, of dull egoism, of clashing interests, of gloomy vice and secret
crimes, in that lowest hell of senseless and abnormal life" (II, 11).

But although the novel to some extent recalls the sentimental hu-
manitarianism of the writer's first period, it shows a new maturity
in the treatment of social injustice and the attitude of both its vic-

tims and its would-be reformers. He now permits the supposedly sacred ideals of a group of "fresh young people filled with ardent love for all humanity" — an obvious reference to such groups as the Petrashevsky circle with which Dostoevsky himself had been associated — to be convincingly "debunked" by the villain of the novel, who is himself a disillusioned idealist.

Where Prince Valkovsky, the probing villain, is the evil genius of the novel, the narrator is a young writer clearly modeled on Dostoevsky himself. "You are poor," the prince gibes at him, "you ask your publisher for money in advance, you pay your trivial debts, with what's left you live for six months on tea, and shiver in your garret while you wait for your next novel to [write itself] for your publisher's magazine" (II, 10). Dostoevsky's own novel, *Poor Folk,* is repeatedly mentioned in the course of the story. The narrator reads it to his admiring foster family; it moves the heroine to tears; and it forms the background for the narrator's and the heroine's abortive romance.

Beginning with a review of the events of the year just past, the narrator tells of two grotesque figures that attracted his attention in the coffeehouse where he was wont to spend his leisure in reading the Russian magazines. An old man and his mangy dog, apparently right out of "some page of Hoffmann," had filled him with a sense of mingled revulsion and attraction. The decrepit ancient, whose "death-like face" bore "the stamp of eighty years, and his disgusting dog" proved to be habitués of the establishment.

In the warmth of the coffeehouse, the dog died quietly at its master's feet, "from old age and perhaps from hunger too." Bowing down gently, the old man pressed his pale cheek to the animal's dead face, then left the coffeehouse, followed by the narrator — only to expire in his turn in the bitter cold of the street. The narrator learns on inquiry that the dead man was a Russian subject of foreign birth, Jeremy Smith by name. Since he himself needs a lodging, he promptly moves into Smith's deserted rooms. There no visitors disturb him except for phantom figures of the dead man and his dog — forewarnings of what he calls *"mysterious horror... something like the anguish of people who are afraid of the dead"* (I, 10).

In a double flashback unfolding in two separate time frames, the reader now learns that the narrator, an orphan, had been brought up in the country by a respectable small landowner, Nikolay Sergeevich Ikhmenyev, with whose only daughter, Natasha, three years younger than himself, he had been childishly in love, as she was with him. But on leaving the Ikhmenyev household to complete his studies in St. Petersburg and launch out as a writer, he had lost Natasha's promised hand because of his lack of success and fortune and, still more, because of the passionate love she had meanwhile conceived for another suitor. "Thin, yellow, and sunken in the face," the melancholy narrator is still deeply in love with Natasha, but is prepared to make any sacrifice to ensure her happiness.

The Ikhmenyev family has meanwhile come down in the world. The adjoining estate belonged to a reactionary member of the ruling class, Prince Peter Alexandrovich Valkovsky, "one of those brilliant representatives of aristocratic Petersburg society who rarely made their appearance in the provinces, but produce an extraordinary sensation when they do" (I, 3). Needing a steward for his estate, the prince had employed his neighbor Ikhmenyev, whose administration had proved so satisfactory that he was even entrusted, "to teach him some sense," with the governance of the prince's nineteen-year-old son, Prince Alexey Petrovich, known as Alyosha.

Perhaps somewhat implausibly, the otherwise lucid and well-balanced Natasha had fallen madly in love with this flighty young man; but his father, the prince, had frowned on such an unequal alliance, if only because he had destined his son for a wealthy heiress whose fortune he was hoping to bring under his own control. These and other developments had ruined the previously harmonious relationship between the prince and Natasha's father. In what appeared to have been a radical personality transformation, the prince had changed from a suave, charming aristocrat into a cunning, greedy, corrupt, depraved man, from whose evil power the weak and honest found no escape. Ikhmenyev was now accused of betraying his employer's trust and diverting funds into his own pocket. Village gossip now had it that the "unprincipled" Natasha had "bewitched" the prince's young son.

Beset on every hand, Ikhmenyev had found no recourse but to resign his stewardship, take his case to the courts, and move to St. Petersburg to await the outcome. There Natasha, her hopes of matrimony checkmated, had abandoned her respectable family and gone to live openly with her aristocratic lover — a stunning blow to the outraged Ikhmenyev, who considered himself doubly "insulted and injured" by his daughter's living out of wedlock with the son of his deadly personal enemy.

Natasha's love for the fickle young prince was, however, that of a woman possessed. Admitting that she loved him "in an evil way," she confessed to the long-suffering narrator that she had to cling to the young man because, in her words, *"He'll forget me if I'm not continually with him....* If he didn't see me for a week he'd fall in love with someone else and forget me, and then when he saw me he'd be at my feet again" (I, 8). Despite Alyosha's good-natured promise to marry her when circumstances permit, Natasha has decided that matrimony would not, in any case, suit his temperament. "If he's going to be unhappy from being married, why make him unhappy?" she asks rhetorically, realizing full well that her attitude is inflicting infinite torment on her beloved father as well as the faithful narrator.

Alyosha, still subject at bottom to his father's guidance, succeeds in breaking loose from Natasha's clinging presence, and his resources are drained away in repeated philanderings. Forced now to find humbler lodgings, sell her clothing, and seek some kind of work to earn a living, Natasha nevertheless opens her arms to Alyosha each time he returns to her. "There was a sort of infinite bliss in forgiving and being merciful; as though in the very process of forgiving Alyosha she found a peculiar, subtle charm" (I, 14). The perceptive narrator notices "a look of martyrdom, tenderness, patience in her smile" each time Natasha relates her acts of pardon to him.

These events gradually begin to tie in with the story of the late Jeremy Smith. Eventually there appears at Smith's lugubrious lodging, now that of the narrator, a half-wild little creature, "not like a human being," who has come to visit her "grandfather." The narrator is intrigued by this early teenage waif, who, it will eventually turn out, carries in her bosom — both figuratively and literally — the secret of Prince Valkovsky's scandalous past. She is in fact Valkovsky's legitimate daughter, though this relationship will not come to light until the final pages of the novel.

With the help of a disreputable but good-hearted and exuberant friend named Masloboev, the narrator rescues the young girl from the clutches of a procuress. The child's horrendous experiences in this den of prostitution, coming on top of prolonged deprivation and ill-treatment, precipitate a serious illness, through which she is nursed by the narrator. Though seemingly appreciative of his attentions, the girl remains remote and mistrustful. "Her gentle, tender heart showed itself in glimpses," the narrator noticed, "in spite of her aloofness and evident mistrust" (II, 8). But it seemed as though she were deliberately trying to aggravate a secret wound, as though she actually enjoyed the pain of her *"egoism of suffering"* (IV, 4).

Only when the narrator himself suffers a nervous attack does the child openly reveal her affection, ministering to him through the night and even authorizing him to call her "Nellie," the name her mother had given her. "All the feeling which she had repressed for so long broke out at once, in an uncontrollable outburst, and I understood the strange stubbornness of a heart that... masked its feeling, the more harshly, the more stubbornly as the need for expression and utterance grew stronger, till the inevitable outburst came, when the whole being forgot itself and gave itself up to the craving for love, to gratitude, to affection and to tears. She sobbed till she became hysterical" (I, 11). This scene prepares the way for the unlocking of the secret of Nellie's past life, her liberation from her inner torment, and the conquering of her "egoism of suffering."

Revealing that her grandfather's dog had previously belonged to her mother — who had been cruelly repudiated and cursed by old Jeremy Smith — Nellie succinctly notes that "he didn't forgive mother, but when the dog died he died too" (II, 11). The mother's "fearful story," the narrator learns, was that of

a woman abandoned and living on after the wreck of her happiness, sick, worn out and forsaken by everyone, rejected by the last creature to whom she could look — her father, once wronged by her and crazed by intolerable sufferings and humiliations. It was the story of a woman driven to despair, wandering through the cold, filthy streets of Petersburg, begging alms with the little girl whom she regarded as a baby; of a woman who lay dying for months in a damp cellar, while her father, refusing to forgive her to the last moment of her life, and only at the last moment relenting, hastened to forgive her only to find a cold corpse instead of the woman he loved above everything on earth. (II, 11)

Gradually the pieces of Nellie's story fall into place, and one notes a parallel with the situation between the lovelorn Natasha and her father, Ikhmenyev. Years earlier, Nellie's mother had been seduced by none other that the sinister Prince Valkovsky, who had also persuaded her to steal certain documents proving that he, the prince, owed money to her father, Jeremy Smith. Though he had made a promise of marriage to the unfortunate woman, the prince had basely yet all too characteristically abandoned her on the eve of Nellie's birth. Her own father had cursed her, and, after having been forced into bankruptcy, had spent the rest of his life in suffering and humiliation, refusing to forgive his daughter until it was too late.

The last part of *The Insulted and Injured* brings the definitive rupture between Natasha and her flighty lover, whom she surrenders to the wealthy heiress Prince Valkovsky has chosen for him — actually, a generous and thoroughly agreeable young girl. In her confession to the narrator, Natasha gives the impression that she, too, is en-

joying "the egoism of her suffering." The perspicacious narrator
observes "that she was lacerating her own wounds on purpose, impelled to this by a sort of yearning, the yearning of despair and
suffering... and how often that is so with a heart that has suffered
a great loss" (IV, 6).

The cynical and corrupt Valkovsky, having first deprived Natasha
of his son, now attempts to palm her off on a lecherous old count.
Churlishly, he offers her ten thousand rubles by way of compensation for her father, who has meanwhile lost his lawsuit against the
powerful prince. But he has reckoned without the intervention of
the devoted narrator, who suddenly emerges from the wings to spit
in Valkovsky's face and slap him on the cheek with all his might. The
base Valkovsky, "seeing there were two of us... took to his heels,
snatching up the roll of notes from the table" (IV, 6).

The narrator now hits upon a means of effecting a reconciliation
between Natasha and her parents. Little Nellie is persuaded to go to
Ikhmenyev, tell him the story of her own life, and point out to him
that it is now Natasha who, like Nellie's mother, remains "insulted
and injured, alone and helpless, with no one to protect her from
the insults of her enemy" (IV, 6). Nellie's heartrending account of
how her grandfather had refused to forgive her mother, even while
she lay dying of tuberculosis in a dark hovel, works the miracle.
Ikhmenyev unconditionally forgives his daughter, who returns home
for a melodramatic scene of harmony restored.

Nellie herself, however, will soon succumb to a chronic heart ail-
ment. An epilogue, largely made up of comments about publishers,
critics, and the effects of stress and strain on the creative writer, informs one also that Nellie in reality is Prince Valkovsky's legitimate
daughter. On her own deathbed, Nellie surrenders to the narrator
the locket she wears around her neck and, with it, a letter that reveals the child's legitimacy and, if used earlier, would have released
her from a life of starvation and humiliation. Nellie, however, had
refrained from following her mother's injunction to confront the
prince with the evidence of his perfidy. "Nellie had not done her
mother's bidding. She knew all, but she had not gone to the Prince,
and had died unforgiving."

Old-fashioned and ultramodern elements are inseparably blended
in *The Insulted and Injured.* The emphasis on suspense, mystery,
and villainy belong to the traditional Gothic style of fiction that
Dostoevsky had enjoyed in his youth. But the novel also offers fas-
cinatingly modern psychological observations on the phenomena of
sadomasochism, on father–daughter similarities and inherited traits,

and on father–son dissimilarities that have resisted the influence of paternal imprinting.

Ikhmenyev, a very exemplar of worth and integrity, shares with his daughter Natasha — who, too, is a serious girl of sterling moral qualities — both an essential benevolence and a formidable stubbornness. Ikhmenyev, Dostoevsky writes, was "one of those very simplehearted and naively Romantic men who ... if they give their affection to someone (sometimes only God knows why) surrender themselves heart and soul, sometimes stretching their attachment to comic lengths" (I, 3). Natasha, too, has "that characteristic of good-natured people, perhaps inherited from her father — the habit of thinking highly of people, of persistently thinking them better than they really are, warmly exaggerating everything good in them" — an explanation, perhaps, of her otherwise incongruous love for the fickle Alyosha.

Similarly, Ikhmenyev at first sees Prince Valkovsky as a model of gentility, and is rudely shocked when he finds himself faced instead with a suspicious and cunning fortune hunter. "A disappointment is always in store for such people," Dostoevsky warns. "It is best for them to stay quietly in their corners and not go out into the world" (II, 6). In like manner, Ikhmenyev refuses to believe his daughter Natasha is anything but an angelic and obedient child, and is crushed on finding she has grown into a thoroughly mature, ardent, and passionate woman with a will of her own.

Though father and daughter bear a moral resemblance to each other, Natasha is the more complex personality and shows more perspicacity in analyzing the paternal psyche than he can bring to the understanding of his own daughter. Natasha sees into the old man's wounded resentment of her love for Alyosha: "A father's love is jealous, too ... He'll insist on an impossible atonement.... We shall have to work out our future happiness by suffering; pay for it somehow by fresh miseries. Everything is purified by suffering.... Oh ... how much pain there is in the world!" (I, 15).

Natasha understands, too, that only continued suffering will soften her father's heart; so she bides her time, awaiting the propitious moment when he will be ready to forgive. His pride, egoism, and wounded self-esteem must first be overcome before he will be ready to pardon and to love his daughter once again. Until then, he will masochistically intensify his own misery, even as he sadistically anathematizes his beloved daughter. Natasha's own egoism and pride impel her to humiliate her father, and his humiliation in turn imbues her with feelings of masochistic self-abasement and self-torment. Both are victims of an emotional dualism that makes them eager to inflict reciprocal suffering. Only a long process of purification through suffering can resolve the conflict between these two similar beings.

In the relationship of the two Valkovskys, on the other hand, one sees a process of willful imprinting by a wicked father on a weak son, a process that determines the boy's social behavior. The prince, who wears a "filthy mask," is another of Dostoevsky's Jekyll-and-Hyde types and has been likened to Svidrigaylov in *Crime and Punishment*. "The light in his eyes was ... twofold, Dostoevsky writes, "and together with the mild friendly radiance there were flashes that were cruel, mistrustful, searching and spiteful" (II, 2).

It had been said of Prince Valkovsky that "though he was so elegant and decorous in society he sometimes was fond of ... secret debauchery, of loathsome and mysterious vices." Exclusively interested in wealth, position, and self-gratification, totally indifferent to the fate of his victims, Valkovsky believes that "at the root of all human virtues lies the completest egoism ... and the more virtuous anything is, the more egoism there is in it" (III, 10).

Unlike Ikhmenyev, who is consistent through and through, Valkovsky has a "double" nature. At one moment the narrator describes him as "some sort of huge reptile, some huge spider" — images that in Dostoevsky's repertory represent evil; yet at the next moment we find this villain enunciating truths to which Dostoevsky himself not only subscribes but would later turn to account in his macabre 1873 story *Bobok* (see chapter 15). "If it were possible," says the prince, "for every one of us to describe all his secret thoughts, without hesitating to disclose what he ... would not on any account tell other people ... what, indeed, he is even at times afraid to confess to himself, the world would be filled with such a stench that we should all be suffocated."

Valkovsky has imprinted in his naive son's mind his own disregard for human obligations, his own ingrained principles of maximum self-interest. Playing with people for the sake of personal advantage is the only sport in which he engages with his son. The weak and trusting Alyosha, "too simple for his age and [with] no notion of real life" (I, 9), is a puppet in his father's hands, yielding to the slightest pressure and blind to the corruption of the man who remains "a humane father in his imagination." Valkovsky is perfectly content that his frivolous, inconstant, and self-complacent son should remain timid of heart and socially irresponsible. So much the more easily will he manipulate the characters on the stage his son is treading.

The figure of Nellie, the proud beggar girl, who so loved her
mother that she accepted a life of misery in deference to her mother's
principles — even when disobeying her dying wishes — affords the
reader numerous insights into the psychology of the "insulted and
injured" parent whose hurt is transmitted to the child. How deep
are the wounds unknowingly inflicted by parents on their own offspring. How dangerous it is for parents to allow their own egoism,
pride, contempt, vengefulness, or fierce intransigence to be transferred to their children. Because Nellie's mother was naive and
disillusioned, because she nurtured inextinguishable hatred for her
seducer, and because she mistrusted humanity at large, she sadistically condemned her daughter, too, to a life of misery and torment
in the streets of St. Petersburg.

When the narrator first encountered Nellie at the door of her
dead grandfather's flat, she struck him as "short, thin, and as pale
as though she had just had some terrible illness [and with] great,
shining black eyes." Later, after having given her shelter and care,
he gains a fuller appreciation of Nellie's features:

With her flashing black eyes, which looked somehow foreign, her thick, disheveled black hair, and her mute, fixed, enigmatic gaze, the little creature
might well have attracted the notice of anyone who passed her in the street.
The expression in her eyes was particularly striking. There was the light
of intelligence in them, and at the same time an inquisitorial mistrust, even
suspicion.... She seemed ... to be suffering from some wasting, chronic disease that was gradually and relentlessly destroying her. Her pale, thin face
had an unnatural sallow, bilious tinge. But in spite of all the ugliness of
poverty and illness, she was positively pretty. Her eyebrows were strongly
marked, delicate and beautiful ... and her lips were exquisitely formed with
a peculiar proud bold line, but they were pale and colorless. (II, 3)

Dostoevsky excels in delineating Nellie's inward traits of intelligence, mistrust, suspicion, and pride. He expertly probes the sources
of the child's moral and psychological difficulties, moving from
her wounded sensibility in early childhood to the masochistic self-
laceration of her adolescence. Though Nellie deeply needs affection
and love, the dominant traits in her personality are suspicion and
hatred. She is a too-mature child, one who "understood many things
that some men do not attain to in long years of their smooth and
carefully guarded lives" (II, 110). Only gradually does she begin to
respond to the kindness and generosity of the narrator, who is somewhat at a loss to handle her shifting moods but does understand that
only kindness and gentleness will soften and tame her savage spirit.

This abused child in fact is animated by a fierce pride and scorn of her former oppressors. With flashing eyes she rips and tears the skirt the procuress had given her. The embittered young girl will accept only a dress of her own fashioning, only a garment she herself has worked for and earned. Obsession with the need to "do something for her living" explains her half-defiant, half-loving gesture in doing the narrator's housework even in the midst of her debilitating illness. Uncertain how to respond to his kindness and compassion, she seems oppressed at times by his very hospitality. Pretended hatred masks her love for him. Her rancor is a cloak for tenderness. She invents gestures of defiance, inflicting pain on herself as well as the narrator, as though she wished that neither of them should ever succeed in healing her hurt.

"This aggravation of suffering and this reveling in it I could understand," writes the narrator. "It is the enjoyment of many of the insulted and injured, oppressed by destiny and smarting under the sense of injustice." Such insights, characteristic of the mature Dostoevsky, guarantee the place of *The Insulted and Injured* among literary works of high rank.

6

The Idiot (1868)

As the first of Dostoevsky's great novels to be written outside of his Russian homeland, *The Idiot* did not flow easily despite the relative stabilization of the author's emotional condition in the wake of his marriage to Anna Grigorievna early in 1867. No fewer than eight attempts preceded his final embodiment of the Christian ideal of the "perfect man" in the person of Prince Myshkin, the central figure in this complex tale of cruelty, passion, masochistic self-torment, and redeeming love.

The title of the novel does less than justice to the mentality of the good-natured young prince, an epileptic who, though certainly naive and inexperienced, is blessed with at least normal intelligence as well as extraordinary sensitivity and psychological insight. The alert reader may already have noted a kind of precursor in the more superficial Prince Aleksey (Alyosha) in *The Insulted and Injured,* a young man whose face the heroine could not contemplate "without being moved; *no one else* [had] such an expression." And just as Alyosha, incapable of choosing between Natasha and the young heiress selected by his father, preferred that "all three [should] love each other," Prince Myshkin, too, cannot understand why he should not be able to "love two persons at once... with two different kinds of love" (IV, 9).

Although *The Idiot* is now universally recognized as one of Dostoevsky's most powerful and perceptive works, it was virtually ignored by the critics on its original appearance. Russia, at that time, was a prey to growing political tensions as the pace of internal reform slackened and revolutionary activity gained momentum. Few readers could spare attention for the universal themes of Dostoevsky's novel, the struggle between love and hate, between good and evil, and the place of the righteous man in a society ruled by self-interest, vanity, and greed.

Despite the complexity of the main characters and their interrela-

tionships, the essential content of *The Idiot* may be readily grasped
if one focuses one's attention on its primary features and disregards
the many secondary figures who contribute to the novel's extraordinary richness and depth. Two kinds of love-rivalry form the core
of the story: the rivalry between two women for the love of Prince
Myshkin — who would gladly have married both of them if it were
possible — and a rivalry between the prince and his friend Rogozhin,
a reckless, violent contender for the hand of one of the two women.

The reader makes the acquaintance of the two male rivals, whose
lives are to become inextricably intertwined, in a compartment of
the train from Warsaw to St. Petersburg. One of them, the turbulent
Rogozhin,

> was a short man of about twenty-seven with curly hair that was almost
> black and a pair of tiny, but fiery, gray eyes. His nose was broad and flat
> and he had high cheekbones; his thin lips were continually curled into a sort
> of insolent, sarcastic, and even malicious smile, but his forehead was high
> and well-shaped.... The most striking thing about his face was its deathly
> pallor, which, in spite of his rather sturdy build, gave the young man a
> look of utter exhaustion and, at the same time, of something agonizingly
> passionate, which seemed to be out of keeping with his coarse and insolent
> smile and his surly and self-satisfied expression. (I, 1)

Such was the physical appearance of Parfyon Rogozhin, an extremely wealthy though coarse and uncouth representative of
St. Petersburg's prosperous merchant class — an exemplar of the
power of money and, still more, a plaything of his own violent
passions.

The second traveler, the prince, was also

> a young man of about twenty-six or twenty-seven, slightly above medium
> height, with very thick, fair hair, hollow cheeks, and a thin pointed and
> almost white little beard. His eyes were large, blue, and piercing, and there
> was something gentle but heavy in their look, something of that strange ex-
> pression which makes people realize at the first glance that they are dealing
> with an epileptic. The young man's face, however, was pleasant, sensitive,
> and lean, though colorless. (I, 1)

This is Prince Leo Nikolayevich Myshkin, last of the ruined family
of the Myshkins — "an historic name.... You'll find it in Karamzin's
history," a fellow traveler observes.

Prince Myshkin has been undergoing treatment for epilepsy in
a Swiss clinic and is now returning to St. Petersburg to establish
contact with a distant relative, Princess Myshkin, and her husband,

General Yepanchin. This elderly couple, the reader learns, has been blessed with three beautiful and talented daughters, Alexandra, Adelaide, and the twenty-year-old Aglaya, a passionate young woman who will later become engaged to the prince.

The name of the prince's other inamorata-to-be, Nastasya Filippovna Barashkov, also comes up in the course of conversation in the railway coach. This mysteriously glamorous woman is described as "a well-born lady...a princess of a kind." Rogozhin, it turns out, actually knows her. Seeing her for the first time at a ballet performance, he had impulsively bought her a pair of earrings with "a diamond the size of a nut in each of them." Expansively, he now invites the prince to meet this celebrated beauty, and the prince accepts — warning, however, that "I've been ill since I was a child and I have no knowledge at all of women." "If that is so," Rogozhin replies with apparently unconscious insight, "then you are a regular holy fool, Prince, and such as you God loves" (I, 1).

Only gradually does the reader learn something of Nastasya Filippovna's background and personality. An orphan raised, educated, and then seduced by a wealthy landowner named Totsky — by whom, moreover, she is still maintained in the most opulent style — this beautiful and mettlesome young woman is now eating her heart out in the position of an elegant demimondaine whose "benefactor" would like to shed her so that he can marry one of General Yepanchin's daughters. Totsky and the general — who, apparently, has also enjoyed Nastasya's favors — are now conniving to palm her off, with sufficient sums of hush money, on the general's secretary, Ganya Ivolgin — an idea that has no appeal for Ganya and arouses the young woman's scornful mirth.

The prince himself conceives an obsessive interest in Nastasya Filippovna on the very day of his arrival in Petersburg. Chancing upon her photograph — which he kisses surreptitiously — he is struck by "the extraordinary beauty of her face and by something else in it. There was a sort of immense pride and scorn, almost hatred, in that face, and, at the same time, also something trusting, something wonderfully good-natured; this striking contrast seemed almost to arouse in him a feeling of compassion" (I, 7).

Later on that eventful day, Prince Myshkin encounters the controversial lady during a tempestuous family scene in Ganya's home, only to meet her again at an evening party in her magnificently appointed apartment. In the course of this soirée, the cynical, artful hostess thoroughly exposes the bestial venality of her guests. The prince, however, sees her as "a paragon of perfection," and she, for

her part, is profoundly struck by his strange appearance and behavior. "The prince means a lot to me," she declares, "for he is the
first man... [in] whom I can believe as a true and loyal friend. He
believed in me at first sight, and I believed in him" (I, 14).

Guided and supported by Myshkin, Nastasya astounds the company by melodramatically announcing her rejection of Ganya's
marriage offer, at the same time releasing Totsky from all further
obligation toward her and declaring her intention to "start a new
life." The parallel to the biblical story of Christ and Mary Magdalene
is clearly no accident.

To cap this already hysterical scene, Rogozhin now enters with
the large sum of money he has promised Nastasya Filippovna in
return for her favors — and, in addition, now offers her a pledge
of marriage. But here a totally unexpected impediment arises in the
person of Prince Myshkin, who, amid the stares and snickers of
the other guests, presents himself as an alternative candidate for
Nastasya's hand. This incongruity is too much even for Nastasya
herself, who, with mingled mirth and insolence, mocks the meek
and gentle prince. "And how can you be thinking of marriage," she
taunts, "when you want a nurse to look after you yourself!"

"You're quite right," the prince replies in a trembling, timid voice,
yet with an air of profound conviction. "I know nothing and I've
seen nothing... I'm nothing, but you've suffered and emerged pure
out of such a hell.... I won't let anyone say a bad word against
you, Nastasya Filippovna" (I, 15). Knowing well the importance
of money in the society in which he finds himself, Prince Myshkin
produces a letter that reveals for the first time that he is the heir to
a large fortune.

Nastasya Filippovna's biting, self-tormenting cynicism breaks all
bounds as her dream of "really being a princess" seems about to be
realized. "Is it worth while having such a husband?" she asks with
devastating frankness. "A million and a half, and a prince, and, I'm
told, an idiot into the bargain. What could be better?... You're too
late, Rogozhin! Take away your money; I'm marrying the prince
and I'm richer than you!" (I, 16). A look of unspeakable suffering
appears on Rogozhin's face and elicits similar suffering on the part
of Myshkin, to whom Rogozhin shouts savagely, "Give her up!"
From this point on, the two friends of a day will also be implacable
rivals for Nastasya's hand.

That mercurial lady decides, however, that she will decline Myshkin's offer of protection and marriage, suggesting rather spitefully
that he marry Aglaya, the general's daughter — with whom she

knows that Ganya is in love. Though she herself has apparently made up her mind to yield to Rogozhin's brutal demands, she continues to torture him with repeated desertions and escapades as the date of their wedding approaches. To Myshkin, who returns to Petersburg after a six months' absence to settle his inheritance, the humiliated Rogozhin confides that Nastasya Filippovna treats him "just as if she were changing her shoes." Yet he refuses to renounce his claim to the temperamental creature, even though he realizes full well that she can never love him and, in fact, can and does love the prince.

The two friends and rivals have a painful interview in Rogozhin's gloomy apartment, situated in the depths of an ancient, dismal, and shadowy house that accurately reflects the young man's somberly convoluted personality. While talking, Prince Myshkin absentmindedly picks up a knife lying on the table — an object that will become the symbol both of Rogozhin's sexuality and of the enmity between the two men.[1] Twice, Rogozhin snatches the knife in anger from Myshkin's hands; twice, later in the novel, he will insanely turn it against the two persons he loves most dearly, Nastasya Filippovna and the prince himself.

In a contrasting gesture that typifies the ambivalence of his attitude, Rogozhin then suggests that the two exchange the crosses around their necks in sign of a fraternal bonding. As they do so, however, the prince observes with painful surprise "that the old mistrust, the old bitter and almost sardonic smile still lingered on the face of his newly adopted brother" (II, 14). As Myshkin prepares to leave the gloomy apartment, Rogozhin, tormented by jealousy, refuses to embrace him — but then again suddenly changes his behavior, clasping his rival in his arms and generously assuring him that Nastasya Filippovna is his.

Musing absentmindedly as he wanders the streets of St. Petersburg, Myshkin gradually realizes that "the other" — i.e., Rogozhin — is actually following him. Three times he turns suddenly and glimpses Rogozhin's burning eyes in the shifting, anonymous crowd. Finally, Rogozhin attacks with his knife; but Myshkin's life is saved by an epileptic seizure that catches his would-be murderer off guard and paralyzes his arm. The forgiving, Christlike Myshkin, remembering only the man with whom he had exchanged crosses and expunging from his mind the man who has tried to kill him, attempts to share the burden of guilt with his rival.

In the meantime, the prince's tender heart has also begun to "ache with sweet pain" for the passionate and proud Aglaya Yepanchin. That young girl, although she respects and even loves Myshkin for

his "noble simplicity of mind" and "boundless trustfulness," taunts
him as cruelly as did Nastasya Filippovna. Culminating a scene of
bitter rivalry between Aglaya and the socially outcast Nastasya Filippovna, the two hysterical women stand in expectation of the prince's
choice between them. But the prince, loving both of them as he does,
is unable to take a position and merely reproves Aglaya for having
mortally offended her rival.

Furious, Aglaya departs, vowing never to see the prince again.
Nastasya for her part falls into a dead faint, and the compassionate
prince attempts to care for the unconscious woman who, to him,
appears as a sick, pathetic child. Stroking her head and passing his
hands tenderly over her cheeks, he caresses her with the same gestures he will use at the end of the novel in trying to comfort the
crazed and murderous Rogozhin.

Myshkin is now determined that he himself will marry Nastasya
Filippovna, who, in a state of obvious distraction, refrains from men-
tioning Rogozhin and in fact prepares for her wedding to the prince.
On the day of the ceremony, however, she undergoes another revulsion of feeling and, from the very steps of the church, rushes madly
into Rogozhin's arms, beseeching him to carry her off. Although the
abandoned prince accepts this shocking development with apparent
calm, he is filled with sinister forebodings as he betakes himself to
Rogozhin's gloomy apartment, where there now occurs one of the
most grisly scenes in all literature.

Lying on the bed in the semidarkness of Rogozhin's lodging is the
lifeless body of the beautiful Nastasya Filippovna, whose heart her
unpredictable lover has pierced "three or four inches — just under
the left breast" with the knife of the earlier scenes. And now, instead
of quarreling or moving to summon the authorities, the two men in
a trancelike ballet prepare a makeshift bed on which they will spend
the night together in the presence of the corpse.

As their long vigil ends and day breaks, Rogozhin bursts into loud
mutterings, screams, and laughter, shouting in incoherent terror as
he is felled by brain fever. "Then," Dostoevsky writes, "the prince
stretched out his trembling hand and gently touched his head and
his hair, stroking them and stroking his cheeks" in an attempt to
soothe his rage and suffering. At last, the exhausted prince "lay
down on the cushion...and pressed his face against Rogozhin's
pale and motionless face; tears flowed from his eyes on Rogozhin's
cheeks, but perhaps he no longer noticed his own tears and knew
nothing about them" (IV, 11). The neighbors found Rogozhin unconscious and in a raging fever, while Myshkin, immobile and silent,

could no longer recognize anyone or understand the questions put to him.

Two months later, the reader learns from a concluding chapter that neatly wraps up the destinies of all the characters, Rogozhin was sentenced to fifteen years of hard labor in Siberia, while Myshkin, reduced to permanent idiocy, was back in the Swiss clinic from which he had emerged at the beginning of the novel.

His characters' downward path to mental disorder and outright madness has been brilliantly portrayed by Dostoevsky, in scenes of increasing intensity that document the progressive disablement of the three victims. When Nastasya Filippovna emerges from her fainting spell (IV, 8), her crazed, distorted face and incoherent babbling already betray a deterioration of her mental condition, which will be dramatically manifested on her wedding day. The inflammation of the brain that affects Rogozhin over a two-month period seems to foreshadow a transformation of the criminal's heart and soul that is not unlike Raskolnikov's in *Crime and Punishment*. Myshkin's final lapse into feeblemindedness is followed, according to the Swiss physician, by the total breakdown of his mental faculties.

This crescendo of madness eventually culminates and resolves itself in the stabbing of Nastasya Filippovna and the virtual transposition of souls experienced by Rogozhin and Myshkin as their individual bodies, hearts, and minds are merged in the lugubrious deathwatch. A scarcely less sinister fate, in Dostoevsky's terms, befalls the novel's fourth main character, Aglaya. She, too, is mentally disturbed, a victim of "obsessions," and the author, who has not concealed his hatred of Catholicism ("Catholicism is the same as an unchristian religion! ... Roman Catholicism is even worse than atheism"), allows her to fall a prey to a Catholic priest who gains ascendancy over her mind "to a fanatical degree."

These four characters, each suffering from some type and degree of mental disorder, have frequently been paired off in such a way as to contrast the two women and the two men. Nastasya Filippovna, for example, has been seen as one of Dostoevsky's typical "infernal" and "inhuman" women, modeled on Polina Suslova and poles apart from the more or less beatific Aglaya, whose love for Myshkin seems rather better attuned to human needs. Both women, however, are endowed with highly complex characters that resist schematic classification.

Nastasya Filippovna is a "badly used woman" (IV, 9), one of Dostoevsky's orphans, born for misery and unhappiness yet capable, at the same time, of serving as a reincarnation of the biblical Mary

Magdalene. Recalling other Dostoevskian characters who masochistically seek to intensify their own suffering, she "seems to derive
some dreadful, unnatural pleasure from this continual consciousness of shame." With her "flashing eyes" and her thirst for pain and
distress, the rebellious and hate-filled woman stands out among the
exemplars of self-commiseration and the "egoism of suffering" so
often met with in Dostoevsky's works of both earlier and later date.

And yet this brilliant and remarkable woman defies any too-facile
analysis. Shamed and outraged by her long-standing profanation at
the hands of the cynical Totsky, insecure yet inexorable where her
own desires are concerned, Nastasya Filippovna was "quite capable," Dostoevsky writes, "of ruining herself by running the risk of
being sent to Siberia to serve a sentence for murder, so long as she
could vent her spite on a man to whom she had such an inhuman
aversion" (I, 4). She still holds an eccentric and savage ascendancy
over Totsky, who had once desired but now fears her, sensing in her
eyes "the presence of some deep and mysterious darkness."

Other characters describe Nastasya Filippovna as "restless,"
"short-tempered," "sarcastic," "double-faced," or a "typically Russian woman," one who treats the men in her life "like dirt yet loves
them in her own way." Elements of duality are everywhere apparent
in her emotional makeup; she passes easily from harshness to play-
fulness, from sympathetic pity to demented ruthlessness. She lacks
refinement yet loves luxury — "a barbarous mixture of two tastes"
(I, 13). It takes the extraordinary sensibility of Prince Myshkin, the
"idiot," to perceive the rift in Nastasya Filippovna's personality and
try to heal it and make her *whole*.

Aglaya, whose name implies "ardent," shares some of Nastasya's
"infernal" willfulness, caprice, and sarcasm, but, compared with
Nastasya, seems all of a piece. A brilliant young lady with excellent
qualities of heart and mind, she seemed, like so many of Dostoevsky's secondary characters, to have been born for happiness. Her
future, the Yepanchin family had decided, "was not to be an ordinary one, but an embodiment of the ideal of heaven on earth.
Aglaya's future husband was to be a model of perfection and a
paragon of all virtues, not to mention his great wealth." Generous
and enthusiastic, Aglaya shows understanding in most situations,
but her love for Myshkin is that of a woman who can feel no
sympathy for a rival.

Nastasya Filippovna sees in Aglaya the person she herself would
like to be. It is to her that Nastasya tries to surrender the man to
whom she despairs of ever truly belonging. But where the "insulted

and injured" Nastasya Filippovna knows that her personal destiny must be a tragic one, the wealthy and pampered Aglaya expects to make her own free choices in life — though she too, in the end, will be sacrificed, a victim of her own inexperience and naïveté.

If Aglaya and Nastasya Filippovna share common traits and yet are pitted against each other as the novel progresses, the dual elements in the personalities of Myshkin and Rogozhin are similarly counterpoised until in the end they somehow exchange them reciprocally. It is significant that Dostoevsky originally conceived the pair as a single, contradictory character and that it was only in the final version of the novel that he undertook to present them as two separate beings.

The innocent and endearing Myshkin is bathed in almost Christlike luminosity as he moves through the dark world of abominations that surround him. Good-natured, frank, and courteous with all, he nevertheless is restlessly and constantly preoccupied with his personal quest. He wears the aura of one who has heard "some mysterious call to go somewhere, [to keep] going for a long, long time..., reach the line where sky and earth met and find the key to the whole mystery...and discover a new life, a life a thousand times more splendid...than ours" (I, 5). A fellow nobleman reproaches him for his naïveté: "It is not easy to achieve heaven on earth, and you do seem to count on it a little: heaven is a difficult matter, Prince, much more difficult than it seems to your excellent heart." But Myshkin imperturbably pursues his mysterious calls, promptings, and subtle subjective sensations.

Always sensitive to the plight of the mortified, Myshkin intervenes to receive blows intended for others, and knows how to humble himself before the humblest. "When I saw your portrait this morning," he tells Nastasya Filippovna, "I seem to have recognized a face I knew well. I felt at once as though you had called me" (I, 16). Uncannily, he seems to penetrate the secret sorrow of this tarnished woman, and to understand that she deserves to be pitied rather than scorned.

With his childlike nature, the prince is passive, patient, and "awfully fond of donkeys," because they are "hardworking, strong... and long-suffering." When first released from the Swiss clinic, he was characterized as a grown-up "only in face and figure"; in development, soul, character, and perhaps also in intelligence, it was said, he was "a real child...and would...stay like that even if [he] lived to be sixty."

His companions in life had always been children, and he finds a kind of alter ego in the thirteen-year-old Kolya, Ganya Ivolgin's younger brother, who, with all his immaturity, is possessed of a superior natural endowment in intellect and will. Myshkin himself acknowledges that his frequent fits of epilepsy have almost made an idiot of him; but "what sort of idiot am I," he asks, "when I know myself that people take me for an idiot?" (I, 6).

Apparently both ageless and sexless, Prince Myshkin has even been described as a "cherub" — that is, an angelic being of a superior order.[2] But a cherub is also a hybrid creature — a dichromatic composite, often depicted with birds' wings and a human or animal face. And Prince Myshkin also has a share in the "animality" or earthiness of Rogozhin, who represents the coarse and impetuous aspects of nature itself. Where the cherub, as an attendant upon the divine throne, is associated with light, Rogozhin is a chthonic or subterranean type of personality who seems rooted in the nether world of the dead. He lives in a dark and gloomy abode whose rooms and corridors run into each other in an endless succession suggestive of the intercommunicating chambers of Hades.

Rogozhin, indeed, seems verily endowed with some of the power of that fallen angel, the Devil. From their very first meeting, he sees straight into Myshkin's soul, and, drawn to what he sees, becomes the prince's mysterious alter ego. Rogozhin's deathly pallor suggests long residence in the nether world, where one grows pale from lack of light (the cherub's light). But Myshkin, too, with his fair hair, almost white beard, and dreamy eyes, has a "colorless" face that may be seen as that of either an angel or a devil.

Aggressive and exuding a heavy sexuality, the inscrutable Rogozhin either maintains an enigmatic silence or expresses himself in an obscure idiom contrasting with the simplicity and clarity of Myshkin's utterance. Like Raskolnikov — and like the Devil himself — Rogozhin wears a contemptuous sneer for the humanity he despises. Forbidding and pitiless, he never quite emerges from the shadowy darkness of his realm; nor does his personality ever fully define itself.

Rogozhin's mysterious figure has something in common with the chthonian rites of ancient mysteries, with their phallic symbols and obscene gestures. The deities of Greece's Eleusinian mysteries were Pluto and Demeter, the latter an earth-goddess of the underworld, the former not so much a god of the dead as the "wealthy one" or the "giver of wealth" — a figure strikingly akin to that of Rogozhin as the bringer of money to Nastasya Filippovna.

For all their extreme differences, then, Myshkin and Rogozhin mysteriously complement each other and are as intensely linked as communicating vessels in a laboratory. Myshkin, "innocent...as an angel," feels his dual nature so strongly that he openly identifies himself with the criminal Rogozhin: "You...raised your hand against me...(which God averted)...we were both guilty!" (III, 3). The assumption of guilt by an innocent person with an occult desire for punishment is a recurrent Dostoevskian theme; but Myshkin's identification with Rogozhin is quite different in character. Here the innocent man is striving to hasten a process of osmosis that will equalize the concentration of guilt in the hearts of the two men.

Myshkin's sought-for identity with his alter ego is stressed again when, after Rogozhin's attempt on his life, he tells his would-be murderer: "I know perfectly well what you had been through that day, just as if it had been myself!" (III, 3). He tries to draw closer to his enemy, anastomose with him as in a union of bodily organs, force their differences and similarities into intercommunication. He seems to know that he has become indispensable to Rogozhin and that it is impossible that they should not face their final destiny together.

In sacred art, Christ, the angels, and the archangels are depicted as triumphing over the Devil despite his innumerable temptations. Seen from a like standpoint, Myshkin, "a knight-errant, a virgin," one "bewitched by [the] fantastic, demonic beauty [of Nastasya Filippovna]" (IV, 9), was unable to resist the temptation inseparable from her very personality. The harlot does not allow the idiot to triumph over the Devil. It is Rogozhin, uncharacteristically in league with the Lord, who saves his friend by snatching his bride from his arm.

"The Lord has preserved the babe himself and has saved him from the abyss," sighs one of the guests at the unfinished wedding (IV, 10). Having once snatched away and murdered the temptress, however, Rogozhin falls prey to Myshkin's very weakness. His mad screams on the night of their vigil were perhaps no different from "the wild shriek of 'the spirit that stunned and cast down' the unhappy [epileptic]" (IV, 7). Perhaps the chthonic Rogozhin had exorcised his own evil spirit and passed it on to the cherubic Myshkin. Embracing each other, the angel and the Devil may thus achieve a total inosculation.

One need not conclude, as do some commentators, that the evil forces represented by Rogozhin are permitted to triumph over the good ones incarnated in Prince Myshkin. The novel's conclusion, cheerless though it is, should not imbue the reader with what one writer has felt as a "sense of frustration [because] a magnificent spiritual idea has been refuted in the end by evil forces."[3] Rather, the concluding chapter of *The Idiot* suggests that the two protagonists have attained to that basic unity which joins together different beings, and that the spiritual idea embodied in the "positively good" man has rubbed off onto Rogozhin as well.

Dostoevsky must have been convinced that the Lord may choose among an infinitude of ways in conveying to humankind the necessity for the continuity of good. The struggle between Myshkin's spirituality and Rogozhin's physicality ends with the former flowing into the latter in an almost physical and psychic identity of opposites. Rogozhin, having absorbed one of Myshkin's dominant qualities — dreaminess — hears his sentence to fifteen years' hard labor in Siberia "grimly, silently, and 'dreamily' " (IV, 12; note Dostoevsky's stress on the word that applies to Myshkin, "dreamily").

Is not this an indication that Rogozhin is being gradually transformed spiritually into the prince, that those fifteen years will prepare the way for his redemption, now that his soul has been freed from the evil spirit that possessed it? Will not Rogozhin succeed in drawing closer to the ideal of Christian love embodied in his opposite?

Still, *The Idiot* remains a tragic novel. Prince Myshkin's Christian compassion, wisdom, and love are challenged by sinful passions and frequently set at naught by the venal ambitions of the ruling Russian aristocracy. Dostoevsky believed that the essence of religious feeling persisted inextinguishably in the Russian heart, and that the fundamental Christian concept of God's rejoicing in man could be embodied in the representation of a "positively good" human being. Nevertheless, he wrote to a correspondent, "I don't think there can be anything harder than that, especially in our time" (*Letters*, II, 297). *The Idiot* remains a stupendous monument to an endeavor that may have lain beyond human strength.

7

The Devils (1871–72)

Sinister gloom and throbbing anxiety pervade the pages of Dostoevsky's most overtly antirevolutionary novel, a work in which devils swarm and the only angelic figure, a crippled, half-demented woman, is ill-equipped to combat their evil machinations. *The Devils* (also known as *The Possessed*) vividly articulates the novelist's loathing of nihilism, terrorism, and the Russian revolutionary movement with which he himself had once been associated but whose later development he saw as fraught with nothing but disaster. In his caustic depiction of a slice of Russian provincial society, Dostoevsky denounces not only the terrorists who are shaking the foundations of Alexander II's regime but also the Russian aristocracy that, in his view, has opened the floodgates by its slavish capitulation to Western ideas.

Suggested in part by the 1869 political murder of a Moscow student by followers of the terrorist Sergey G. Nechaev, the sprawling, complex yet gripping plot of *The Devils* embodies elements of revolutionary conspiracy, crime, and, at a deeper level, the curse of atheism and its implications. For Dostoevsky, the denial of God that underlies the socialists' demand for violent change spells a vital threat to the religious and spiritual development not only of Russia but of the entire world.

In his zealous determination to expose the errors of the contemporary revolutionary movement, Dostoevsky indicted not only the young nihilists of Alexander II's reign but, retroactively, the more idealistic, sentimental reformers and revolutionaries of his own youth. This man who had undergone the searing experiences of trial, condemnation, and exile saw in the nihilism of his young contemporaries an attitude that could lead only to crime and destruction. Once the mechanism of terror is unleashed, he felt, it can no longer be stopped and destruction becomes an almost automatic process.

What might otherwise be dismissed as a mere reactionary polemic is redeemed, from both a literary and a human standpoint, by its author's imaginative and narrative gift and, above all, by the metaphysical dimension with which he endows it. The whole subject of "nonbeing" is masterfully developed in a series of brilliant forays into the uncanny workings of the human mind. Dostoevsky's proclaimed atheists exist on a metaphysical as well as an earthbound plane, and confront the ugly realities of killing and death under the self-deluding guise of vindicators of the future society.

The action of the novel centers in an "unremarkable town" of Russia. Stepan Trofimovich Verkhovensky, a handsome, aging, sensitive idealist, will serve as the link between the older and younger generations. Himself a relic of the idealistic, Westernizing movement of the 1830s and 1840s, he is also the father of a young contemporary nihilist, Peter Stepanovich Verkhovensky, a cynical, ruthless, manipulative revolutionary who is cut out to be the novel's villain.

Bemoaning what he sees as Russia's parasitism on the world scene, the elder Verkhovensky is depressed by the social injustices prevailing in the country he holds responsible for his own frustrations and failures. "The best thing for mankind," he rhetorically affirms, "would be for all Russians to be annihilated" (II, 1, II). To his townsfolk, Stepan Trofimovich poses as a police-tracked, persecuted man in exile — in reality a purely imaginary status, but one that greatly flatters his own vanity. In sum, Dostoevsky writes with tongue in cheek, Verkhovensky is an intelligent, gifted man "with no special academic achievements... in fact no achievements at all [as is] so often the case with our learned men in Russia."

Stepan Trofimovich is the household pet of an extremely wealthy, aristocratic lady, Varvara Petrovna Stavrogin, who, two decades earlier, had entrusted to him the education and intellectual development of her only son, Nikolay — a complex, ambiguous figure around whom much of the novel's action will center. Verkhovensky, the reader is told, gratefully "threw himself into the arms of [Mrs. Stavrogin's friendship] and nestled there for twenty years." Increasingly parasitic, vain, negligent, and inefficient Verkhovensky over the years had gradually slipped into a kind of champagne alcoholism, at the same time developing a hypersensitivity to esthetic values. He had even declared on one occasion that art and beauty were more important than the emancipation of the serfs.

Although the circle of liberal and atheistic friends that clustered around Mrs. Stavrogin and the elderly Verkhovensky was locally regarded as a hotbed of freethinking and vice, Dostoevsky is far from taking them seriously and assures the reader that in reality the guests were "just enjoying a pleasant, innocent Russian pastime — liberal blather." Stepan Trofimovich and his liberal friends are, however, outraged by the Slavophil views of one member of the circle, the gloomy and taciturn Shatov, a serf by birth and a former socialist who has been converted to patriotism and religion. "[A] man who has no country has no God either," Shatov declares. "... Those who cease to understand the people of their own country and lose contact with them also lose the faith of their forefathers and become godless or indifferent" (I, 1, IX).

This Shatov — who will serve to some extent as Dostoevsky's own mouthpiece — had been in Geneva, three years before the opening of the novel, and had there married a Russian girl, although the two had lived together for only three weeks and then "parted like free people." Shatov also has a sister, Dasha, who, unlike her saturnine brother, enjoys the good graces of Mrs. Stavrogin. That magnanimous lady, in fact, has even arranged for her to marry old Stepan Trofimovich in order to resolve a pressing situation brought about for the girl by one of the "whims" of her son Nikolay.

Though Mrs. Stavrogin had always doted on this pampered young man, she had apparently chosen the wrong tutor to develop her son's mind and character. Stepan Verkhovensky, it would seem, had upset his pupil's nerves by his strange pedagogical methods, among them a practice of awakening the ten-year-old boy during the night to pour out to him the secrets of his own soul as the two sobbed in each other's arms. Puny, pale, and strangely withdrawn, Nikolay had eventually been sent away to boarding school and had later become known for his powerful physique, elegance, and social grace — until he spoiled the impression by commencing to mingle with the dregs of St. Petersburg society. Assuming a character marked by savage recklessness and inexplicable brutality, he for some time led a sordid slum life out of sheer eccentricity and contrariness.

Now, after prolonged travels abroad, Nikolay Stavrogin, bored and satiated, has returned to his home town on what the local gossips believe to be some "confidential, secret assignment." Captivated by this idea, the governor's wife lavishes attention on this "man of the most mysterious connections in a most mysterious world and ... certainly in town on some mysterious mission" (II, 5, 1). Half the local ladies adore the young man, while the other half cry out for his blood; but all alike are fascinated by an individual who is described as "elegant without affectation, not too talkative, very modest, and at the same time bold and self-reliant."

Stavrogin's looks, indeed, are almost excessively remarkable: "His handsome head of black hair was somehow a bit too black, his light eyes were perhaps too steady, his complexion too smooth and delicate, and his cheeks too rosy and healthy; his teeth were like pearls and his lips like coral. This sounds like a strikingly beautiful face, but in reality it was repulsive rather than beautiful. His face reminded some people of a mask" (I, 2, I). Although his social demeanor was ordinarily impeccable, when "the beast suddenly unsheathed his claws," the townspeople were stunned by his outrageous behavior. While excusing himself "dreamily" and "absentmindedly" for doing "stupid things," he never showed the slightest regret for even his most shocking actions. His frozen smile radiated nothing but superficial amiability and self-assurance.

In Paris, Nikolay had drawn close to the proud and beautiful Liza Drozdov, the daughter of one of his mother's friends. With the girl and her mother he had gone on to Switzerland, where, however, the high-spirited, quick-tempered Liza had taken offense at his behavior and a rupture had occurred despite the fact that the pair were actually much in love. Liza, in the hope of making Nikolay jealous, had begun to display an interest in Stepan Verkhovensky's son Peter; but instead of becoming rivals, the two young men, Nikolay and Peter, had become fast friends.

Nikolay in due course returned to Russia, and Liza, greatly subdued, had ceased to mention his name or to permit her mother to do so. She herself has now returned to the "unremarkable town," accompanied by a new, official fiancé — who, as it happens, is the first to notice that behind her ostensible hatred for Nikolay there still smolder sparks of a violent love.

Peter Verkhovensky, the self-promoting radical, has also returned to his father's town after having become involved in the drafting of a seditious proclamation, but escaped to Switzerland before his trial. Visits by this glib, insolent iconoclast are a source of acute distress to his old-fashioned humanist father, who lies prostrate on the sofa, pale as death, his head wrapped in a vinegar-soaked cloth. The elder Verkhovensky does, however, persist in believing that his son is really a kind, sensitive, well-meaning boy whose problems arise merely from immaturity and sentimentality. Projecting his own idealism onto his son, he imagines that what fascinates the latter is not the actual program of the socialists (to whom he refers as "squealing demons") but only its emotional appeal, its mystic religious aspects, and its romanticism.

In spite of Peter's supposed revolutionary past, the town gossips soon observe that he, like his friend Stavrogin, is warmly welcomed in the mansion of the governor. This dignitary, Andrey Antonovich von Lembke by name, is a stupid man over whose equally stupid wife Peter soon gains an "uncannily strong influence." In effect, he subjugates her "by frantically toadying... to her dreams of gaining great influence over society and impressing high government circles. He became part of her schemes... and he entangled her from head to foot in a web of the crudest flattery. Finally he became as indispensable to her as the air she breathed" (III, 2, II).

Still another acquaintance from the Swiss period is Alexey Kirilov, who is described as "a brilliant construction engineer" but impresses the reader as a gloomy, dreamy, absentminded eccentric who happens to live in the same depressing house as the Slavophile, Shatov. Kirilov, who is doing research on the growing incidence of suicides in Russia, denies the existence of morality and has become an advocate of "total destruction" in the name of what he calls "the ultimate good." The reasons most people dare not kill themselves, Kirilov claims, are found in two "superstitions:" pain and the next world. "Real freedom," he maintains, "will come when it doesn't make any difference whether you live or not."

The house in which Shatov and Kirilov have their separate quarters belongs to an overblown, red-faced drunkard, Captain Lebyatkin, with whom the wealthy Stavrogin also maintains an eccentric connection. With Lebyatkin lives his lame, gentle, half-demented sister, Maria, an "extraordinary dreamer" who is regularly beaten by her insensitive brother. This Maria, who proves to be the victim of another of Stavrogin's "whims," had ostensibly been "sold" to the eccentric aristocrat during the obscure period of his life in St. Petersburg. Stavrogin, it would appear, had even gone through the form of a legal marriage to the unfortunate cripple, not out of love but out of sheer perversity and wrongheadedness.

Maria did, however, at times awaken his chivalrous instincts. In her defense, Stavrogin on one occasion had actually tossed a bully from a second-story window; and such were his apparent consideration and respect that the poor cripple deluded herself with dreams of a Prince Charming who would even give her a child. But the deceitfulness and inhumanity displayed by Stavrogin at other times had been directly responsible for the helpless Maria's dementia and would ultimately lead to her martyrdom.

Stavrogin's strange role in the lives of these dissimilar people is highlighted by a philosophic debate with Kirilov, the engineer. While Kirilov makes the case for suicide, Stavrogin poses as the defender of order, logic, and even religion. Kirilov is bent on committing suicide in spite of a conviction that all things in life are good. The only reason humans are bad, he maintains, is that they have not been taught they are all good. Startlingly, Stavrogin retorts, "He who tried to teach that was crucified." But Kirilov insists: "He'll come and his name is man-god." "God-man?" questions Stavrogin. "No," replies Kirilov, "man-god — that's the great difference." While Stavrogin attempts without success to goad Kirilov into acknowledging the existence of God, Kirilov's evasiveness suggests that Stavrogin himself may be Kirilov's man-god: "Remember the part you've played in my life, Stavrogin," he admonishes (II, 1, V).

The part played by Stavrogin in the lives of the revolutionist Peter Verkhovensky and the reactionary Shatov is equally significant. Each of these characters, in fact, attempts to name Stavrogin as his "leader," despite their membership in diametrically opposed camps. Stavrogin himself, thus far, has remained outside the revolutionary movement, although he had, "accidentally and out of boredom," written a charter to govern the reorganization of secret revolutionary cells. Peter, however, ingratiatingly insists that Stavrogin should be the one to raise the banner of their "common cause." "You're more romantic and mysterious than ever and that's useful," he says. "...You're the leader, the force; I'm only at your side, a sort of secretary."

Peter's idea, he tells Stavrogin, is to form a two-man "central committee" composed simply of "you and me, and we'll soon have as many chains of command and branches and cells as we wish." Stavrogin, who realizes that his "secretary" is deluding himself about the potential extent of their power, offers him the diabolical suggestion — inspired, no doubt, by Dostoevsky's reading of the Nechaev affair — that the best "cementing" of the entire structure would be achieved by binding any four members of a cell in the killing of a fifth. The brotherhood of henchmen would thus be indissolubly linked in a collective spilling of blood, a new kind of consanguinity.

Shatov, who will eventually become the victim of this fiendish gambit, also expresses undying devotion to Stavrogin, paying extravagant tribute to the strength he sees beneath the latter's ambiguity and dandyism. On an earlier occasion, when Stavrogin had publicly revealed his marriage to Maria Lebyatkin, Shatov had gone up to him and struck him in the face, to his own and everyone else's surprise. "I did it because of your degradation — for your lies!" Shatov explains. "It wasn't to punish you — I didn't know I'd hit you...I did it because you've meant so much to me...I [won't] be able to prevent myself from kissing the spots where your feet have trodden when you leave...I can't tear you out of my heart, Nikolay Stavrogin."

Dismayed, however, by the senselessness and cruelty of Nikolay's unconsummated marriage, Shatov reproaches his friend for seeking to satisfy his perverse "passion for remorse" and "laceration of the nerves." Ambiguously, Stavrogin admits that he knew "more or less...why I married her then and why I'm willing to accept *punishment now*" — another recurrence of the familiar Dostoevskian motif of crime and expiation (II, 1, VI).

Nikolay is aware that Shatov has by this time become the target of Peter Verkhovensky's revolutionary schemes. For Shatov, at one time, had belonged to Verkhovensky's secret society, and, in that capacity, had been made responsible for the safeguarding of a secret printing press. Peter had, however, assured him that he could resign from the society as soon as the press was turned over to another member; but this, Stavrogin now tells him, was actually a lie. According to Stavrogin, not only Shatov's life but his own, too, is in danger; for though he himself had never actually belonged to the society, he is considered too informed a person to be allowed to leave the group, and a death sentence has accordingly been passed on him, too.

Shatov is horrified to learn that Stavrogin, too, is involved in this "stupid organization of flunkies," and is appalled by the seeds of self-destruction Stavrogin is cultivating within himself. "You seem to consider me some sort of sun and yourself as a bug in comparison," Stavrogin protests. In reality, Stavrogin knows better than anyone that the entire secret organization is essentially nothing but one man, the fanatic, maniacal Peter Verkhovensky, and that it is Peter alone who has passed the death sentences on both Shatov and himself.

Stavrogin and Shatov are linked not only humanly, through Shatov's sister, and ideologically, through the Slavophilism Stavrogin has inculcated in Shatov, but also on a religious and metaphysical plane. In the past, Shatov had been deeply influenced by Stavrogin's Russian Orthodox convictions. "A Russian can't be godless," Stavrogin had then contended. "As soon as he becomes godless, he ceases to be a Russian."

To Shatov it had appeared that Stavrogin alone was capable of raising the banner of "the completely new word" — that is, the renewal and resurrection of the God-bearing Russian nation. But now, Shatov laments, it is rumored that Stavrogin has turned away from

Christ and joined a secret society dedicated not to political renewal but to the practice of bestial sensuality and the abuse of children. If such rumors should prove true, Shatov declares, he would kill Stavrogin on the spot.

In one of the novel's most gripping and meaningful dialogues, these two men peer into each other's dark souls where light seems unable to penetrate. Again, as in the scene with Kirilov, Stavrogin probes Shatov's mind, attempting to learn whether his trembling interlocutor does believe in God. Shatov dares not answer. "I believe in Russia and in the Russian Orthodox Church," he mumbles. " . . . I believe in the body of Christ . . . I believe that His new coming will take place in Russia. . . . " "But," Stavrogin interrupts insistently, "In God? Do you believe in God?" "I — I *shall* believe in God," Shatov miserably replies.

Stavrogin, for his part, has lost his ability to distinguish good from evil. He is unable to answer when Shatov asks him whether he finds equal pleasure in the extremes of debauchery and of heroism, such as giving one's life for the good of humankind. Shatov accuses Stavrogin of sensuality and cruelty. "Kiss the earth — drench it with your tears and ask for forgiveness!" he shouts (II, 1, VII) in words reminiscent of Sonia's in *Crime and Punishment*. In a last-ditch effort to convert his friend to the principle of good, Shatov, in Christlike tones, urges the idle aristocrat to find God through labor, give up his possessions, and seek guidance from the holy man Tikhon, who lives in a monastery just outside the town.

Stavrogin does in fact call on Tikhon, and it is to him that he confesses the heinous sin that weighs upon his conscience — the rape of a young girl, which had been followed by her suicide. This crucial incident is related in a chapter that Dostoevsky excised from the original text of his novel, but which is now included in most editions under the title "At Tikhon's: Stavrogin's Confession."

Still another character who looks up to Stavrogin as his "sun" is the drunken Captain Lebyatkin, who declares that his benefactor (and brother-in-law) has "played such an important part in my life." Whether out of remorse or from contrariness, Stavrogin has pumped money into the Lebyatkin household, money that the captain dissipates on drink and then beats his sister all the more vigorously. Lebyatkin, too, has been drawn by Peter Verkhovensky into his "movement" of "crazy fellows . . . possessed by demons," and, as he reveals to Stavrogin, has been given the assignment of distributing subversive leaflets "for money." Entering with spirit into Peter's game, Lebyatkin has also informed on other members of the society, though not, of course, on Stavrogin, who serves as his financial "milk cow" (II, 2, II).

Peter himself, meanwhile, is deliberately driving his father, Stepan Trofimovich Verkhovensky, to despair with his reproaches for allegedly "milking" his patroness, Mrs. Stavrogin, and helping to cover up "another man's sins" by his betrothal to Dasha. The distraught father goes to the length of laying a curse on his son; but even he does not realize that Peter is planning to involve him in a "certain scandal" that will, in due course, subject the old man to public disgrace, the confiscation of his papers, and a lonely, pathetic flight into the unknown.

Peter is also considering how to take advantage of Kirilov's announced determination to commit suicide as a means of showing that he does not fear death. Before shooting himself, Peter decides, Kirilov must leave a note, to be dictated by Peter himself, in which he will assume responsibility for the horrendous crime that Peter is now on the verge of organizing. This crime is to be the murder of the unsuspecting Shatov, supposedly as a punishment for disloyalty to the "movement."

A so-called cell meeting now takes place in the home of one of the conspirators, Virginsky, where fifteen guests are assembled for the ostensible purpose of celebrating the birthday of their host. In satirizing this gathering of small-town nihilists, with its confused, mysterious, and somewhat romantic air, Dostoevsky permits himself some touches of genuine humor. With autobiographical overtones he describes the participants as "either belong[ing] to that bilious type full of frustrated romantic aspirations and pride, or to the type filled with the first impulse of generous youth" (II, 7, 1). All of them, he makes clear, are carried away by their imaginations and vastly exaggerate their collective power and influence.

Dead silence falls upon the meeting at the appearance of Stavrogin and Peter, who are sarcastically described as "the flower of the reddest liberalism in our ancient town." All present believe that Peter is an emissary from abroad, and that he has been vested with special authority to organize five-member cells throughout the province. All of them share the delusive belief that theirs is "only one among hundreds and thousands of similar fives scattered through Russia, all controlled by some vast, mysterious central organization that maintain[s] close contact with the European and worldwide revolutionary movements" (II, 7, I).

Shatov and Kirilov sit silent during this so-called conference, while Peter, paring his nails as he sprawls at the head of the table, displays an ostentatious contempt for the assembled company. The "long-eared" Shigalov, whom Dostoevsky had earlier caricatured as the gloomiest, most scowling progressive imaginable — even though he claimed to be privy to the day and hour when Utopia would settle on the province — asks for the floor in order to expound his system for world organization. "I started out with the idea of unrestricted freedom," Shigalov declares, "and I have arrived at unrestricted despotism."

Shigalov's ideas, as Dostoevsky ironically elaborates them, include "organized obedience" and "a great spy system [in which] each member of the government watches all the others" — concepts that have been seen as prophetic of the post-1917 Soviet police state. The ensuing debate attains its climax with Shigalov's assertion that "there's no longer any cure for the world and the only way is the radical measure of chopping off a hundred million heads." This cure-all is enthusiastically seconded by Peter Verkhovensky, who calls on all humankind to "reach a new religion to replace the old one."

Peter now insists that each of the guests declare his preference as between the "slow solution" for social evolution — i.e., the writing of social novels, bureaucratic reforms, etc. — and "quick action" regardless of methods. From the assembled company he squeezes a declaration of readiness for immediate political action — the "quick solution."

There follows a still more momentous question. "If each of us knew that plans for a political murder were afoot," Peter asks, "would he...go and inform, or would he stay quietly at home ready to face the consequences?" As the individual guests begin to swear silence, the doomed Shatov, calling Peter a "low schemer [and] traitor," rises and leaves the meeting. Some of those present observe that Stavrogin, too, has avoided answering Peter's question. "We have compromised ourselves," they shout, "and you haven't!" "And what do I care?" Stavrogin jeers as he laughingly departs, followed sheepishly by Peter — who, as one of the guests points out, himself "didn't answer the question — he only asked it" (II, 7, II).

Groveling at Stavrogin's feet, Peter now admits his own weakness and begs his friend's help in stirring up political unrest. "Only ten cells...throughout Russia and no one will be able to touch me," he urges. "Don't you really believe that we two are quite enough?...in the West they have the pope and we — we will have you!" Crawling as though before an idol and kissing his hand, Peter tries to flatter his divinity. "You are the leader, the sun, I'm your worm," he protests.

" ... I need you. Without you, I'm a zero, a fly in a glass jar, a bottled thought, a Columbus without America."

Stavrogin already suspects that Peter's alleged socialism cloaks a mere thirst for power and destruction; and he finds corroboration in the latter's apocalyptic vision of a Russia that, "will be shrouded in mist and the earth will weep for its old gods — and it is then that we shall use ... the fairy-tale prince — you!" Stavrogin, according to Peter, will become the New Truth; but he has only three days to accept his "mission." Crudely yet cleverly, he intimates that unless Stavrogin in fact becomes the new messiah, a horrible crime will be committed against Maria and Lebyatkin. Peter thus employs against its author the very idea that Stavrogin had originally planted in his mind — the idea, namely, of binding cell members with the "cement" of spilled blood.

Preparations are meanwhile going forward for a gala benefit to be sponsored by the governor's wife, notwithstanding such sinister portents as a threatened cholera epidemic, incendiary fires in other towns and villages, and a doubling in the incidence of robberies and murders. The governor learns with dismay that pamphlets inciting to violence, identical to those seized in another province, have been found in a local factory. But Mrs. von Lembke's "literary matinee" and evening ball proceed on schedule, though they will end in a fiasco equal to that of the cell meeting and underscore the novelist's contempt for the upper crust of Russian society as well as the revolutionists.

The intended highlight of this gala event, which will develop into one of the more memorable scenes in Dostoevsky's fiction, was to be the participation of the "great writer" Karmazinov — a grotesque caricature of Ivan Turgenev, Dostoevsky's on-and-off friend, literary rival, and ideological opponent. Earlier in the novel, Dostoevsky had described the pompous Karmazinov as one of those "mediocre talents who are taken for near geniuses during their lifetimes [but who] vanish from people's minds as soon as they are dead" (I, 3, II).

Everything Dostoevsky hates in Turgenev, the Westernizer, is summed up in Karmazinov's comment to Peter Verkhovensky: "Holy Russia is a poor wooden, and ... dangerous country. ... Everything here is doomed. Russia ... has no future. I have become a foreigner and I'm proud of it" (II, 6, V). Karmazinov, in Dostoevsky's words, is no more than an "emigrating rat."

Karmazinov's tedious oration precipitates a riotous debacle of this literary gala, one of several converging events that bring the story to a sensational climax. Fires break out in the quarter beyond the river;

their origin is subsequently traced to Fedka, an ex-convict employed by Peter Verkhovensky, and to three factory workers acting "for reasons unknown." Captain Lebyatkin and the crippled Maria are found dead and are thought at first to have been victims of the conflagration, though it is later discovered that they had been robbed and murdered even before its outbreak.

For Stavrogin and for Liza, his former lady love, the night is also a fateful one. In conformity with a plan devised by the ubiquitous Peter, Liza has now broken with her official fiancé and is about to elope with none other than Stavrogin. But though the latter now avows his genuine love and begs Liza to remain with him, she hysterically mocks him and his former beliefs, sarcastically inquiring whether they should not perhaps go somewhere where they could be "resurrected." Refusing to be his "sympathizing nurse," she bitterly denounces him. "I've always imagined that you'd take me to some place where there lived a huge, vicious, man-sized spider and that we'd spend the rest of our lives staring at it in fear. And that's how we'd spend our days of mutual love. You'd better ask dear little Dasha, she'll go with you wherever you wish."

This loverly duet is interrupted by the appearance of Peter himself with news of the just discovered death of Maria and Lebyatkin — an event that, of course, conveniently releases Stavrogin from his mysterious involvement with that unlucky pair. To Liza's point-blank question whether Stavrogin himself is guilty of the Lebyatkins' murder, "I didn't kill them and I was against the killing," he honestly replies, "but I knew that they were going to be killed and I didn't stop the killers" (II, 3, II). Such an acknowledgment of indirect complicity brings the reader very close to an idea that lies at the heart of Dostoevsky's greatest novel, *The Brothers Karamazov*.

With nerves already strained to the breaking point, Liza now rushes off to the quarter where the fires are raging, determined to catch a glimpse of the murder victims. Out of the smoky gloom emerges a much disoriented Stepan Verkhovensky, dressed, the reader is told, "for travel." He kneels to Liza, his former pupil, by way of taking farewell of the world and all his past. "Let's forgive them, Liza," he babbles, "and we shall be free forever and ever. To settle one's accounts with the world and to become truly free — *il faut pardonner, pardonner, et pardonner!* ... I'm running to try to find Russia!"

Liza makes the sign of the cross over Stepan, but by now the violence of the crowd on this night of horrors is threatening her own safety. Recognized as Stavrogin's sweetheart and therefore, perhaps, an accomplice in the crime against the Lebyatkins, she is thrown to the ground and fatally trampled by the mob.

The climax of the novel — for still further sensations are to come — finds Peter assembling his local group of five and, with supreme disregard for truth, accusing the absent Shatov of having informed against them and thus incurred the penalty of death. The date of the execution has already been set, and Peter already has in mind the note he will dictate to Kirilov, the intended suicide, in which he will state that it was he who killed Shatov before killing himself.

The brainwashed members of the cell, though fully convinced that the doomed Shatov deserves his fate, are aware that they, too, are mere pawns in Peter's hands. They move in a climate of irrational violence and, like Liza, are obsessed by the frightening image of a spider — "they felt like so many flies caught in the web of some huge spider" (III, 4, II). Momentarily caught off balance by news that Stavrogin has lately fled to St. Petersburg, Peter nevertheless retains a firm grasp on his puppets. His next victim is Fedka, who had carried out the Lebyatkin crime at Peter's behest but is now found dead in his turn.

While these outrageous crimes are unfolding, Shatov has become absorbed in caring for his estranged wife, who has unexpectedly returned from abroad — not, however, to resume their former "stupid relationship," as she calls it, but to seek aid and shelter for the delivery of a baby fathered (of course) by Stavrogin. Devoting himself to mother and infant with touching submissiveness, the all-forgiving Shatov is rudely summoned from his moment of happiness to meet the conspirators and yield custody of the printing press. At a sinister, deserted spot in the vast park of the Stavrogins' country estate, Peter shoots Shatov in the forehead and the others dump his corpse into a nearby pond.

The horror of this unjust killing unleashes a hysterical reaction on the part of one of the conspirators, but Peter's cold command calls the group to order: "Now your immediate aim must be to bring about the collapse both of the state and of the moral standards it represents. Then there will be no one left but us, and we will have been groomed in advance to take over power." Playing remorselessly upon the naïveté of these easily influenced young men who do not even know whether they have been acting alone or in concert with other revolutionary groups, Peter now coolly punctures any illusions by revealing that their "five" is actually the only one in existence. Yet he remains certain that none of his disillusioned youths will talk.

Three days later, the local authorities receive orders from Moscow to arrest Peter Verkhovensky; but he, by then, is back in St. Petersburg, concealing his identity under an assumed name. Before leaving, he had managed to extract the hoped-for suicide note from Kirilov, though only after a further strenuous discussion on the subject of free will and God — in the course of which Kirilov had reaffirmed what he described as "an obligation to shoot myself because the supreme gesture of free will is to kill oneself.... I am the first man in history to refuse to invent God" (III, 6, II).

Relieving the sense of horror that pervades the later chapters of *The Devils* is a moving account of the last days of old Stepan Verkhovensky, who, after having written a romantic letter of farewell to his fiancée Dasha and received the blessing of Liza, sets out proudly on foot along "the old road, black and scarred with ruts and planted with willows on each side, [which] uncoiled before him in an endless thread." When death finds him soon afterward, he is under the care of a woman of the people who sells Bibles. It is of her that he begs a reading of the passage (in Luke 8:32–37) "about the demons going into the pigs and getting drowned, the lot of them" — a passage that also serves as the novel's epigraph.

The ultimate self-destruction of Dostoevsky's devils — except for Peter Verkhovensky himself — is recounted in an epilogue to the three-part novel. Mary Shatov and her baby die within three days of her husband's murder. Stavrogin hangs himself. Kirilov's body is found with the gun still in the suicide's hand; but the note he has written at Peter Verkhovensky's behest does not prevent the arrest of the other conspirators, who willingly cooperate with the authorities as a relief from their own remorse. One of them, sobbing and "squealing," falls to the ground before the authorities in sign of repentance. The "squealing" of this conspirator turned informer is deliberately made to echo the squealing of the pigs in the biblical parable.

Do demons have a place in the chain of historical causation? Will humans sometimes perform political acts because a devil stirs within them? Many of Dostoevsky's characters are "possessed" by demons, and it is in this way that he explains the possibility, even the prevalence, of such monstrous conspiracies as that of Stavrogin and Verkhovensky or, in real life, of Nechaev or even his own former associates of the Petrashevsky circle. He seems convinced that such phenomena are neither accidental nor isolated, that they grow directly from the ensnarement of Russia's intelligentsia by the devil who lures them away from the primordial foundations of Russian life.

Conversely, can humans be impelled to act, or to change their course of action, by heeding the voice and will of God? In *Crime and Punishment,* the reading of a passage from the New Testament marks a turning point in Raskolnikov's life. Likewise in *The Devils,* a Gospel reading enables old Stepan Verkhovensky to surmount a lifelong "stumbling block" to his belief in God. Hearing the "wonderful, extraordinary passage" from the Gospel of St. Luke — a passage that gains a special resonance from its repeated evocation in the novel — Verkhovensky feels his former liberal atheism yielding before the once scorned religion of the Russian masses. His eyes miraculously open on a vision of the devils who are sowing the seeds of destruction in the belly of Great Mother Russia:

Those devils or demons coming out of the sick and entering into the swine — they are all the festering sores, all the poisonous vapors, all the filth, all the demons and the petty devils accumulated for centuries and centuries in our great, dear, sick Russia.... But the Great Idea and the Great Will protects her from up above, just as it did that other madman possessed by demons; and all those demons, all that filth festering on the surface, will themselves beg to be allowed to enter the swine. Indeed, they may have entered them already! It's *us,* us and the others — my son Peter and those around him; we'll hurl ourselves from the cliff into the sea ... and all of us, mad and raving, will drown and it will serve us right because that's all we're fit for. But the sick man will recover and will sit at the feet of Jesus and they will look at him in surprise. (III, 7, II)

Old Stepan Verkhovensky explicitly identifies his country with the man of the biblical parallel, the man whose name was "Legion" because of the great number of demons that had entered into him. The exorcism performed by Jesus causes the swine, into which the demons have passed, to run headlong to their death in the lake of Gennaseret (the Sea of Galilee). *"Tiens, un lac!"* exclaims the dying, semidelirious Stepan. "Oh God, to think I hadn't noticed it!" (III, 7, II). For Stepan, "all those demons" are simply *"us,* us and the others — my son Peter and those around him." He numbers himself, too, among those unhappy men who are "possessed" by devils, for he knows that when God was driven from his heart, it was the demon who triumphantly entered. With the death of God, Stepan, too, had been condemned to make his solitary way through Russia's history, along a path strewn with the victims of the demoniacs.

If, indeed, a hierarchy could be established among these noxious

spirits, young Peter Verkhovensky, the archvillain, would surely rank
as the grim leader of the apostate angels. He is the one who lusts for
absolute control, even though it means the apocalyptic destruction
of his own country. Supreme incarnation of the spirit of evil, Peter
epitomizes the infection of Great Russia. Unscrupulous, base, cynical, and fantastical — a "provincial Robespierre," in the words of
one critic — Peter dons a deceitful mask in order to create an aura of
naïveté that serves only to mislead and ensnare. His feigned simplicity is in reality the deepest cunning. He uses a cold logic bordering
on madness; he turns speech and men into knives; he is prepared to
use all forms of infamy and violence to attain his ends.

The power that Peter Verkhovensky seeks for himself would give
him dominion over a kingdom of hell, a kingdom where the system of destruction advocated by Shigalov would realize its worst
excesses under the scepter of Stavrogin, a splendid and despotic
messiah. Intent on harnessing Stavrogin's charismatic power for his
own sinister ends, Peter seeks to create a twofold gravitational center toward which the demons will swarm. But the supreme irony
is attained when Stavrogin, who has seen through Peter's machinations and manipulations, angrily turns him out of his house with the
words, "to hell with you now; go to hell!" (III, 3, II).

Stavrogin, another terrifying creature, as immobile and taciturn as
Peter is mercurial and talkative, is a thinking devil with a penetrating
intelligence. Skillful, secretive, and efficient, he, too, has legions of
demons at his command. He, too, is capable of the worst crimes and
the vilest debauchery. He, too, possesses astonishing energy and will.
With his profound inhumanity, he wreaks havoc in the lives of those
who come too close to him, and his human relationships inevitably
end in disaster because he is confusedly sane in his insanity and mad
in his sanity.

Ambiguous and unpredictable, Stavrogin disconcerts by actions
that he himself seems not to understand nor to be able to explain.
His perversions, however, are voluntary, and are aimed at obtaining
fresh experiences as a matter of intellectual curiosity. His behavior
calls to mind the "cursed poets," Paul Verlaine and Arthur Rimbaud,
whose homosexual relationship, to take one example, was inspired
by a mutual determination to reject the natural order and see life in a
different light. To such men, it seems that everything is permissible
because they choose to obey no moral code. Their very extrava-
gance serves to cultivate a certain desperate wisdom, even though
its by-product is spiritual torment. Like Raskolnikov in *Crime and
Punishment,* they consider themselves free to transgress, to challenge

God, society, and their own inner consciences; to them, they feel, is permitted the willful performance of acts beyond good and evil.

If Stavrogin is attracted both by beauty and by vice, by sublimity and degradation, and if he has lost the ability to distinguish good from evil, the reason, Dostoevsky implies, is that he has turned his face away from his "great, dear, sick Russia." Liza ruefully reminds him that he has lost his faith in God and therefore will not be "resurrected." And yet Stavrogin is capable of probing the souls of others, questioning their belief in the existence of God, as though he realized that his own life was arid and meaningless, and that he must seek an answer for himself. Equally capable of noble action and of beastly brutality, Stavrogin seems to wonder about this contradiction in himself, as though tragically apprehending the duality of a God who could be seen as universal creator of both good and evil.

Like Peter, Stavrogin wears a mask, but it is one of a different fashioning. His cold, listless smile, his pale, stern, frozen face, and his affected lethargy make him look like "a wax statue." Beyond the mask, however, Maria Lebyatkin at least perceives a suffering and empty heart. Maria, in fact, is the only character who sees Stavrogin *plain,* closed up in the anguish of his insoluble conflict and oppressed with the sense of nothingness that will ultimately lead to his own suicide. Discerning in her dark prince a "relative" of Christ, a man with an imprint of holiness, Maria asks his permission to kneel in veneration of his obscure majesty.

Like Christ, Stavrogin preaches ideas that arouse others to action and sometimes to destruction, even while he himself remains aloof. Like Christ's, his is a perverse mystique. The opposing forces that clash within Stavrogin's monstrous universe seem, to his perverted mind, to be equally legitimate, and it is this duality and ambiguity that preserves him from becoming a full-blown incarnation of evil. He is, in sum, a defecting angel as well as a watered-down devil.

The novel's other suicide — the spare, wiry Kirilov, whose "black, lusterless eyes" suggest the nether world of the dead — offers another blend of mystical and outright pathological elements. As central to the plot as are Stavrogin and Peter Verkhovensky, Kirilov is perhaps the most modern of Dostoevsky's devils, the most complete embodiment of the underlying oneness of love and death, Eros and Thanatos. Kirilov loves life and children, yet he is ready to commit suicide purely as an act of will, an assertion of the ability to destroy the fear of pain and to abolish an unbearable God.

Having once overcome his dread of death and fear of the beyond, Kirilov expects to set the example of a future society of those who

dare. Dazzled by what he considers the logic of his theory, carried
away by his expectation of humankind's progressive development,
Kirilov feels a strange joy in his freedom from the anguish caused by
transcendent nothingness. He is grateful for the reminder of his own
approaching liberation that is transmitted to him by the crawling of
a spider — the symbol of nothingness that threads the novel.

Kirilov experiences moments of supreme joy when he suddenly
feels the presence of "eternal harmony in all its perfection" — not
in a future, eternal life but in the "present, eternal life ... when time
suddenly stops and becomes eternal." Eagerly would he share his
sensation of timelessness with the humanity of the future. "When
man attains happiness, there will be no more time because there
will be no need for it," he announces. In a startlingly contemporary
formulation, he voices the idea that "time is not a thing, it's an idea.
It will vanish from the mind" (II, 1, V).

"Possessed" as he is by the idea of a man-god who will transform
humankind and history, Kirilov is attracted by Stavrogin's coldness,
impassivity, and amorality because he believes that it is just such an
indifference to life and death, when achieved on a wide scale, that
will usher in the age of the man-god. Since his fellow demons are
unable either to accept or to refute his theories, he holds to the conviction that if humans can only succeed in putting God (or the gods)
to death, everything will be permitted them. Precariously poised between two universes, the sacred and the man-centered, his highest
aspiration is to bring about the negation of a God invented by man
in order to validate the concept of a man-god. Through Kirilov, it
may be suggested, the reader may better understand Dostoevsky's
own need for Christ, the man, as an indispensable support if he is
to accept — that is, "invent" — the existence of God.

Having once proved his impious theory to the world, Kirilov will
supposedly be happy — but only in the same manner as the Roman
Emperor Caligula, whose frustrated wish for happiness, combined
with an insane pride, had transformed an idealistic young man into
a life-destructive, self-destructive maniac. Caligula, too, had wished
to compete with the gods, and the origin of his madness, if one
is to follow Albert Camus's well-known interpretation, lies in the
perception that "men die and are not happy."

Kirilov's correlative maxim is that "man is unhappy because he
doesn't know he's happy" (II, 1, V). By rejecting the fiction of the
gods, Caligula believes he has achieved complete freedom and independence; his cruelty and wild despotic caprices can be seen as an
attempt to exercise what he sees as the attributes of divinity. Kirilov,

similarly, exclaims: "For three years I've searched for the attributes of my divinity and I've found it — my free will! This is all I have at my disposal to show my independence and the terrifying new freedom I have gained" (III, 6, II).

Kirilov's purely gratuitous act of self-destruction, without external motivation and undertaken simply as a proof that he could exercise his free will, can be read as a kind of suicidal revenge on his own youthful illusions. Dostoevsky had long reflected on the phenomenon of suicide, and would express a special comprehension and hope for the salvation of the souls of suicides, who were considered in the Russian folk tradition as "unclean" and rejected by the earth.[1]

Neither Caligula nor Kirilov, the two self-appointed avengers of human destiny, succeeded in proving that humans can become gods. The impious Kirilov abolished from his heart the God he found so intolerable, but in the depths of his conscience one must suppose there remained a tormenting void similar to Stavrogin's. Unlike Stavrogin, whose suicide was the result of anguish and a sense of nothingness, Kirilov, believing he could remodel the world through the judicious exercise of human reason and free will, committed suicide through intellectual hubris.

Nor is Shatov, the one holdout against the devils' sway, serene in his Christian faith. His very name indicates that he is "shaky," "unstable," or "uncertain," much like his alter ego, the pre-Siberian Dostoevsky. In the past, Shatov had fanatically accepted liberalism as infallible truth. Now, a reformed radical, he adheres with equal ferocity to his new creed, preaching that the Russians will be God's chosen people, and that Russian nationalism, autocracy, and Orthodoxy will pave the way for the new messiah.

Shatov, too, would eliminate the gods — that is, all the particular gods of other peoples, in order to adore exclusively the God of Russia. For Shatov, the problem of the revolution is essentially a question of religion and Slavophilism. Although he holds that socialism is preferable to Roman Catholicism, he nevertheless condemns it as a form of atheism because in seeking to base society on science and reason it runs counter to the Russian Orthodox spirit.

And yet, for Dostoevsky, the strange character of Shatov seems to emit a gleam of hope for the salvation of the tortured world. Shatov's attitude reflects an immense capacity for love and pardon, revealed in his devotion to Stavrogin, to Maria, and to the adulterous wife who gives birth to Stavrogin's child in the humble asylum of Shatov's home. Incarnating as it does the novelist's ideal of uni-

versal pardon, Shatov's personal behavior would set an example
for humanity to follow in achieving the final redemption of all. His
tragedy, like Dostoevsky's own, is that he is unable to say whether
he really believes in God.

In this novel, Dostoevsky's nihilists are devils of destruction and
despotism. They act not on behalf of Russia's "poor folk," but
as subversives goaded on by their inner demons to wreak reckless
and relentless annihilation. Beguiled, "possessed" recruits in Satan's
army, they doom themselves and all of Russia. Harbingers of the
demoniacal socialist ideas coming from the West to undermine the
Russian nation — as Dostoevsky sees it — each of the members of
Peter Verkhovensky's fearsome crew is closed in his mad, ferocious
cult of evil; each seems to have within him an attendant power who
speaks the inconsequent language of demoniacs.

Only the crippled Maria Lebyatkin, Dostoevsky's purest, most
innocent, and almost mythic figure, with her "quiet, gentle gray
eyes...and dreamy...trusting...cheerful gaze," speaks a consistent language of biblical inspiration. An archetypal personage, she
may be seen as Dostoevsky's Madwoman of Sweet Russia, brutal-
ized and martyrized by the raging fanaticism and fury that whip
the land, a woman whose legendary story has been enacted and
reenacted throughout history. She may also be associated with the
lineage of mythology's "lame heroes," ranging from the ancient
Greek figures of Hephaestus, Achilles, and Oedipus to the more
modern Cinderella.

In some of her half-demented utterings, Maria communicates il-
luminating messages. Her eyes see through matter, plunge through
debris and reality; her sight is endowed with extrahuman power.
Captain Lebyatkin brutalizes her, but she refers to him compassionately as her "servant." She knows that in using his savage *physical*
force to beat her, he is trying to escape the *moral* power of his victim, whose "servant" he rightly is — a concept that will be more
fully developed in *The Brothers Karamazov.*

Piercing the mystery of Stavrogin's duality, Maria curses him because she imagines he is impersonating her Prince Charming. "I'm
my prince's wife," she cries out, "and I'm not afraid of your knife!"
But Stavrogin is unarmed. It is Maria's divine flash of vision that
permits her to see the knife that is concealed in Fedka's boot and
will ultimately be plunged into her own throat.

Maria's very vulnerability endows her with a peculiar kind of
spiritual nobility, through which she is able to exercise a singular dominion over those who are stronger and saner than she. Stavrogin,

alternating between his diabolic impulses and his desire to protect Maria, finds himself in bondage to the moral influence of the demented woman. His pity for her arouses a sense of shared personal guilt, and he comes to identify with her passive suffering. Maria, indeed, seems to set the characters around her before a mirror, or, better, she opposes the mirror of "insanity" to the logic of the "sane." The reflections truly test the conscience of sane society, its standards of rationality. The "irrational" questions Maria puts to the faces in the mirror can only be answered in kind, for men who brutalize the mentally unsound must surely be insane themselves.

This complex, somber, and structurally untidy masterpiece has been seen as a "political melodrama"; as a "poetic" novel, powerful as any religious work; as the "most prophetic," and, according to André Gide, the "most powerful" and "most admirable" of all Dostoevsky's works. Regardless of the rank assigned *The Devils* in the totality of Dostoevsky's oeuvre, this powerful novel deserves to be read with attention, and as a whole. Filmed versions, inevitably, can capture only fragments of its intellectual burden, as has been seen again in the apocalyptic film by Polish director Andrzej Wajda, in which Dostoevsky's demons became the vehicle for cinematic denunciation of the Soviet system.

8

A Raw Youth (1875)

After *The Devils,* Dostoevsky was to produce only one more novel before beginning work on his final masterpiece, *The Brothers Karamazov.* *A Raw Youth* (also known as *The Adolescent*) was coolly received on its publication in 1875 and continues to be overshadowed by its author's greater works. With action alternating between the palaces and hovels of St. Petersburg, the novel teems with characters whose very multiplicity dissipates the reader's involvement. A plethora of subplots involving swindling, blackmail, gambling, and unwanted pregnancies may easily create an impression that the uncentered life of the hero is totally taken up with sideshows. Yet in spite of manifest shortcomings, *A Raw Youth,* with its moving treatment of a young man's search for paternal affection, stands virtually alone as a nineteenth-century Russian example of the Bildungsroman or novel of personal development.

A story rich in autobiographical overtones is related by the "Raw Youth" himself, a young man whose complicated family ties demand the reader's close attention. Twenty-two years old at the time of his narration, Arkady Dolgoruky is nominally the son of an elderly religious pilgrim, Makar Ivanovich Dolgoruky by name, who had at one time been a serf in the household of Arkady's real father, the aristocratic Andrey Petrovich Versilov. Arkady's mother, Sofia or Sonia Andreyevna, had also been a serf on the Versilov property, and, at the age of eighteen, had married the then fifty-year-old Makar in compliance with the wishes of her dying father. Six months after the marriage, however, she had given her love — "through servility," as her seducer cynically put it — to the handsome and glamorous Versilov, the master of the estate, who was then twenty-five years of age, a widower with two young children. Sonia had borne him two more children, Arkady and a girl, Lizaveta, both of whom, however, acknowledged the technical paternity of the elderly Makar.

Years later, Versilov in talking to his illegitimate son characterized Sonia as "one of those 'defenseless' people whom one does not fall in love with...but whom one suddenly pities for their gentleness....One pities them and grows fond of them." Arkady readily understands how his simple, pure-hearted mother, despite her rigid ideas about the sanctity of marriage, could have succumbed to his father's fascination, his "society polish," and his "air of worldly superciliousness" (I, 1, V).

Versilov, however, is a highly complex character, one whose seemingly contradictory actions often baffle those around him. After seducing Makar's wife, the mercurial landowner had promptly confessed the whole affair to the offended husband, at the same time making it clear that he intended to keep his new conquest. Sobbing on his serf's shoulder, the master, as a self-styled man of honor, had not only offered Makar a substantial sum of money but had stated that if Makar refused, he would restore his wife and let them have the money as a gift. Makar, while accepting the money and in effect "bequeathing" Sonia to her lover, had set the money aside for his wife's future benefit. Skeptical about the master's long-term intentions, he had even begged Versilov to marry Sonia after his own death — since he obviously could not do so earlier — and Versilov had given his word "as a nobleman" that he would comply with Makar's wishes.

A period of almost two decades precedes the actual opening of the story. Versilov, a highly neurotic personality who suffered from spleen and boredom — notwithstanding his professed belief in the mission of the Russian people — had wandered over western Europe in Sonia's company. The "typical melancholy of the Russian nobleman" had perhaps been enhanced in his case by a feeling of oppression arising from the social "unworthiness" of his family. While "dragging [Sonia] about with him," he had kept up a formal correspondence with Makar, who, though he had previously never left his village over a period of fifty years, had taken up a pilgrim's staff and was now wandering through Russia's towns and monasteries, preaching his faith in God and collecting money for the building of a church.

Makar's spirit, unlike Versilov's, had become light and joyous. At rare intervals he turned up at home and stayed with his wife, who always had her own rooms apart from Versilov's. Versilov, at first alarmed by these visits, had gradually come to wonder how Sonia ever could have preferred him to this handsome, stately, and serene old peasant.

The children, meanwhile, had been separated and, to a great

extent, left to fend for themselves. Arkady had grown up feeling like an outcast. "When I was born my mother was still young and good-looking, and therefore necessary to Versilov; and a screaming child, of course, was always a nuisance, especially when they were traveling" (I, 1, VI). Having no real family, he had developed into a "contemptible urchin"; one of his teachers had described him as "filled with ideas of vengeance and civic rights." Mercilessly taunted at Moscow's aristocratic Touchard boarding school, where his illegitimacy was common knowledge, Arkady had become "mistrustful, sullen and reserved . . . ready to find fault, and given to blaming others." Although basically good-hearted, he had inherited his father's suspicious nature and an inclination to see evil everywhere; and he also had his father's capacity to "keep up a passive hatred and underground resentment . . . for years" (II, 9, I).

Like many Dostoevskian characters, Arkady took a perverse pride and satisfaction in humiliating himself. "Perhaps from my earliest childhood [I had] one characteristic: if I were ill-treated, absolutely wronged and insulted to the last degree, I always showed at once an irresistible desire to submit passively to the insult, and even to accept more than my assailant wanted to inflict on me, as though I would say, 'All right, you have humiliated me, so I will humiliate myself even more, and enjoy it!' " (II, 9, I).

Until he was nineteen, Arkady scarcely saw his mother except on two or three brief occasions, the most notable of which had been her visit to the Touchard school — an event so painful that the boy had suppressed it in his mind and remembered it only years later after an accident in which his head had struck the pavement. Lying unconscious on the sidewalk, he relived the experience as though he were again receiving his mother's visit, his "eyes cast down, but with a great air of dignity."

Embarrassed and "disgraced" by her old dress, her coarse, working-class hands, her even coarser shoes, and her terribly thin face, he had contemptuously ignored her presents of oranges, gingerbread cakes, and French bread. At the end of their agonizing visit, Sonia had given her son a handkerchief into which she had tied four almost worthless coins. After making the sign of the cross over him and whispering a prayer, she had made the boy a prolonged low bow that caused him to shudder with embarrassment. Thrusting the handkerchief into his little box of belongings, he had allowed six months to elapse before suddenly feeling the urge to kiss it. "Mother, mother," he had whispered, "show yourself to me just this once, come to me if only in a dream, just that I may tell you how I love you, may hug you and kiss your blue eyes, and tell you that I'm not ashamed of you now" (II, 9, II).

While grappling with his mixed emotions toward his mother, Arkady had also made ineffectual efforts to win a place in the heart of his father, Versilov — who, on his side, was cruelly neglecting his offspring. "This cold, proud man, careless and disdainful of me," wrote the unwanted child, "after bringing me into the world and packing me off to strangers, knew nothing of me at all ... perhaps he had only a vague and confused idea of my existence." Arkady's own confused "dreams" were always colored by this dashing father of whom he did not know whether he "hated him or loved him" (I, 1, VII).

As a man of power and charisma, Versilov is surrounded in the boy's mind by a mystical aura that is denied to his saintly mother. Yet while his mother is unvaryingly dignified in her humility, his father at times displays a disconcerting will to self-abasement. Arkady hears strange stories about the public humiliations and calumnies to which Versilov has been subjected, and determines to protect the "imagined" man against all his enemies. "Of course, I proposed to assist this man secretly without display or excitement, without expecting his praise or his embraces. ... Was it his fault that I had fallen in love with him and had created a fantastical idea of him?" The emotionally rudderless Arkady is prepared at one and the same time to lay down his life for his beloved father's interests or to leave the hated parent forever.

By the time Arkady had reached the age of nineteen, the slothful Versilov had already dissipated three inherited fortunes and was living with his family in St. Petersburg in a state of poverty verging on destitution. Arkady, summoned to the capital as the story opens, is placed in a humiliating situation as paid companion to the wealthy old Prince Sokolsky. In the course of trying to "amuse" his elderly patron, he is profoundly impressed by the beauty and charm of the prince's only daughter, the widowed but still youthful Katerina Nikolaevna Ahmakova.

This proud, strong-willed lady, who "knows how to look haughty and crush one with a glance" (II, 4, I), is modeled once again on Polina Suslova, Dostoevsky's temperamental inamorata of the 1860s. She and Versilov had at one time been in close intimacy, but a mutual hatred had since sprung up between them. Not only does Ahmakova now believe herself to hate Versilov; she fears his power over her, for she believes him to be in possession of a compromising letter she once wrote that might deprive her of her father's favor and thus reduce her to poverty. The letter that fills Ahmakova with such anxiety tickles the reader's curiosity through chapter after chapter as it moves from Versilov's possession into that of the suicide Kraft, is then sewn up in Arkady's pocket lining and ultimately falls into the hands of Arkady's former schoolmate, the extortionist Lambert.

So smitten is Arkady by Katerina Nikolaevna's charms that he radically transforms his life-style, from that of a vagabond consorting with criminal apprentices to that of a dandy who runs up bills with tailors, opens an account at a celebrated restaurant, and practices his French with his coiffeur. Beginning in a whirl in which his soul is "singing with joy," he soon becomes a pitiful, indebted derelict at the gambling tables. Yet he continues to find sustenance in the image of the beautiful lady. "I have gained a treasure," the indigent young man confesses to his idol, "the thought of your perfection." Shyly, he keeps his eyes cast down and dares not look at her during their "rendezvous": "To look at her meant to be flooded with radiance, joy, and happiness, and I did not want to be happy," he confesses (II, 4, I).

The fact that both father and son are enamored of the same lady provides one of the structural centers of this somewhat amorphous novel. Eventually the reader learns that Versilov had actually desired to marry Ahmakova, had even sought Sonia's permission to do so, but that their affair had ended in a rupture full of rankling bitterness when the jealous and haughty Ahmakova had discovered Sonia's existence. Ahmakova nevertheless remained an obsession in Versilov's mind. He is still bound to her by a mysterious link that Arkady attempts to understand while Versilov, apparently loving and hating Ahmakova in equal measure, disguises with blasé irony his deep emotions and real despair.

Arkady, in a halfhearted rebellion against paternal authority, at one time flings an ultimatum to his mother to choose between Versilov and himself. But Sonia, unequal to such a challenge, simply turns pale and her voice fails her at the thought of leaving Versilov. It is the son who leaves home, but the rupture does not prevent his father from visiting him in the humble "coffin" where he finds lodging. The situation he has created leaves the ordinarily loquacious Arkady at a loss for words with which to define his emotions: "Nothing in the world would have induced me to go to him first, and not from obstinacy, but just from love of him; a sort of jealous love — I can't express it" (II, 1, II).

Arkady's emotions reach a climax at the end of one paternal visit when the candle accidentally goes out as he accompanies his father to the door. "Then I clutched his hand. It was pitch dark. He started but said nothing. I stooped over his hand and kissed it greedily several times, many times. 'My darling boy, why do you love me so much?' he said, but... his voice quivered, there was a ring of something quite new in it as though it were not he who spoke." Arkady runs back upstairs: "I threw myself on my bed, buried my face in the pillow and cried and cried. It was the first time I had cried since I was in Touchard's [school]. My sobs were so violent, and I was so happy."

Yet every conversation with Versilov leaves Arkady more troubled and, at the same time, more attracted by his father's secrecy and the strange meekness that seems totally out of keeping with the personality of this independent and egotistical aristocrat. Versilov's powers of accommodation, his resiliency and elasticity are almost superhuman. "There's no crushing me," he tells his son proudly, "no destroying me, no surprising me. I've as many lives as a cat. I can with perfect convenience experience two opposite feelings at one and the same time, and not, of course, through my own will" (II, 1, III).

Since Versilov preferred calling on his son in his "coffin," Arkady only rarely visited his mother, until the fall that brought recall of the Touchard school visit and resulted in his transfer to Versilov's own bed at home. Crying from ill humor, the irritable, emotionally undisciplined youth worries his mother and hates the doctor who is called in to treat him. On the fourth day of his convalescence, lying in bed in the midst of a profound stillness, he is mystified by hearing words pronounced in a half-whisper: "Lord Jesus Christ, have mercy upon us."

Rising with difficulty, Arkady makes his way to his mother's bedroom and there finds "a very gray-headed old man, with a big and very white beard, and it was clear that he had been sitting there a long time." This is Makar Ivanovich Dolgoruky, Arkady's legal father, who has come to stay with the Versilovs between pilgrimages. Arkady stares in astonishment at this old man, whose laughter, "the surest test of the human heart," makes a deep impression upon him because it is so infectious, good-hearted, and indeed "irresistible." Gradually engaging Arkady in a discussion of life, death, love, and mystery, Makar communicates to the boy a sense of his own holiness. In this old pilgrim, the "raw youth" finally discerns the "seemliness" for which he has been searching all his life — that is, a decorous and fitting "gaiety of heart." New horizons open before Arkady's eyes: "My whole soul seemed to be leaping for joy, and

a new light seemed penetrating to my heart.... It was ... an instant
of new hope and new strength" (III, 1, III).

In this man of the Russian people, Arkady finds serenity and con-
solation. Lacking a supportive real father, caught up in a senseless
tangle of events and intrigues, troubled by shapeless dreams that reveal his latent sexuality, the emotionally disturbed adolescent finds
help and solace in the venerable peasant. Makar, to Arkady's perception, is the very incarnation of Love. His benignity endows him with
the precious gift of "seemliness," a quality mentioned in St. Paul's
First Epistle to the Corinthians and defined by Arkady as "extraordinary pureheartedness and ... freedom from amour propre; one felt
instinctively that he [Makar] had an almost sinless heart. He had
'gaiety' of heart, therefore 'seemliness' " (III, 3, I).

As Arkady grows increasingly oppressed by what he considers his
own loathsomeness and lack of "seemliness," he remembers how he
used to find pleasure in what disgusted him because he had "the soul
of a spider" — again, Dostoevsky's symbol for evil or nothingness.
Within his corrupt heart, Arkady realizes, he carries the same debilitating duality as his father. "I have marveled a thousand times," he
declares, "at that faculty in man (and in the Russian, I believe, more
especially) of cherishing in his soul his loftiest ideal side by side with
the most abject baseness, and all quite sincerely" (III, 3, I).

But the admirable Makar, who is himself quite free of these
schizophrenic traits, has come to the Versilovs' because it is time
for him to die. By his death, Sonia's matrimonial tie is dissolved,
and the reader expects that Versilov will now fulfill his responsibility toward his faithful companion. Katerina Ahmakova, who by
now acknowledges her own love for this man who knows "every
secret of her soul," also looks forward to emotional release through
Versilov's marriage.

Makar's death also eased the relationship between Arkady and
his real father, who now "talked like two friends in the highest
and fullest sense of the word," loved each other, and felt happy
together. Versilov has promised to tell his expectant son the full
story of his liaison with Ahmakova; but the youth's assumption
that his father has now ceased to love this fascinating woman proves
wholly illusory. Versilov, as will become apparent in the novel's later
chapters, is in fact consumed by a romantic and irrational passion
for their common idol.

A catastrophe approaches as Versilov, returning from an un-
explained absence, brings Sonia a nosegay for her birthday — a
seemingly innocuous gesture that, however, is followed by a scene

of uncontrollable violence, culminating in the smashing by Versilov of Makar's precious religious icon. Versilov's strange words, uttered in a voice not his own, strike dread to Arkady's heart. "I feel as though I were split in two," the older man confides; "yes, I am really split in two mentally, and I'm horribly afraid of it. It's just as though one's second self were standing beside one; one is sensible and rational oneself, but the other self is impelled to do something perfectly senseless... ; and suddenly you notice that you are longing to do that amusing thing... against your will" (III, 10, II).

Versilov's diabolic second self, the reader learns, had, after Makar's death, made a formal offer of marriage to Katerina Ahmakova, which she had refused. He had thus broken his promise to Makar, given as a nobleman and a man of honor, to wed Sonia if she became a widow. And, in addition, the man who had told his son that he "could not get on without [Christ]" had vindictively broken the icon as a way of putting a symbolic end to his life. Thus this European *par excellence* had forcibly rejected the two primordial symbols of his Mother Russia: Sonia, and Makar's icon.

Arkady convinces himself that he personally has an obligation to save Versilov, bring him back to Sonia, and destroy the illusions of this man who is "spellbound by sorcery." In his heart, however, he simply wishes to shame Ahmakova, because he himself is in love with her and therefore jealous of his father. He, too, now hates and loves this creature who characterizes herself as "one of the most gloomy characters among modern women" (III, 6, III), and whose behavior, in the end, actually deprives Versilov at least temporarily of his sanity.

In the novel's conclusion, Versilov is seen recovering from madness. His "ideal" side has now become more marked; he never leaves Sonia's side, and Arkady loves him more than ever. Versilov has apparently forgotten Ahmakova, whose name he never mentions; but neither does he say anything further about marrying Arkady's mother. For the "raw youth" himself, a new life has also begun. The realities of life have by this time given him the strength of character without which he would not have "confessed all this to the reader." "As I finish my narrative and write the last lines," Arkady concludes, "I suddenly feel by the very process of recalling and recording, I have reeducated myself" (III, 13, III).

Arkady Dolgoruky epitomizes, for Dostoevsky, the plight of Russian youth in his own time. The life of this uprooted male adolescent, Dostoevsky feels, might have been less awkward, more meaningful and successful had the very foundations of Russian society not been undermined by the sinister influence of European ideas. Arkady is a troubled youth of Russia's troubled times, but he is also a mythic figure as well, the timeless youngster engaged in an everlasting dialogue of the deaf with the society in which he lives.

As the reader knows, Arkady has two fathers, the venerable, spiritual, and completely Russian Makar, and the dissipated, dissatisfied "European" Versilov. Makar, his nominal "nonfather," played the role of a listener. He never wearied of hearing his "nonson" talk on a variety of subjects, "realizing though a 'youth' I was immeasurably superior to him in education." To his real father, on the other hand, Arkady's voice repeatedly cries out: "I wanted the whole of Versilov, I wanted a father" (I, 6, IV); but the man remained unfathomable.

As a small child, Arkady had sought Versilov's love and attention, had longed passionately to be at his side, yet had been permitted only to catch brief glimpses of the handsome nobleman getting into his carriage and driving off while the boy gazed in wondering admiration. Versilov, thirty-seven years old at that time, had been a dashing figure with his jet black hair, his face of even pallor, his moustache and whiskers, dark glowing eyes, and gleaming teeth. (Critics have compared his mystical aura to that of Stavrogin in *The Devils*.) The father's smile had rejoiced the child's heart, but Versilov had remained shrouded in mystery. In his own mind, Arkady had set him on a cloud-capped pinnacle so high that any attempt to reach him was doomed to failure.

In the Touchard boarding school, Arkady's instinct for male bonding again was thwarted. He longed to return home to his adored father, yet fear restrained him and he had to submit instead to the physical and psychological ordeals inflicted by his schoolmates. "Besides being a lackey, I was a coward, too, and my real development began!" Later, as he will recall in a conversation with his father, his behavior at the boarding school was still childishly infatuated: "When I got into bed and pulled the quilt over me, I began thinking of you at once ... only of you, no one else; ... I dreamed about you too. I used always to be passionately imagining that you would walk in, and I would rush up to you and you would take me out of that place, and bring me home with you ... and ... that we should not part again — that was the chief thing!" (I, 6, IV).

Awakening both his father's and his own latent memories, Arkady poignantly reminisces: "I can see you now as you were then, handsome and flourishing ... how much older and less good-looking you have grown in these years." Versilov's reply is like a mirror flashed before Arkady's eyes: "Yes! yes! I remember it all now ... you were such a charming boy then, a thoughtful boy even, and, I assure you...you have changed for the worse in the course of these nine years" (I, 6, III).

Both father and son are yearning to show their love, but both seem frozen in a stiffness that arrests their souls. "Will you never give me a real warm kiss, as a child kisses its father?" asks Versilov, with a strange quiver in his voice. Arkady kisses him fervently, but, as he tells us, "I had never kissed him before in my life, I never could have conceived that he would like me to" (II, 5, III).

As a young adult, Arkady often loses patience with his father and deliberately insults him; yet after the fact his heart aches and he feels he has "cut off a piece of [his own] flesh." Fascinated by Versilov's insight, he shudders inwardly at his father's capacity to read his own feelings and divine the workings of his mind. "He knew beforehand every gesture I made, every feeling I had felt....I found in him...such a marvelous faculty for guessing what I meant from half a word" (II, 5, III). At the same time, Arkady is perplexed and exasperated, unable to understand, "if he so well understood one thing, why was it he utterly failed to understand something else."

During the period when Arkady had fallen into frivolity and foppery, squandering whatever money he earned, his father showed no curiosity about his son's eccentric behavior. Arkady was at a loss to understand why his father did not check his dissipation. "If he had said one word I should have perhaps pulled up," he writes (II, 1, III). Again Arkady's refrain is heard: "All my life I had wanted Versilov himself, the whole man, the father, and...this idea had become part of myself. Was it possible that so subtle a man could be so crude and so stupid?" (I, 7, IV).

In spite of transitory frictions, the symbiosis of father and son is so strong at times that they react in the same way and even love the same woman, adopting similar behavior as though they were doubles. As Arkady attempts to draw his father into the secret of his passion, he blushes, squeezes his father's hand — "which he had somehow seized and was unconsciously holding" — as he eagerly seeks an entrée into the subject of "intimacies." Shyly, he begins: "It's utterly out of the question for a son to speak to his father...of his relations with a woman, even if they are of the purest! In fact, the purer they are the greater the obligation of silence."

Faltering in his attempts to broach this delicate matter, Arkady relies on Versilov's guidance, but the father shies away from "meddling" in his son's life, protesting that "all such saving counsels and warnings are simply an intrusion into another person's conscience, at another person's expense" (II, 5, II). Versilov, in fact, is unequipped to provide the paternal advice Arkady seeks. "I'm a wretched raw youth, and I don't know... what is good and what is evil," Arkady protests. "Had you given me the tiniest hint of the right road, I should have... been eager to take the right path. But you only drove me to fury." Defensively and evasively, Versilov retorts, as though seeking to wash his hands of responsibility: "*Cher enfant,* I always foresaw that, one way or another, we should understand each other" (II, 5, II).

Arkady, like youth in general, needs and seeks discipline, basic truths, parental authority, and a father image that will provide a code of conduct. "Since I was entirely made up of other people's ideas," he laments, "where could I find principles of my own when they were needed to form independent decisions? I had no guide at all" (II, 7, II). Indeed, the central issue in this father–son relationship is not, as some assert, a rebellion against parental and paternal authority but a positive search for just such a stabilizing influence.

The dazzling figure of Versilov, the predatory male whom Arkady subconsciously imitates by dressing like a dandy and hiring a smart coachman, leaves the son without a firm foundation on which to base his life. In the absence of such paternal discipline, the only method Arkady finds to "reeducate" himself is that of shaping his autobiography. "I am dreadfully sorry," he writes apologetically, "that I have... in this narrative allowed myself to take up a disrespectful and superior attitude in regard to Versilov.... I regret a great deal I have written... but I will not cross out [sentences and pages] or correct a single word" (III, 13, I).

The factor that prevented Versilov from becoming a true father to Arkady, and a true husband to Sonia, was the emotional dualism that turned itself inward with regard to his family but exploded outward in his fierce passion for Katerina Ahmakova. Versilov's all-consuming love for that seductive lady, whom Arkady also desires if only in imitation of his adored father, gives rise to both love and hatred between father and son. This so-called displaced Oedipal competition, in which an adolescent and his adult rival crave the same love object, has been studied elsewhere in all its complexities.[1]

Separated from his father by a seemingly impassable gulf, Arkady fails also to find a compensating mother figure in Sonia. Indeed, he nurtures similar love/hate feelings toward this refined though low-born serf-woman, whose pale, anemic face "had a look of simplicity, but by no means of stupidity" and whose eyes "shone with a gentle and serene light" (I, 6, I). His emotions toward his mother, mixed as are his father's toward him, find vent in behavior that often belies his true feelings. "I was haunted by the soft look in my mother's eyes, her dear eyes which had been watching me so timidly," he writes. "... Of late I had been very rude at home, to her especially. I had a desire to be rude to Versilov, but not daring, in my contemptible way tormented her instead" (I, 4, III).

While Versilov speaks familiarly with his grown son, his mother, fearing some outburst on Arkady's part, always addresses him deferentially, even imploringly, when the three are together. During Arkady's convalescence from his accident, "she, poor darling, thought I was crying from tenderness, [and] stooped down and began kissing me. I restrained myself and endured it, but at that instant I positively hated her. But I always loved my mother, and at that very time I loved her and did not hate her at all, but it happened as it always does — that the one you love best you treat worst" (III, 1, I).

Acknowledging her patience, love, and delicacy of heart, Arkady still seems unable to esteem his mother. Irritated by her "everlasting submissiveness," her feelings of shame and inferiority, and her extreme, shrinking modesty, he recalls with a sense of guilt how he himself had experienced a similar feeling of shame at her very existence. "Mother," he says, "do you remember how you came to me at Touchard's and I would not recognize you?" Sonia, eager to excuse her son, replies, "I remember, my own; I have been bad to you all your life. You were my own child, and I was a stranger to you" (II, 8, IV). There are strong similarities between mother and son. "She hated displaying her feelings," Arkady writes, "and in that she was like me." Often they communicated merely through glances.

Arkady's guilt feelings toward his mother, in combination with his jealous competitiveness toward his father, spurs him to vociferous championship of the former against the latter. "Mother, if you don't want to stay with a husband who may take another wife tomorrow, remember you have a son who promises to be a dutiful son to you for ever; remember, and let us go away, only on condition that it is 'either he, or I' " (I, 6, IV).

Could the mother and "dutiful son" have worked out a meaningful existence together if Sonia had indeed chosen to leave Versilov? This mother who recognized her state of sin by making a low bow before her young son, this submissive woman who publicly humiliates herself, is one with whom Arkady does come to identify, yet their relationship is so suffused with guilt on both sides that it seems doomed from the start.

Sonia is especially loath to speak to her son about Makar, so that the relationship among the three remains unresolved to the end. The Oedipal triangle formed by these three emblematic figures — including the mother who "all her life, in fear and trembling and reverence... had honored her legal husband, the monk" (III, 1, III) — seems to transcend mundane concepts and take on almost mythical proportions.

The figure of the venerable Makar, one of the most remarkable in Russian literature, introduces us to still another dimension of Dostoevsky's multifaceted novel. Dostoevsky himself once told his wife that at least four novels were contained in essence in this one work. The book that recounts Arkady's coming of age may also be read as another Bildungsroman or "Education of Makar Dolgoruky" — a novel, that is, of the sociopsychological development of a Russian pilgrim.

In seeking personal fulfillment in a society that provided few models, Makar had insisted on his right to break away from established traditions and feed his mind on better things. Despite his servile origin, he had always been obstinately concerned with his honor and dignity and was fired by a determination to rise above his rank. As one of nineteenth-century Russia's intelligent house serfs, he had found a place at the center of his master's private, spiritual, and intellectual existence and had even taken an interest in the evolving concerns of the landed gentry as a group. Versilov, aware of the differences between Makar and his other serfs, had feared his silence and somber character, to him more frightening than the behavior of an actually violent man.

Though deeply offended by the relationship that had developed between his wife and his master, the self-controlled Makar had not directly revolted against his destiny but had decided instead to base his life on alternate values of his own choosing. Instead of futilely nursing his private susceptibilities, he exhibited the supreme good taste of a man of self-respect who had achieved purity of heart and freedom from malice. His choice lay in the ascetic life: he would carry Christ through Russia, making his spiritual progress through deep and spontaneous prayer. Sincerely pardoning his wife, he had detached himself from his own social group, set himself apart from humanity, and become completely absorbed in the deepening of his inner self. His rejection of conformism and subordination had given him such spiritual authority that he could show warm, deep, and disinterested love for others — even for those whose conduct had scandalously affronted him.

Handsome, tall, weather-beaten, serious in demeanor and noble in character, Makar maintains his stately bearing as he wanders over Russia in a spirit of renunciation. A supreme self-made outcast, he knows that "in the desert a man strengthens himself for every great deed" (III, 3, II). Versilov marvels at his benign serenity, evenness of temper, complete absence of conceit, and capacity for "talking sense" without any "silly servantish profundity."

Having once decided to devote his life to God and to his own inner reality, Makar had cast off the gloom of his early days and become suffused with spiritual brightness and joy. His purification and transformation lend him a saintly ecstasy that causes others to venerate him. Where Makar treads, the most violent human passions are appeased; his calm gentleness echoes the harmony of the universe. His love embraces "everyone and everything"; rather than point a finger at transgressors, he veils and pardons their wickedness, canceling from his mind the weight of the world's evil in order to give himself to rapturous contemplation of the good.

Nor does Makar's immersion in God preclude original views on worldly matters. With Arkady he shares his ideas on old age, on how elderly persons should die, and on the mystery that, the raw youth falsely imagines, has been "effaced by science." Makar accepts the advances of science, but, in terms that still have relevance, absorbs them into a religious worldview from which he deduces science's limitations as well as its possibilities.

It is from such processes of purification and transformation that Makar's true greatness emerges. His spiritual ascendancy makes a mockery of Arkady's obsession with "money" as a form of "despotic power" (I, 5, III). Arkady's original "idea," as expounded early in the book, had been to make himself "as rich as Rothschild," and it was for that reason that he had cut himself off from society with "obstinacy and perseverance" (read hubris and arrogance) in a futile attempt to reach "the foremost place." But this obsession had simply made his life weak and meaningless, putting him at the mercy of everyone.

Makar, in contrast, had also cut himself off from society, but had emerged as a radiant, majestic figure, endowed not only with personal power but with strength to provide anchorage for others. Recognizing Makar's power, Arkady, in a thought reminiscent of one of Pascal's, sees him as one who "has a firm footing in life, while we all of us have no firm standpoint at all" (III, 2, III).

In contrast with Makar Devushkin of *Poor Folk,* Makar Dolgoruky of *A Raw Youth* attains a spiritual power and definite moral ascendancy over the other characters in the novel; whereas the earlier Makar is doomed to remain a lowly scribe at the bottom of the sociobureaucratic scale, incapable of rising to the symbolic dimensions of his later namesake.

It is true that both these characters have to deal with a tension between the need for external dignity, for self-respect, and the craving for inner satisfaction of their spiritual needs. Both are symbols of the Russian people, and each takes on a life of his own under Dostoevsky's pen, which highlights their individual attributes even while they remain true to the Russian type. Both Makars give us insight into the culture in which Dostoevsky lived and breathed. But their human behavior is radically different. It is only Makar the pilgrim who succeeds in transforming himself and transcending his society, attaining to an integrated physical and spiritual maturity as the reward of a lifelong quest for his inner self.

Where *Poor Folk* depicts a man concerned about his worn-out boots and dangling buttons — a man incapable of transforming himself authentically and profoundly — *A Raw Youth* may be read as a study of the growth of an archetypal hero. Wrenching himself free from the constricting norms of tradition, even though it causes him pain and allows others to refer to him as a "tramp," Makar roams through his homeland and develops himself both on an existential level and in a spiritual context. He becomes, for Dostoevsky, a perfect Russian model of a man whose inner and outer development allows him to live fully on multiple levels, in harmony with his ego or conscious domain and also in equilibrium with the transpersonal entity we call deity.

Part 3

Long Tales and Novellas

If Dostoevsky had written nothing else but the six short novels [*The Double, Uncle's Dream, The Village of Stepanchikovo and Its Inhabitants, Notes from Underground, The Gambler, The Eternal Husband*], his name would no doubt still deserve a preeminent place in the history of the world's narrative literature.

—Thomas Mann,
preface to *The Short Novels of Dostoevsky*

Courtesy of the artist, Tullio Pericoli

9

The Double (1846)

Some of Dostoevsky's most significant characterizations and themes are developed in his six short novels. Among them are the paranoiac split personality whose double materializes before his incredulous eyes; the decrepit dotard with his impossible marital dream; the "perfectly good man" confronted with the despotic hypocrite in the microcosmic village of Stepanchikovo; the unloved, unloving "underground man" in his miserable mouse hole; the gambler whose ardor and vitality are focused on the treacherous revolutions of a roulette wheel; and, lastly, the respectable "eternal husband" who finds himself inexorably linked with his eternal rival.

The Double, which was written immediately after *Poor Folk,* is the earliest and probably the best known of Dostoevsky's short novels, not only because of its intrinsic fascination but also because its central figure has lent itself inexhaustibly to caricature by graphic artists. The pathologically ambivalent hero, Mr. Yakov Petrovich Golyadkin, offers a reflection of Dostoevsky's own agitated self as he existed in the mid-1840s. Just before completing the story, in February 1846, Feodor had written to his brother Mikhail: "My health is terribly unstrung; my nerves are sick and I'm afraid of a nervous fever.... I can't live in an orderly way, I'm so dissolute" (*Letters,* I, 123).

Accentuating Dostoevsky's internal turbulence was a feeling of dismay about the implications of the rigid bureaucratic order then prevailing in St. Petersburg government offices — a stultifying hierarchical system that smothered any aspirations to bureaucratic or social advancement such as those imputed to the "hero" of his story. In this novel, he chose to employ the Gothic device of the supernatural double as a means of exploring the attitudes, toward himself and others, of an abnormally shy, paranoiac petty employee who is subject to delusions.[1]

In an inept rebellion against the prevailing bureaucratic social

order, the "ambitious" but pitifully weak Mr. Golyadkin becomes
a victim of acute guilt feelings, mental distress, and a breakdown of
his own psyche. In striving to assert himself in the real world, he is
brought face-to-face with himself in the conviction that he has actually become two people.[2] In reality a purely psychic phenomenon,
his inseparable doppelgänger paces alongside him, indistinguishable
from the real Golyadkin, although inevitably one of them must be
displaced by the other.

To twentieth-century readers, the progression from the splitting
of Golyadkin's personality to the appearance of his actual double
seems masterfully handled, even though Dostoevsky's contemporaries apparently had difficulty in determining whether the double
was a hallucination or really existed side by side with Golyadkin
himself.

As one who insists upon his own genuineness and sincerity and
"wears a mask only at masked balls," Golyadkin has been tormented
by a suppressed desire to distinguish himself socially, at the same
time straining to conceal those aspects of his character that he himself is unwilling to acknowledge. There is a part of his own nature
that he disapproves of, fears, and cannot bear to contemplate. He is,
in fact, the perfect example of the type that Luigi Pirandello so ad-
mirably portrayed in Naked Masks: the character divided between
what he would like others to believe about him and what he really is.

The opening of Dostoevsky's haunting story finds Mr. Golyadkin engaged in ludicrous preparations to make an appearance at
the birthday party of a young lady named Clara Olsufyevna, the
daughter of a high official who has been Golyadkin's "benefactor
and patron" but has no idea of receiving him socially. Thus far,
Golyadkin has been frustrated in his desire to make a good social impression, obtain a promotion, and sue for Clara Olsufyevna's hand.
Yet he truly believes himself deserving of esteem and recognition,
attributing his lack of success thus far not to personal incapacity
but to persecution by members of his entourage.

To convey him to the festive event, Golyadkin procures a hired
blue hackney carriage decorated with a heraldic device. Petrushka,
the servant, is outfitted in old, oversized livery adorned with tarnished gold lace. Golyadkin's own formal clothing is carefully
pressed and perfumed. On the way to the party, however, he becomes conscious of an irresistible need to visit his doctor, for the
heroic deed he is about to perform has filled the timid man with
justified trepidation.

Having concluded the medical visit, where his abnormal behavior has been duly noted by the bemused physician, Golyadkin proceeds to the birthday party but is immediately turned away by the butler, who has had orders not to admit him. Returning humiliated to his blue carriage, he feels an irrational desire "to sink through the ground or hide himself, together with his carriage, in a mouse hole" (151) in defiance of all the laws of physics — an anticipation of the "mouse hole" to be met again in *Notes from Underground.*

After gathering courage for a second, bolder attempt to gain admission, Golyadkin barges straight into the refreshment room, proceeds thence to the drawing room, where he finds himself face-to-face with Clara, and astonishes himself and the entire gathering by his eccentric behavior. Crimson with the realization that he could never hope to achieve any kind of "social status" in this high-toned milieu, he tries to behave as though the situation had nothing to do with him, as though he were not the person who is about to be ejected.

It is here that the reader may discern the psychological origins of the "double" who will shortly begin tormenting this unhappy and uninvited guest. Crushed like an "utter insect," Golyadkin is summarily excluded from the sumptuous fête and breaks into flight to escape his "enemies." And now the wretched Mr. Golyadkin "senior" — the original Mr. Golyadkin — taking leave of himself, involuntarily stands to one side to make room for the "junior" who suddenly looms up beside him.

Once the double has materialized, the reader is privileged to observe the lengthy process whereby Golyadkin finally recognizes the stranger as "none other than himself." Over the ensuing days, his "infamous twin" and ignominious rival gradually supplants the original Mr. Golyadkin both at home and in the office — even obtaining Clara's consent to an elopement. His double having thus demonstrated that the original Mr. Golyadkin was nothing but a counterfeit, the weak and trembling senior is left out in the cold, both physically and morally. "[A] mere mosquito, if one could have existed in such weather in St. Petersburg, could very easily have knocked him down with one of its wings" (249).

Devastated by these fateful events, Golyadkin in due course is carried off to an insane asylum while his double pursues the carriage with cries of farewell. Finally, Mr. Golyadkin sinks into total madness and unconsciousness — at which his double vanishes.

Although the original subtitle of the novel was *The Adventures of Mr. Golyadkin,* in a revised version of 1866 it was changed to *A Poem of St. Petersburg.* Indeed, *The Double* may be read as a dramatic poem unfolding in the streets of the capital, not unlike the "story of St. Petersburg" narrated in Pushkin's famous poem about a "little hero" who is pursued through the city's streets by the statue of the "Bronze Horseman," Peter the Great.

Matching the main characters in Dostoevsky's "poem" are its two principal scenes of action, the one real and familiar, the other ideal and fanciful: the dirty green, smoke-begrimed, dusty domain of the downtrodden Golyadkin, and, in sharpest contrast, the fashionable drawing room of a Petersburg privy councillor, the ambiance to which he aspires but where he cannot realistically hope for acceptance.

The "real" place and time are established in Dostoevsky's opening sentence. In his bed at 8 A.M., the simple, uncomplicated Yakov Petrovich Golyadkin — who is, after all, a familiar Petersburg type — wakes from the slumber of the satisfied: a "sleepy, short-sighted, rather bald figure... of such insignificant character that nobody at all would have found it in the least remarkable." Scrutinizing himself in his mirror, the owner of the figure was "evidently quite satisfied with all he saw there" (127). The mirror will continue to play tricks on Mr. Golyadkin, projecting its reflection onto doorways that the hero will mistake for mirrors because his double is bewilderingly standing in them.

Mr. Golyadkin's awakening places the reader in the midst of one of Dostoevsky's typical evocations of the Petersburg scene, in which the city and its attributes are repeatedly personified. "[T]he dull, dirty, gray autumn day peered into the room at him through the cloudy windowpanes with a grimace so sour and bad-tempered that Mr. Golyadkin could no longer have the slightest doubt: he was not in some far-distant realm but in the capital" (127). Having duly peered into this gray soup, Mr. Golyadkin regales himself with an assortment of colors — actually a description of some ruble notes — in which lurks another personification. A shabby green wallet extracted from under some old yellowed papers reveals a "packet of green, gray, blue, red and rainbow-colored paper... [which] seemed to look back at Mr. Golyadkin in a friendly and approving fashion" (128).

A third personification is embodied in the samovar, which "was now raging and hissing fiercely, almost beside itself with anger and threatening to boil over any minute, gabbling away in its strange gibberish, lisping and babbling" (128–29). Complementary to the samovar is the comic figure of the servant, Petrushka, with his silly smile and ill-fitting livery, holding a gold-laced hat trimmed with green feathers and armed with a lackey's sword in a leather scabbard.

Mr. Golyadkin's good spirits quickly desert him as his hired carriage clatters, jingles, and creaks toward the home of Clara's father. Over his face comes a strangely anxious expression. He squeezes into the darkest corner of the hackney, for he has been espied by two young clerks who work in the same government department. They impudently point at him and loudly call him by name, to the chagrin of Golyadkin, who tries always to present himself with dignity and good breeding.

When Mr. Golyadkin's own department head catches sight of him from another carriage and stares incredulously, Golyadkin blushes to the roots of his hair, tormented all the while by nagging uncertainties about how he should conduct himself, whether he should pretend he is not himself but someone who looks strikingly like him, etc. The psychological roots of his "double" experience are already beginning to implant themselves in Mr. Golyadkin's mind. Before determining to speak to his doctor, he changes course several times or does just the opposite of what he intends — behavior that parallels the social ineptitude that is manifested in muttered words, vacuous smiles, blushes, and confusion ending in eloquent silence.

Like Dostoevsky himself, Golyadkin really prefers peace and quiet to the fashionable hubbub; he loathes gossip and scandalmongering. But even while reaffirming his social values in his conversation with the doctor, he is undergoing a strange transformation: "His gray eyes had a curious shine, his lips twitched, every muscle and every feature of his face seemed to be in fluid motion. He was shaking from head to foot.... His lips trembled, his chin quivered, and our hero unexpectedly burst into tears." "I have bitter enemies who have sworn to ruin me," he tells the doctor in a frightened whisper (138–39).

His fears proliferate in opulent literary imagery as Mr. Golyadkin makes his successive approaches to the privy councillor's residence. On the first sally, he gains an impression that "everything whatever in Olsufi Ivanovich's house was staring at him through the windows" (personification), and he knows that "if he turned round he would die on the spot" (hyperbole) (151). At his second attempt to gain entrance, he oscillates between running like a rabbit (simile) and barging straight in.

Having once chosen the latter course, in a scene of pathetic humor he invites Clara to dance, sways, raises a leg, executes a kind of shuffle, then a kind of stamp, then stumbles (164). His next sensation is that of his overcoat being put on him and his hat pulled down over his eyes. Mr. Golyadkin is being reduced to a grotesque puppet costumed for the stage, passing down the dark stairs and into the cold courtyard, where he breaks into flight to escape the hail of social opprobrium, the shrieks of alarmed old women, the gasps and exclamations of the ladies, and his own chief's annihilating stare.

Nothing could be more dramatic than this humiliated man's attempts to run away from himself, hide from himself, free himself of the creature that is now gestating within him and seeking delivery at the cost of so much psychic pain.

He stopped dead in the middle of the pavement and stood there motionless as though turned to stone; in those moments he died and disappeared off the face of the earth; then suddenly he would tear himself away from the spot like a madman and run, run without a backward glance, as though trying to escape from some pursuit or an even more horrible disaster.... Suddenly his whole body quivered, and involuntarily he leaped to one side.... It seemed to him that just now...somebody had been standing there, close to him, by his side...and — an extraordinary thing! — had even said something to him, something...not altogether understandable. (167)

Was it the wind's complaint? "The wind seemed to wail its long-drawn-out lament still more dolefully and drearily, like an importunate beggar whining for a copper coin" (168). The rainy, snowy November night churns around him in images that complement the personification of the grimacing, bad-tempered day in the opening chapter:

It was a terrible night.... The wind howled in the empty streets, whipping the black water of the Fontanka higher than the mooring-rings...which in their turn echoed its wailing with the thin piercing squeak that makes up the endless whining, creaking concert so familiar to every inhabitant of St. Petersburg.... Jets of rainwater, broken off by the wind, prick[ed] and cut the wretched Mr. Golyadkin's face like thousands of pins and needles. In the nocturnal quiet, broken only by the distant rumble of coaches, the howl of the wind and the squeaking of the swinging street lamps, the splash and murmur of the water running from every roof, porch, gutter, and cornice on to the granite flags of the pavement had a dismal sound. (165–66)

As the wind, the rain, and the river continue their mockery, the wretched Mr. Golyadkin turns sharply to look at the stranger who has just passed him: "He turned about as though he had been twitched from behind, or as though the wind had whirled him round like a weathercock" (169).

The long, suspenseful drama of this meeting on a St. Petersburg street is temporarily resolved as Golyadkin falls into unconsciousness and awakens in his bed at eight the following morning, a mirror image of the novel's opening sentence. Henceforth, his portrait will be a double one, for there are now two persons in the dingy green room. "[T]he man now sitting opposite Mr. Golyadkin was Mr. Golyadkin's horror, he was Golyadkin's shame, he was Mr. Golyadkin's nightmare . . . ; in short, he was Mr. Golyadkin himself [and] nobody would have taken it on himself to say which was the old and which the new, which was the original and which the copy" (177).

Mr. Golyadkin's new guest at first exhibits familiar pangs of conscience and guilt feelings that actually elicit an upsurge of sympathy on the part of his involuntary host. Reluctant to try to evict the intruder by force, Mr. Golyadkin senior searches for "the politest way of showing the scoundrel the door"; but then, surprisingly, the meek, submissive double turns into a rude hypocrite, for he, too, has a split personality! To the confused Golyadkin, it appears that "people wearing masks have ceased to be a rarity . . . and . . . it is difficult nowadays to recognize the man under the mask" (199).

Shaken by his double's outlandish behavior, Golyadkin spends many a miserable night as the imagined victim of a universal conspiracy. Even his medicine is personified as an enemy: "The dark, reddish, disgusting-looking liquid shone with a evil gleam in Mr. Golyadkin's eyes." His nightmares feature "a certain person renowned for his ugliness and his satirical propensities," or "a certain person notorious for his disloyalty and swinish impulses." Armies of doubles haunt his dreams, "stretching out in a long file like a string of geese."

The double, meanwhile, has taken possession of Golyadkin's desk at the office and is doing excellent work, surpassing the highest expectations of his department head. His colleagues clearly prefer the new Golyadkin to the old one, and Mr. Golyadkin senior now realizes how foolish he has been in allowing himself to be used "as a doormat for people to wipe their dirty boots on." Yet in reproaching himself for his own baseness and cowardice, he feels "a kind of profound, indeed almost voluptuous satisfaction" (209) — a foretaste of the masochism described in such later works as *Notes from Underground* and *The Eternal Husband*.

The denouement of the story finds Mr. Golyadkin once again on a Petersburg street. "The weather was abominable: there had been a thaw, snow was falling thickly and it was raining as well —

everything exactly as it was in the middle of that terrible, never-to-be-forgotten night when all Mr. Golyadkin's troubles had begun" (266). Once again, the mirror is held up to reflect two similar nights; and this, in turn, will be followed by still another mirror image.

Before being bundled off to the mental asylum, the sodden Mr. Golyadkin huddles for hours in Olsufi Ivanovich's courtyard awaiting the signal from Clara — who is now to elope with his double — while groups of people peer out of the windows at him. "Our hero would most gladly have crept then and there into some little mouse hole among the logs and crouched there in peace" — the same little mouse hole into which he would have liked to disappear with his hired carriage earlier in the story. Once again, the reader previews the melancholy domain of Dostoevsky's "underground man" in *Notes from Underground.*

The Double disappointed its readers when it appeared on the heels of *Poor Folk* in 1846, and Dostoevsky was dismayed by its poor reception after his assurances to Mikhail that it was "turning out superbly" and would be his "chef d'oeuvre" (*Letters,* I, 118). Playing with his character while the work was still progress, he had cheerfully reported: "*Yakov Petrovich Golyadkin* is standing quite firm in character. A horrible scoundrel, he's unapproachable; refuses to move ahead at all, claiming that after all, he's not yet ready and that he's fine for the meanwhile just as things are.... He absolutely refuses to finish his career earlier than mid-November.... And he's putting me, his creator, in an extremely bad situation" (*Letters,* I, 113–14).

But by April 1846, after publication, the author writes: "Dear brother...everyone is displeased with me for Golyadkin" (*Letters,* I, 124). In fact, this experiment in the domain of the pathologically grotesque had been fully successful neither in style nor in characterization. It was, perhaps, too derivative and at the same time too original to be fully appreciated in its own era. Yet it has since been pointed out that, over and above its considerable literary merit, some of its episodes read almost like extracts from the classic studies of schizophrenia written half a century later.[3]

10

Uncle's Dream and The Village of Stepanchikovo and Its Inhabitants (1859)

Thomas Mann dismissed *Uncle's Dream,* Dostoevsky's earliest publication after his release from prison, as "too long-drawn-out for its content, a farce, whose tragic conclusion, the story of the tubercular young schoolmaster, is filled with unbearable sentimentalism derived from the early influence of Charles Dickens upon Dostoevsky's work."[1] The weakness of this mildly entertaining comedy of manners may be explained by the fact that Dostoevsky, struggling desperately to recommence his literary career and terribly fearful of the censorship, did not at that time dare write anything more challenging than what he called this "little thing of sky-blue mildness and remarkable innocence" (Letter of September 14, 1873).

Subtitled *From the Annals of Mordasov,* the novella chronicles the remarkable goings-on in a nondescript provincial town in connection with the visit of the elderly Prince K., a figure so worn-out and decrepit that he looked as though he might "drop to pieces." The reader is assured, however, that the prince's false wig, moustache, and magnificent black whiskers, his rouged and powdered face, his one glass eye and his false teeth, the corset he wears to compensate for a lost rib, and his artificial left leg suffice to hold together this "corpse worked by mechanism" (241). People whispered that the prince was "off his head," but so, to some extent, are most of the characters in the story.

Rumors of a plot are set in motion apropos the prince's ceremonial call at the home of Mrs. Marya Alexandrovna Moskalev, a provincial lioness and "the leading lady in Mordasov," a woman of whom everyone is afraid — "and that is just what she wants," Dostoevsky explains. The novelist clearly welcomes the opportunity for a satire

on small-town gossip, backbiting, and petty power struggles such as
he had come to know too well during his residence in Semipalatinsk.
"The instinct of provincial newsmongers sometimes approaches
the miraculous," he writes.

It is founded on the closest and most interested study of one another, pursued through many years. Every provincial lives, as it were, under a glass
case. There is no possibility of concealing anything from your excellent fellow citizens. They know you by heart, they even know what you don't know
about yourself. The provincial ought, one would think, by his very nature to
be a psychologist and a specialist on human nature. That is why I have been
sometimes genuinely amazed at meeting in the provinces not psychologists
and specialists on human nature, but a very great number of asses. (271)

Though "the greatest gossip in the world or at any rate in Mordasov," Marya Alexandrovna is at the same time very reserved about
secrets, telling them "only in extreme cases...to her most intimate
female friends." In general, she confines herself to frightening people
with hints about what she knows and thus keeping them in a state
of continual apprehension. "That is intelligence, that is diplomacy!"
Dostoevsky exclaims with caustic irony.

Marya Alexandrovna's current and all-too-mercenary objective is
to secure Prince K.'s estate as an inheritance for her daughter Zina.
To this end, she seeks to enlist her husband's cooperation in impressing the prince. Dostoevsky describes this husband of Mordasov's
"leading lady" with scathing humor: "Afanasy Matveyitch...was
a man of very presentable exterior, and indeed of very correct
principles....He was extraordinarily dignified...but his dignified
air and presentability only lasted till the minute when he began to
speak" (227). It was only his wife's genius that had enabled Afanasy
to keep his position in government service, and on his retirement his
"incompetence and absolute uselessness" had led his wife to remove
him to their country place, two-and-one-half miles out of town.

For Thomas Mann, the figure that "saves the novel" was the
Moskalevs' daughter, the lovely Zinaida (Zina) Afanasyevna, the
very type of the proud, high-principled Russian girl. Beautiful, well-
educated, bold, and unapproachable, Zina is "one of those women
who excite general enthusiasm and wonder whenever they appear
in society" — yet, at twenty-three, she is still unmarried.

Zina is being courted at the moment by a distant relative of Prince
K. by the name of Pavel Alexandrovitch Mozglyakov — a dandi-
fied Petersburg bureaucrat, young and not bad looking though "not
quite sound in the upper storey." But without absolutely rejecting

the young man's advances, Zina still remains faithful to Vasya, the impoverished and ailing local schoolteacher. That unfortunate individual, proud and haughty like Zina herself — "a fellow who could talk of nothing but that cursed Shakespeare," according to Marya Alexandrovna — is dying of consumption; but Zina is determined that even after his death she will remain single and refuse any marriage offers that may be contrived by her nagging mother.

Marya Alexandrovna, however, has come to believe that marriage to the decrepit prince would furnish her daughter with wealth, a title, and even the prospect of an early widowhood assuring her the freedom and independence she so much covets. Perhaps the older woman sees in such a marriage a vicarious realization of her own romantic aspirations, which center in the idea of Spain, the place of all good: "Spain, where there is the Alhambra and the Guadalquivir, not this wretched, miserable river here with its unseemly name" (257). One is reminded of Dostoevsky's own yearning to escape to Italy from Semipalatinsk on the River Irtish.

But Zina sees through her mother's schemes and has nothing but contempt for her ingenious machinations. So Marya Alexandrovna changes her tactics and hypocritically appeals to her daughter's sense of self-sacrifice. Marriage to the dotard prince, she asserts, will be an act of compassion and devotion. "Look at it from a lofty, indeed from a Christian point of view, my child! ... You said yourself ... that you would like to be a Sister of Mercy. ... This old man has suffered too ... warm his heart, and you will be doing an act godly and virtuous! ... What troubles you most is that it is all for the sake of money, as though it were some sale or purchase. Well, renounce the money if money is so hateful to you. Keep only what is barely necessary for yourself, and give away the rest" (259–60).

Although Zina finally gives her reluctant consent, a new complication arises because young Mozglyakov, listening at the keyhole and learning that he himself is definitively rejected, resolves to frustrate the scheme by letting the whole town know how the two women are tricking his kinsman, the prince. But Marya Alexandrovna is a better tactician than the gullible Mozglyakov, and neatly checkmates him with an appeal to his own romantic proclivities. Zina, she tells him, in reality is deeply in love with him, and if he will only behave nobly — that is, step aside to permit her advantageous marriage to the prince — her love for him will, of course, "rise up again with irresistible force."

"Meet her at some ball," Marya Alexandrovna advises, "and in the midst of this gay festival you alone mournful, melancholy, pale,

leaning somewhere against a column...watch her in the whirl of
the ball. She dances. Around you flow the intoxicating strains of
Strauss and the scintillating wit of the highest society — while you
stand alone, pale and crushed by your passion" (291). The image
flatters Mozglyakov's vanity and romantic disposition, all the more
so because Spain, the very land of romance, is also included in
the picture. "For the Prince's health," Marya Alexandrovna promises, "Zina will go...to Spain — to Spain where there are myrtles,
lemons, where the sky is blue, where one cannot live without loving: the land of roses, where kisses...float in the air.... At last
[the prince] will die.... Tell me: whom would Zina marry if not
you?" (291).

With Mozglyakov at least temporarily neutralized by these means,
the crafty Marya Alexandrovna goes to work on the old prince. At
a dinner party in the Moskalev home, successive potations reduce
him to a maudlin state in which, carried away by Zina's bewitch-
ing singing, he falls to his knees and asks her to marry him at
once. Marya Alexandrovna, who plans to kidnap the prince and
detain him in their country home, endeavors to keep him in a state
of continued inebriation; but Zina has meanwhile become ill with
repulsion, and tears of shame gush from her eyes.

Mozglyakov, too, has begun to reflect that the scenario given
him is somewhat unrealistic and that in fact he has been made a
fool of. Now disabused, he proceeds to disabuse the old prince as
well by telling him that he had not really proposed marriage to
Zina but had only dreamed it. Thanking his "nephew" for setting
him right, the prince then announces that he will shortly be going abroad, alone, in order to observe the progress of European
enlightenment.

Marya Alexandrovna, "perhaps for the first time in her life
cowed," screams at her husband to "do something" to detain
the prince. Proud that he has at last been called upon to save a
situation, Afanasy Matveyitch pronounces with dignity the magnificent climactic lines: "Wife! Didn't you perhaps dream it all,
and afterwards when you woke up, you muddled it all to suit
yourself!" (325).

The conclusion of *Uncle's Dream* recounts the "remarkable history of the...solemn downfall of Marya Alexandrovna and all her
family." With the collapse of her despotic rule over local society,
this intriguing woman has decided that she must move away from
Mordasov. Small-town society is, after all, "a mere exhibition of
fictitious qualities, of noble sentiments, a farce, an outer husk of

gold. Remove that husk and you will find a perfect hell under the flowers; a perfect wasp's nest, where you will be devoured to the last bone!" (277).

There is, however, an epilogue. Three years later, the reader encounters Mozglyakov, who has moved to Petersburg and completely forgotten Mordasov and its people, on an expedition to a remote region of his boundless fatherland. Calling on the governor-general of the place, he asks to pay his respects also to the latter's wife — who turns out to be none other than the proud and haughty Zina. Her schoolteacher lover has died, and, contrary to her earlier resolve, Zina has made a very advantageous marriage.

The mother, too, has managed to improve her position. The governor's wife, the reader is told, "had a mamma who lived with her, and...this mamma belonged to the highest society, and was very clever...but...the mamma herself was completely dominated by the daughter, while the general himself simply doted on his spouse" (341). As for Zina's poor father, "they had no conception of his existence in the 'remote region.' "

Replicating Marya Alexandrovna's earlier suggestive image, Mozglyakov in a picturesquely romantic attitude now leans against a column in the ballroom watching Zina dance. "But alas! all his antics, all his striking attitudes, his disillusioned air and all the rest of it were thrown away. Zina completely failed to observe him" (342). Returning exhausted to his lodging, the young man departs next morning, driving out over the boundless deserted plain with its bordering of dark forests, dismayed and crestfallen at the failure of Marya Alexandrovna's prophesies.

In this entertaining tale, Dostoevsky offers a seriocomic illustration of two important if unglamorous truths. Romantic visions like those conjured up by Marya Alexandrovna can seldom stand up against the realities of life; while sincerity and a will to sacrifice, such as one originally encountered in the figure of Zina, may all too readily lose their force or be diverted from their object by hypocrites pursuing baser goals.

In *The Village of Stepanchikovo and Its Inhabitants,* another uncle dreams of marriage. This richly comic novel, sometimes called *The Friend of the Family,* is unique among the works composed by Dostoevsky in the later years of his Siberian residence. As in *Uncle's Dream,* matchmaking and the plotting of advantageous marriages highlight the happenings in the fictional village of Stepanchikovo, a community that has been plunged into confusion by a man whose

behavior is so dismayingly eccentric that many of the inhabitants
believe him to be possessed of the devil.

This fiendish rogue, who bears the name of Foma Fomich Opiskin
and has a noticeable resemblance to Molière's Tartuffe, has joined
with a local widow, the "General's Lady," in a plot to magnify their
joint power and wealth by marrying off the lady's middle-aged and
widowed son, retired Colonel Rostanev, to a semidemented spinster
with a million rubles. The melancholy, submissive bridegroom-
designate, who is evidently intended to embody Dostoevsky's notion
of the "perfectly good man," is reluctant to fall in with their scheme,
because he loves the young and beautiful governess, Nastenka, and
is dismayed at the way she is being persecuted by his mother and
her ally, Foma Fomich.

In a desperate bid to put the situation to rights, Colonel Rostanev
has summoned his nephew from St. Petersburg in the hope that the
latter can win the governess's hand and save her from her persecutors
even though he himself must forego the hope of making her his wife.
This nephew will serve as the narrator of the story and as the one
more or less normal individual among its characters.

Even before reaching Stepanchikovo, the young man begins to
hear disturbing rumors about the devilish Foma Fomich. At first he
tries to defend the unknown man in accordance with the humanitarian principles inculcated by his progressive university education —
principles like those that had inspired Dostoevsky's own works of
the 1840s. Perhaps, the traveler suggests, Foma is really a "gifted
nature" wounded and crushed by suffering? But as soon as he has
a chance to observe the reality of Foma's tyranny over his uncle's
household, his philanthropic feelings give place to a sense of outrage.

Foma Fomich, he learns, had been a vagrant of obscure origins
and had been employed as a reader by the colonel's stepfather, the
late General Krakhotkin. Since the general's death, Foma had maneuvered himself into a position of supreme power in the Rostanev
household, thanks to his own unscrupulousness, the pathological
devotion he had inspired in the general's widow, and the equally
pathological submissiveness of her forty-year-old son. The credulous
and superstitious mother is described by Dostoevsky as a "with-
ered and bilious old woman dressed in black" (78); her principal
confidante, a spinster named Perepelitsyna, is a "dried-up creature
embittered with the world, with tiny, rapacious eyes devoid of eyebrows, paper-thin lips, hands washed in pickled gherkin juice, and
wearing a chignon" (33).

Under the regime of Foma Fomich and the General's Lady, Colonel

Rostanev's home has become a haven — "a veritable Noah's Ark" — for a variety of eccentric toadies, spongers, and hangers-on who are all engaged in exploiting their humble host. The chapter entitled "At Tea" describes a gathering of these personages and their entertainment by a perplexing individual called Yezhevikin who plays the jester and appears to be perversely reveling in his own misery. Though he serves as the official buffoon at the Rostanev tea parties, this personage has been prevented by his enormous pride from taking up residence in the colonel's home, preferring to earn a mere pittance but maintain his personal independence. This rather ambiguous character turns out to be the father of the governess Nastenka, whom he is trying to help by conciliating her powerful persecutors.

The story reaches a climax when Nastenka and Rostanev, in a departure from their usual timid resignation, are seen exchanging a surreptitious kiss in the garden. Foma Fomich and the General's Lady, shouting accusations of depravity, try to seize the opportunity to dishonor and dismiss the pure, innocent governess; but Rostanev, at last losing patience, suddenly grasps Foma Fomich by the shoulders, turns him round like a wisp of straw, and hurls him violently through the French window into the courtyard. There the hypocritical Foma deliberately remains under a pouring rain until rescued by the colonel himself, who promptly reverts to his normally docile and forgiving state of mind and bitterly rues his own loss of self-control. Temporarily chastened though far from repentant, Foma now reverses course and heartily approves the union of Nastenka and Rostanev, thus reconciling the General's Lady as well to the match they had so vehemently opposed. All the characters are now satisfied except Rostanev's very modern fifteen-year-old daughter, Sashenka, who has seen through Foma's cruelty and hypocrisy, and at one point even tried to defend her papa against the satanic intruder by threatening "to tear him to pieces... and shoot him dead on the spot with a pair of pistols" (96). Such measures prove unnecessary, however, since the end of the story finds the household settled in a bizarre "equilibrium" reflecting, perhaps, the paradoxical truth that humanity needs the devil to keep it in balance.[2]

Structurally, the love affair between Nastenka and Rostanev is of no more than secondary interest in this satirical study of the interaction between two archetypal figures. Foma Fomich Opiskin, the Russian Tartuffe, is an insolent, impertinent hypocrite, the very personification of self-righteousness; while Colonel Rostanev incarnates the passive, obliging, reasonable Russian type, a "perfectly good man" and genuine Christian who is habituated to turning the other cheek and reacts against his tormenter only when pushed to the limits of endurance.

Dostoevsky did not underrate the emblematic significance of these two character types. "I consider the novel...to be incomparably superior to *Uncle's Dream,*" he wrote Mikhail. "There are two serious characters there and they are even new, without precedent anywhere.... [The] novel has great shortcomings and the main one, perhaps, is long-windedness...but there are two enormous typical characters that I *have been creating* and *writing down* for five years... —characters that are completely Russian and which until now have been poorly pointed out by Russian literature" (*Letters,* I, 360, 363–64).

The background of Foma Fomich Opiskin is shrouded in mystery, but the reader is told that like Dostoevsky himself he was possessed of monstrous vanity, had once been in government service, and had suffered for an unspecified "just" cause. Trying his hand at literature in Moscow, he had suffered only disappointment, humiliation, and rejection. In the end, he had been obliged to "enter martyrdom" as reader and jester in the service of General Krakhotkin, a position in which he had even gone to the length of portraying "various animals and tableaux vivants" for the general's entertainment. The vicious general had positively enjoyed degrading his flunky for his own amusement.

Since the general's death, however, Foma has worked his way to the top and now tyrannizes over a household that is not even his. "Who knows," writes Dostoevsky, "but that some of these ill-fated outcasts, your clowns and God-forsaken wretches, instead of being cowed by humility, have had their vanity augmented still further by this very humiliation, by the sycophancy, wretchedness and obligation to play the fool enforced upon them, by the extirpation of all individual personality?" (34). Since Foma's meteoric rise has placed him in a position of absolute power, his behavior has changed, just as radically, from that of *jester* to *master.*

Foma's sadistic and tyrannical conduct is clearly the outgrowth of a desire for revenge for past humiliations, and the fundamental maxim of *The Village of Stepanchikovo* is that "a base soul escaping from oppression becomes an oppressor." Foma finds satisfaction in the very act of inflicting suffering. Since he himself was once an abused clown, it flatters him to have a clown of his own in the person of Yezhevikin, Nastenka's father; but whereas Foma may possibly have been sincere in his performance as a groveling flatterer, the reader knows that Yezhevikin plays the fool only for the sake of his daughter's position and runs no risk of assuming abusive power or authority.

Dostoevsky's other "serious character," Colonel Yegor Ilyich Rostanev, is also something of an anomaly, an unresisting, long-suffering, supine product of Dostoevsky's own landowning and military tradition. His excessive deference and consideration for Foma Fomich have been attributed to a deep-seated feeling of inferiority and an urge to hero worship. But just as Foma Fomich is not a simple villain, Rostanev is more than simply a weak hero.[3] They represent two irreconcilable opposites: on the one hand, an insatiable need to dominate, joined with unabashed arrogance; on the other, self-imposed bondage rooted in credulous good nature. The insolent, domineering Foma could not take his sadistic pleasure in browbeating and humiliating Rostanev if the latter were not totally compliant, benign, generous, and wholly lacking in self-regard.

Yet Dostoevsky insists that the colonel's pliancy and weakness do not spring from any want of backbone. It is simply that he is excessively respectful of his neighbor, and of humankind in general, and views with terror the possibility of giving offense or performing a cruel act. "His compliance was born of a shy generosity of spirit, a bashful considerateness of others" (37). It is Rostanev's vocation to sacrifice his own interests for the good of others. His only desire is to "see everybody happy and contented" — as indeed they are at the end of the story, though only after the colonel has for once emerged from his passivity and shown the rascally Foma that there are limits he had better not transgress.

None of Dostoevsky's comments about these two "typical," "completely Russian" characters would support the idea that they were intended as mere caricatures, or that he unreservedly repudiated the conduct of one or endorsed the behavior of the other. Foma Fomich and Colonel Rostanev are an inseparable pair, sharing elements of Dostoevsky's own diabolic/angelic makeup. The vain, egocentric Foma, a member of the Russian intelligentsia who had been "humiliated at his first literary attempt" (35), may even have some affinity with the pre-Siberian Dostoevsky. For all his monstrous vanity, he entertains some excellent ideas ("forests must be preserved, for they retain moisture on the earth's surface") and even enunciates sound ethical principles ("Why not be more gentle, loving and understanding towards your fellow men? Forget yourself, remember others.... Patience, toil, prayer and hope are the precepts I should like to instil into every human heart"). It is this good/bad

Foma Fomich who in the end will shift his portentous weight in
such a way as to reestablish a precarious balance in the Rostanev
household.

Concomitantly, the simple, uneducated Rostanev, landowner and
ex-military man, embodies that intrinsic goodness that Dostoevsky
discovered in the soul of the ordinary Russian during his penal
servitude and later crystallized into one of the elements of his
moral and religious universe. Rostanev practices what Foma merely
preaches. Contrasted with the vociferous, evangelizing Tartuffe is
the guileless believer and genuine Christian. Rostanev's selflessness,
long-suffering, and love of his fellows foreshadow the more fully
developed figures of Prince Myshkin in *The Idiot* and of Alyosha
Karamazov, Dostoevsky's two precocious lovers of all humanity.

As a sustained exercise in comedy, *The Village of Stepanchikovo
and Its Inhabitants* stands alone among Dostoevsky's works. The
novel can, in fact, be read as simply an amusing entertainment with
a typical happy ending, one whose more serious aspects are handled
in a lightly satirical manner all the more remarkable in the light of
Dostoevsky's painfully difficult situation at the time it was written.

11

Notes from Underground (1864)

> Always disposing ourselves to be happy, it is inevitable that we never become so.
>
> — Blaise Pascal, *Thoughts, 5, 2*

If the mountain up which Sisyphus pushed his boulder could be inverted, one might find oneself in the depths of the "mouse hole" where the underground man perpetually contemplates his existential dilemma. Sisyphus, a man of action, and the underground man, a man of inertia, may be coupled in an inverse image. Both are resistants against social conformity, both are "strangers" alienated from their societies, and the life of each is in its own way a reductio ad absurdum.

In an age of reason and scientific determinism, the protagonist of Dostoevsky's *Notes from Underground* is convinced of the irrationality and futility of moral and emotional reactions; yet he cannot help behaving as if some sort of free response to the rigid laws of nature were possible and even meaningful — just as Sisyphus cannot help feeling that although the stone he pushes rolls down again as often as it nears the summit, he is nevertheless achieving superiority over a fixed destiny. From an existential viewpoint, the lucid despair that distinguished both Sisyphus and the underground man infuses their existence with a unique and irreplaceable quality. They both are able to focus, squarely and pitilessly, on the absurd. Each of them puts into practice an existential conception of liberty and moral freedom as a form of personal revolt.

"Perhaps the purpose of man's life on earth," Dostoevsky wrote in *Notes from Underground,* "consists precisely in . . . uninterrupted striving after a goal. That is to say, the purpose is life itself and not the goal." In a recurrence of this Pascalian thought, Dostoevsky tells us elsewhere in the same work that "man is frivolous and unaccountable and perhaps, like a chess player, he enjoys the achieving rather than the goal itself"; that he is a "comical animal" who "loves

the achieving but does not particularly enjoy what he achieves"
(116–17).

This thought rings like a leitmotiv in the two segments of the underground man's confession that make up the substance of *Notes
from Underground*. During his unhappy days at school, the underground man — like the later "raw youth" — had been jeered, baited,
and ostracized by his schoolmates. "I did make a friend once," he
tells us, "but I was already a tyrant at heart and wanted to be the
absolute ruler of his mind.... When I felt I had full possession of
him, I began to hate him and finally rejected him. It was as though
I'd only wanted his total friendship just for sake of winning it and
making him submit to me" (147). Later in the novel, while verbosely
prophesying her doom to Liza, the young prostitute, he says, "I'd
felt that I was turning her soul inside out and breaking her heart and
the more I was convinced of it, the more eager I was to finish what I
had set out to do. It was a game I was playing, and I was altogether
absorbed in it — although, perhaps, it wasn't only the game" (179).

Unlike the mythological Sisyphus, the underground man is, in
Dostoevsky's words, "a real man of the Russian majority" — a despairing, divided victim of those European ideas that the novelist had
come to consider so noxious and inapplicable to Russian conditions.
Indeed, this novel marks the definitive rejection of Dostoevsky's former Western beliefs and a passionate rebuttal of the views of the
French utopian socialists he once had shared. Incensed against his
former political associations, he now protests against what he has
come to see as their oversimplified, naively optimistic visions of the
future.

All that is wrong with the outlook of his former comrades is
symbolized for Dostoevsky by London's Crystal Palace, that bold
construction of metal, glass, and prefabricated parts that had been
built to house the Great Exhibition of 1851. For Dostoevsky, this
imposing edifice has become a kind of metaphor of the man-made
socialist utopia or human ant colony that Nikolay Chernyshevsky
had recently vaunted in his didactic novel, *What Is To Be Done?*,
serialized in *The Contemporary* in March–May 1863. Where Chernyshevsky optimistically postulated a future based on reason — a
world of coherence and solvable problems — Dostoevsky sees such
a world as fundamentally inconsistent with humanity's innermost,
capricious nature.

Dostoevsky does not, of course, deny that man's sometimes senseless and irrational desires are prone to clash with his own best
interests; but he nevertheless insists that human beings must be left

free to choose their course, even if they are bent on choosing irrational and willful self-destruction. For Dostoevsky, Chernyshevsky's positivist doctrines present a vital threat to the personal freedom and individuality that are humanity's most treasured possessions.

It is for similar reasons that the antihero of *Notes from Underground* has renounced all comfort in the "mouse hole" he has chosen to inhabit. His life has become a demonstration that perhaps human beings do not seek only for well-being; perhaps they like suffering just as much; perhaps they actually enjoy being ridiculed and downtrodden. This particular "sick, mean man," who is an ex–civil servant, a liar "out of spite" and an unabashed masochist, has lived for some twenty years in his mouse hole, out of contact with all human feelings. In his "repulsive, evil-smelling nest," he steeps himself in stubborn meanness. Forty years of ignominious humiliation have driven him to imagine the possibility of still further humiliations, the source of "a pleasure that sometimes reaches the highest degree of voluptuousness" (100).

The work is in two parts, a philosophical monologue in which the underground man expounds his misanthropic ideas, and a longer, autobiographical section that affords some insight into their origin and development. This second section, entitled "Brought to Mind by a Fall of Wet Snow," is replete with memories of places, people, and events of Dostoevsky's own lonely days in the Academy of Military Engineering and his place of first employment. In flashbacks that provide a momentary escape from the musty mouse hole, the reader learns about the irrational streak that had characterized the underground man while still "in action."

Even at the age of twenty-four, he had led the gloomy, disorganized, and solitary existence of a recluse, for his own infinite vanity had led him to set impossible standards and regard himself with furious disapproval. "I hated my face," he writes (124). In his morbid fear of appearing ridiculous, he had slavishly adhered to all the external conventions, and was perhaps the only person in his office to look upon himself as a coward and a slave. "I felt that," he explains, "because I was more highly developed than the others" (125). At home, he read avidly in order "to drown out the clamor in me," and at night he indulged in unspecified "vice." "Even then," he confesses, "I carried this hole in the floor in my heart."

Successive episodes illustrate the underground man's careless contempt for others, their rejections of his proffered friendship, and their failure to recognize the superiority of which he himself is so convinced. Determined "either to be a hero or to wallow in the mud," he seeks to demonstrate the impossibility of acting with reason and without caprice. Typical of his attitude is his persistent quest for revenge for an imagined insult that his reason tells him was no insult at all. It is this quest, too, that brings the underground man to a so-called dress shop — actually a brothel — where the action of the second part of the novella begins.

Here he encounters Liza, a girl with "a fresh, young face, rather pale, with straight dark eyebrows and a serious, rather surprised expression." Aware that she is looking at him while he contemplates his face in the mirror — a "revolting" face, ashen, vicious, abject, with disheveled hair — "I don't give a damn," he thinks. "So much the better. The more repulsive she finds me, the better I'll like it" (163). As is his wont, he humiliates the pitiful prostitute even while recognizing that she has aroused his interest. "Shamming so easily coexists with sincere feeling," he muses (170).

Liza accepts his cold, contemptuous invitation to visit him at home, but is dismayed by his erratic behavior and uncontrollable anger — for which, of course, her vulnerability provides an admirable outlet. "I felt that I'd make her pay dearly *for everything*," he tells the reader (192). In cynically humiliating her and crushing her spirit, he is taking revenge for his own frustrations. "I had to vent my spite on someone else," he tells her, "and you happened to be around, so I poured my resentment out on you...I'd been insulted, so I wanted to insult back; I'd been made a doormat, so I wanted to show my power and wipe my feet on someone else."

Yet even in making his confession, the underground man betrays the element of unpredictability Dostoevsky finds in all human beings by bursting into sobs and letting his tears flow uncontrollably. "Of course it was I who suffered most because I realized how loathsome my perverse stupidity was, *even though I couldn't help it*," he tells the reader (194, italics added). "I cannot live without having someone to bully and order around," he tells Liza. "But since nothing can be explained by reasoning," he adds, "why reason?" (198).

Realizing that these outbursts are the product of unhappiness and thirst for revenge, the gentle, understanding Liza stretches out her hands to him, flings her arms about his neck, and bursts into tears of compassion. He feels, for his part, that it would be "terribly awkward for me to lift my head now and look Liza in the eyes. I'm not sure what I was ashamed of, but I was ashamed all right.... Precisely because I was ashamed to look her in the eye, new feeling flashed in my heart — the need to dominate and possess.... How I hated her, and how furiously I was drawn to her at that moment!"

Would the underground man be capable of self-forgetfulness, of performing an act of genuine and unselfish love? "I couldn't fall in love," he says, "because for me loving means bullying and dominating. Even dreaming in my mouse hole, I never visualized love as anything but a struggle, starting with hatred and ending in the subjection of the loved object" (199).

Unable to overcome his impulse to harry and make sport of the unfortunate girl, he slips a five-ruble note into her hand despite his realization that the act of love she has performed was prompted by human sympathy and was not done for material reward. Unnoticed, she drops the note on the table as she leaves the sordid mouse hole. Moved by the loftiness of her gesture, her tormentor runs after her, intending to fall on his knees, kissing her feet and sobbing with remorse; but a new reflection stops him in his tracks.

"Won't I hate her even more tomorrow, just because I've kissed her feet today?" he asks himself. "...Isn't it much better...for her to bear this humiliation...because humiliation is purification." Falling back into his usual cynical egoism, "This insult and humiliation will never be extinguished in her," he thinks. "...My insult will elevate her, purify her through...hatred....I must also add that I was very pleased with my phrase about the beneficent effect of insult, humiliation and hatred, although I...almost fell sick with despair" (201-2).

Liza is Dostoevsky's recurring symbol of those meek and humble ones among the children of God who will one day inherit the earth and dispossess the sinners in their demoniacal pride. The prostitute's untrammeled Christian instincts and capacity for selfless love have hallowed her name, even as the cynical hollowness and egocentricity of the underground man have relegated him to moral decay in his mouse hole.

Can one feel any sympathy or compassion for the dark, ugly, cruel, yet tragic qualities of this "real man of the Russian majority"? Can one commiserate with such a man, who, though clearly possessed of acute intelligence, has been driven by his exaggerated sensitivity into a retreat from which he emerges only to avenge his humiliations by humiliating others? He bears a certain resemblance to another agent of social upheaval, Foma Fomich in *The Village of Stepanchikovo*. Like Foma Fomich, he too finds satisfaction in the act of inflicting suffering; but he is Foma's opposite in that while Foma advances and steadily climbs his totem pole, the underground man retreats ever deeper into the obscurity of his mouse hole. The two are diametrically opposed, as well, in that while Foma Fomich is a grandiloquent humbug, the antisocial paradoxes of the underground man do not lack intellectual cogency. For Thomas Mann, they were the expression of "a new, deeper, and unrhetorical humanity that has passed through all the hells of suffering and of understanding."[1]

The underground man is quite aware of his own distorted personality. He is a profound analyst of his own as well as others' feelings. He does not believe that man tends toward good, but rather that his free will propels him along the paths of temptation and evil. He has chosen to turn in upon himself, retreating in order to store up venom, surrendering to "conscious inertia" as he drinks toasts to his hole under the floor.

When "at home," so to speak, he reveals himself as a frightening and paradoxical combination of intelligence, awareness, and self-consciousness, deriding even his own convictions and life-style because he has lost hope that they serve any purpose. Outside the mouse hole, he is a frightful and tragic amalgam of wickedness, repulsiveness, insolence, cowardice, vileness, and lust, who champions his convictions through self-centered intellectual arguments that are directed against reason itself, his supreme enemy. "Though I said I was green with envy of the normal man," he asserts, "I still wouldn't take his place... although I'll go on envying him" (120).

The basic contradiction in the underground man's nature lies in his refusal, or inability, to reconcile Will and Reason. He could never, he says, live in the Crystal Palace — an edifice based on reason — for suffering there is inconceivable: "Suffering means doubt and denial, and what kind of crystal palace would that be, if people had doubts about it?" (118). Man, he is convinced, is a creature who will never give up real suffering, never renounce his predilection for destruction and chaos. "You can say anything about world history... except one thing[:]... that it is reasonable" (144).

If reason fails, there is still caprice or whim, by which the underground man intends to be guided at his own choice without necessarily seeking either prosperity or suffering. "I'm not advocating suffering any more than well-being," he says. "What I'm for is whim" (118). What can you expect, he asks rhetorically, of such a strange creature as a human being? "You can shower upon him all earthly blessings, drown him in happiness... and even then, out of sheer spite and ingratitude, man will play a dirty trick on you.... What he wants to preserve is precisely his noxious fancies and vulgar trivialities, if only to assure himself that men are still men... and not piano keys simply responding to the laws of nature" (114).

Do these assertions offer a key to the irrationality of some of today's youth, who, though showered with "all earthly blessings," seem obstinately bent on self-destruction? Their rebellion may not be born of "sheer spite and ingratitude," yet they doggedly defy those natural laws that would, if respected, ensure their self-preservation. Are these young people filled with a sense of self-revulsion at having become outlaws, or are they expressing social anger, indignation, outrage, and guilt in the hope of reassuring themselves and others that they are not mere "piano keys"? A quotation from Dostoevsky's later story of *The Gambler* may serve as both illustration and premonition: "If the spirit has passed through a great many sensations, possibly it can no longer be satisfied with them, but grows more excited, and demands more sensations, and stronger and stronger ones, until at length it falls exhausted" (*The Gambler,* 273). May the twentieth century still avoid being labeled the age of fallen and exhausted spirits.

A highly original staged version of *Notes from Underground,* reflecting the mood of ferment then reigning in the Soviet Union, was presented by the Moscow Young Spectator Theater at a festival of "new tendencies" held in Belgrade, Yugoslavia, in 1989. The left area of the theater's proscenium was piled high with broken furniture, old mirrors and trash, and a narrow bed, all seeming to dramatize the sordid existence of the solitary protagonist.

Between invectives addressed to the public, snatches of shameful self-pity, and bursts of violence, the antihero appears to be performing secret rituals in celebration of the Ego. He pokes his finger into his nostril, stuffs and removes wads of cotton from his ears, endlessly pours himself tea, spits into his hand the food he has masticated, laps it up again, and performs acts of autoerotism. Reduced to the state of a caged animal, he runs offstage to open the theater doors, leaves freely but then returns to the stage and, by means of a revolving door, encloses himself once more in his infernal mouse hole simply to vindicate his freedom to be irrationally individualistic.

Liza's initial appearance is bathed in a light of youth and innocence that dissolves into complete nudity as she performs ablutions in a basin while the underground man turns from masochism to dizzying sadism. Alternately he kisses her feet and spews the most abominable and offensive insults. In the end, he twice expels her from the inhospitable mouse hole under a hail of vicious tirades about his sexual impotence. Although this avant-garde version of the novella may have gone beyond Dostoevsky's own intentions, it offered a true flavor of the work to an enthralled audience.[2]

Dostoevsky, in a letter to Mikhail of March 1864, complained that the writing of *Notes from Underground* was proving "much more difficult than I had imagined. But meanwhile it's essential that it be good; *I myself* need that. In its tone it is very strange...; people may not like it; con[sequently], it's essential that poetry soften everything and carry it off" (*Letters,* II, 95). But the "poetry" seems to have gone astray, and as to whether people might like it or not, the underground man confesses in the last chapter that "spinning long yarns about how I poisoned my life through moral disintegration in my musty hole, lack of contact with other men, and spite and vanity is not very interesting" (202).

Yet there can be no question that Dostoevsky succeeded in "carrying it off." For André Gide,[3] *Notes from Underground* is the keystone of Dostoevsky's entire oeuvre, the summit of his career, and the basis of his distinction between the man of action as opposed to the thinking man (cf. "the man of action is... of limited intelligence," *Notes from Underground,* 92). Other commentators have recognized in this novella an overture to the second part of Dostoevsky's creative career, a unique example of his concentrated power of psychological analysis, and a prologue to the five great novels in which he was to contest the moral and spiritual ascendancy of the radical Russian intelligentsia.

"I've at least felt ashamed all the time I've been writing this story, so it is... a punishment and an expiation," the underground man concludes (202) as he returns to the frustrations of his own solitude. Perhaps his cynically presented idea of purification through suffering, and his satire on the sentimental social romanticism of the 1840s,[4] may also belong to the inheritance of Raskolnikov, the repentant sinner of *Crime and Punishment.*

12

The Gambler (1866)

Le jeu est une interrogation de la fortune. Et plus elle refuse de répondre, plus on l'interroge. [Gambling is a questioning of Fortune. And the more she refuses to answer, the more we question.] — (André Suares, *Trois hommes. Pascal — Ibsen — Dostoievski,* 249.)

As the underground man rejected the rigid notion that "twice two makes four" and sought escape in the irrational, so too the gambler takes refuge from mathematical certainty by risking his fortune at roulette, where the flow of fortuitous chances lies outside the laws of logic. The roulette wheel, the reader is informed, is, so to speak, that "delightful little item [that] now and then" says "that twice-two-makes-five" (*Notes from Underground,* 117).

Remembering how *The House of the Dead* had riveted public attention through its graphic portrayal of life in a Siberian prison camp, Dostoevsky was convinced that *The Gambler* must succeed if only by virtue of its detailed and vivid description of the game of roulette. In fact the novel has always been rightly considered one of the author's best short works. Its "main point," Dostoevsky wrote in autobiographical vein,

is that all [the gambler's] life juices, energies, violence, boldness have gone *into roulette.* He is a gambler, and not an ordinary gambler, just as Pushkin's miserly knight is not an ordinary knight. . . . He is a poet in his own way, but the fact is he is ashamed of that poetry, because he feels profoundly its baseness, although the need for *risk* in fact ennobles it in his own eyes. The whole story is a story about his playing roulette in gambling towns. (*Letters,* II, 70).

But the book has also a second, sociohistorical motif in its representation of the uncertainty and emptiness that characterized the existence of the Russian living abroad.[1] "I take a spontaneous nature . . . who has lost his faith and *does not dare to believe,* who revolts against authorities and is afraid of them. He tries to reassure himself with the idea that *there is nothing for him to do* in Russia, and therefore [*sic*] the fierce criticism of people in Russia who call on Russians abroad to return."

To the autobiographical hero of the novel, it is hardly to be wondered at that the richly and multifariously gifted Russian abroad, who has found no reason for existence in his homeland, should waste his strength on vain and pointless passions. In sheer folly, he wantonly exhausts his capital in his devotion to a spinning roulette wheel, which, if it enables him to grow rich without working, will satisfy and justify his innate laziness.

The novel's third important purpose is to present a gallery of portraits of the personality types who frequent the fashionable spas and casinos of Europe. Most notable among these creations is La Baboulenka, a wealthy, imposing, abusive, imperious, brisk, and frisky grandmother of seventy-five who makes a highly dramatic entrance, borne aloft in an armchair by her numerous lackeys. With her strength of character and unsuspected weakness for gambling, she seems to have stepped from the stage of the French boulevard theater to entertain and distract the habitués of Roulettenburg, as Dostoevsky's mythical spa is called.

The realism of her characterization, her acidulous banter with the other protagonists, and her humorous, unsubtle tirades, place her on an artistic level not inferior to that of the proud Polina, an equally unforgettable figure who is directly modeled on Dostoevsky's beloved Polina Suslova. The reader sees Polina firsthand, with Dostoevsky's eyes, and vividly experiences the gambler-narrator's masochistic love, tinged with a touch of sour grapes:

I don't even know what there is attractive about her! And yet she is pretty, she is; I think she's pretty. After all, she drives other men mad as well. She is tall and shapely. Only very thin. I think you could tie her into a knot or fold her in two. Her footprint is long and very narrow — agonizing. Really agonizing. Her hair has a tinge of red. Her eyes are really feline, but how proudly and arrogantly she can use them.... She looked [at the Marquis de Griers] in such a way...that afterwards....I could imagine she had slapped his face — had just done so and stood looking at him.... I was in love with her from that evening. (52, Coulson edition)

Various motifs are woven into the novel, but the action hinges essentially on the two obsessions, or conflicting passions, of love and gambling. Caught by the fever of the game, the hero resembles Dostoevsky himself in his delusive belief that he has discovered an infallible system by which to "beat the wheel." "It is terribly stupid and simple," Dostoevsky himself wrote in one of his letters, "and consists of restraining oneself at every moment, no matter at what phase of the game, and of not losing one's head. That's it, and by following it it's impossible to lose, and you're certain to win" (*Letters,* II, 58). Nevertheless, the novelist warns, reminding the reader once again of the irrationality of human behavior, "you can be as wise as Solomon, with the most iron character and still lose control"; and to his wife, Anna, he confesses in a letter from Homburg, "where the best gambling is": "My efforts are successful every time as long as I have the composure and calculation to follow my system: but as soon as a winning streak starts, I immediately start to take risks; I can't control myself" (*Letters,* II, 233).

Anna did not attempt to curb her husband's passion for gambling; she understood that his encounters with the roulette wheel were not only essential but actually beneficial to a man so harassed by tensions, anxieties, griefs, and worries. The changes of scene, the journeys to the various "Roulettenburgs," and the heightened, intense emotions he experienced at the gaming tables served as an emotional cathartic and a catalyst for his creativity.

As *The Gambler* progresses, the ups and downs of fortune spin as dizzily as the little white ball that twirls and tumbles within the roulette wheel; and the psychology of the player who, thus far, is winning heavily, is minutely analyzed. Then, his pockets bulging with his gains and his gait unsteady, the gambler leaves the casino to devote himself to his other passion: "I only felt a sort of fearful pleasure — the pleasure of success, of conquest, of power.... Likewise, before me there flitted the image of Polina; I kept ... reminding myself that it was to *her* I was going, that it was in *her* presence I would soon be standing, that it was *she* whom I should soon be able to relate and show everything" (274).

Such elation suggests that the moment is approaching when the two contradictory passions — gambling and love — will be reconciled and fused. But Polina, insultingly and crushingly, rejects the gambler and his money — and, in so doing, incidentally resolves his internal conflict. "From the moment when ... I had approached the gaming table and begun to rake in the packets of bank notes, my love for her had entered upon a new plane.... Was I, then, at heart a gambler? Did I, after all, love Polina not so *very* much?" (282). The two obsessions being in fact irreconcilable, Polina has now become his secondary priority.[2]

In the meantime, the gambler's enormous winnings have gained the attention of the beautiful and frivolous Mademoiselle Blanche, who spirits both the man and his money away to Paris — where, in the space of three weeks, she will succeed in spending virtually his entire fortune. The reader is not surprised when the hero, on reappearing, is uncertain where his next meal is to come from. Yet persistent as Sisyphus with his boulder, he uses the handout given him by an old friend to return to the casino, determined to "rise from the dead" by winning another fortune — yet, at the same time, knowing full well that he may again end up "in a worse position than the meanest beggar" (307).

13

The Eternal Husband (1870)

Combien d'hommes ne seraient peut-être pas jaloux, s'ils n'avaient entendu parler de la jalousie, s'ils n'étaient pas persuadés qu'il fallait être jaloux? [How many men would perhaps not be jealous if they had never heard speak of jealousy, if they were not convinced that they *had* to be jealous?] — (André Gide, *Dostoïevski,* 139.)

This eerie story of passion and jealousy is set in what Dostoevsky ironically calls "a paradise for a melancholy man" — in other words, St. Petersburg in summer, when "the dust, the stifling heat, the white nights...always fret the nerves" (345). The "melancholy man" is Alexey Ivanovitch Velchaninov, a comfortable bachelor who is approaching the age of forty and finds himself at a turning point in his life. Having become a prey to extreme sensitivity, nervousness, insomnia, and hypochondria, Velchaninov has lost his former good humor and brightness and the past has taken on a different aspect in his eyes. His vanity, too, has degenerated into a morbid concentration on past sins — sins, he realizes, that despite his "tears of repentance" he would repeat if the same temptations were to be repeated.

One of these "cursed reminiscences" is gradually brought to life by a puzzling series of encounters with a certain "gentleman with crape on his hat," a man whose countenance strikes Velchaninov as familiar and arouses an "undefined and aimless aversion." The first such meeting triggers a peculiar dream about a crime Velchaninov has committed and concealed, a dream that alerts the reader to the man's double nature: "His heart thrilled with horror and misery at what he had done, but there was enjoyment in that thrill" (357).

On awakening, Velchaninov goes to his window and again catches sight of the gentleman with crape on his hat, now stalking mysteriously on the dark, deserted pavement opposite his house. The stranger approaches, and Velchaninov, opening the door to admit him, finally recognizes an old acquaintance named Pavel Pavlovitch

Trusotsky. The visitor tells Velchaninov that he is now in mourning for his wife, Natalya Vassilyevna, to whom he refers as a "precious link" between the two of them. At the conclusion of his nocturnal visit, Velchaninov loudly slams the door, locks it carefully, and spits "as though he had been in contact with something unclean" (368). The events of nine years ago now rise vividly before Velchaninov's mind. For he himself had been the lover of Natalya Vassilyevna, but after a liaison of a year's duration, she had repudiated him. He has since been unable to comprehend the "stupid passion" he had felt for a woman whom he now recalls with indignation and hatred, even though he recognizes that it was he who at one time had idealized her so fantastically. Natalya, he now learns, had actually borne his child, Liza, who is now eight years old and has accompanied Trusotsky, her presumed father, to St. Petersburg.

On a return visit to his old acquaintance, Velchaninov makes the acquaintance of this child. "A little over eight months after you went away, God blessed us with her!" his host sarcastically explains. Velchaninov perceives that the nominal father is cruelly tormenting the child both mentally and physically; yet he apparently loves the little girl and suffers in maltreating her, while she on her part firmly persists in loving her unhappy "father."

Aghast at the conditions in which Liza is living, Velchaninov arranges to carry her off to a friend's country estate, notwithstanding his realization that Trusotsky is planning to use the child as a means of taking revenge upon him. Not only does Trusotsky in fact renege on his promise to visit Liza regularly in the country; he actually allows the little girl to die of a mysterious fever, aggravated by the shame she feels at her rejection by her supposed father.

On two occasions, the two men pass the night together in Velchaninov's flat, where their actions are fraught with mystery and ambiguity. In the first instance, Trusotsky pretends to see the ghost of his late wife, and Velchaninov is roused from sleep by the rustle of "something white" standing over him. On a second such occasion, a stormy night when Trusotsky is again invited to stay at Velchaninov's, the latter becomes ill and his guest displays a strange ambivalence. He first outdoes himself in caring for the sick man, helps him to bed, undresses him, wraps him in a quilt, prepares tea, and spends hours applying hot compresses to his chest. Relieved and touched by these attentions, Velchaninov calls the strange visitor to his bedside to acknowledge that "you are better than I am."

But Velchaninov then falls into a deep sleep and is tormented by another dream, in which phantoms crowd around him while an immobile, mute man with crape on his hat sits at a table in the middle of the room. Awakening just in time, he finds Trusotsky on the point of cutting his throat with a razor. Though he manages to seize and turn the weapon aside, the blade cuts a deep wound in his left hand and will leave a permanent scar that will be of significance at the end of the tale.

As the stronger of the two men, Velchaninov is able to overcome his attacker and tie his arms behind him with the window cords; but when the subdued Trusotsky asks for water, he gently holds the glass to his adversary's lips with his uninjured hand, a gesture of human solidarity corresponding to Trusotsky's earlier ministrations. Once Trusotsky has succeeded in untying himself, he approaches Velchaninov and the two look deeply into one another's eyes before what each believes to be a final parting.

The two men nevertheless meet once again by chance, two years later, at a railway junction where we also catch a glimpse of a provincial shrew who turns out to be the henpecked Trusotsky's new wife. Velchaninov, in a friendly, jocular mood, holds out his right hand to his former friend, who, however, refuses to take it. A dramatic transformation then occurs in both men. Something quivers and bursts in the pale and trembling Velchaninov. Clutching Trusotsky by the shoulder and holding him in a tight, furious grip, he shows the palm of his left hand with its telltale scar. "If I hold out this hand to you," he whispers, "you certainly might take it!"

Trusotsky's lips tremble, his cheeks and chin twitch, and tears suddenly gush from his eyes as he murmurs the name of the dead Liza. As Velchaninov stands stupefied, the shrewish wife screams for Trusotsky to get on the moving train, and the two men are separated forever.

The complex figure of Velchaninov impresses one as highly individualized and even autobiographical, fraught as it is with powerful reminiscences of Dostoevsky's own ambivalence, hypochondria, insomnia, and financial irresponsibility. The masochistic figure of Trusotsky, on the other hand, is universal and eternal in its quality. So, too, is the triangular figure composed by the two men and the dead Natalya — and not less universal is the innocence of the child Liza, a hapless victim of adult intrigues.

Dostoevsky here offers for the reader's special contemplation two human types, one feminine, the other masculine: the woman who is born to become an unfaithful wife, and the male whose sole vocation is to play the "eternal husband" and subject himself to female dominance. Although Natalya Vassilyevna has died of consumption long before the story opens, it is she who provokes the action of the drama and it is her figure that Dostoevsky so vividly revives. Natalya's liaison with Velchaninov might have doomed him, too, to the "eternal husband" category had she not contemptuously dismissed the lover whom she then held in bondage and who was ready to perform the most monstrous, senseless acts to satisfy her slightest caprice.

Like Polina in *The Gambler*, Natalya had "something exceptional — a power of attraction, of enslaving, of dominating" other men (370). Passionate, cruel, and sensual, she forces Velchaninov, like the gambler, to wonder whether he had really loved such a haughty, capricious woman or whether it had been mere infatuation. Yet both Velchaninov and the gambler know full well that if destiny were to set them once again in the path of Natalya or Polina, they would promptly succumb to those unfaithful ladies' fascination.

Nine years have elapsed and Velchaninov has forgotten Natalya's existence by the time the story opens. The deceived masochistic Trusotsky, on the other hand, has all along been planning his revenge as the only way of escape from the distress caused by his wife's infidelity. Simultaneously attracted and repelled by Natalya's former lover, Trusotsky travels to St. Petersburg and purposely stumbles across him five times in the dusty streets before making himself known. Velchaninov is perplexed: is the man looking for him or trying to avoid him? The cuckold and the paramour, it has been pointed out, seem to gravitate toward each other up to the moment of mutual recognition — whereas from that point on, the rival becomes more important, psychologically, to each of them than the woman they shared.[1]

Trusotsky seems incapable of finding an adequate solution to the "eternal" problem that besets him. He suffers from jealousy, yet seems to enjoy his own suffering, and hesitates to conform to the conventional standard requiring that he take vengeance. Though he had loved Natalya, he now seems to love his jealousy per se, and to cherish it no less than he cherishes the memory of his wife. In his quest for suffering through Liza as well, he reminds us of the underground man in his remorseless cultivation of masochistic self-torment.

The Eternal Husband thus presents an extraordinarily penetrating analysis of the contradictory impulses and motivations of a betrayed husband whose deep unconscious promptings urge him to try to kill the rival he has so tenderly cared for. He goes to Velchaninov's apartment "to embrace him and to weep" — that is, to murder him.

Yet whatever hatred he may harbor for his rival is counterbalanced by a strange, mysterious love. He tries to kill, almost unwittingly, without knowing that he wishes to kill. "People...don't know a minute beforehand," Dostoevsky asserts, "whether they'll murder a man or not—as soon as they take a knife in their trembling hands and feel the hot spurt of blood on their fingers they don't stick at cutting your throat, but cut off your head, 'clean off,' as convicts express it" (459).

André Gide pointed out that *The Eternal Husband* takes one far beyond conventional love and hatred, conducting the reader into those deep regions of human solidarity in which Dostoevsky found the secret of happiness.[2] It is a timeless region where men are no longer separated by temporal limitations and personal egoisms, where they are generous in helping those in distress and where the spirit of the Good Samaritan reigns.

Whatever thirst for vengeance stirs within the "eternal husband," whatever distaste he feels for the child fathered by another man, and whatever compulsion he may feel to try to exact vengeance, Trusotsky's behavior is governed by psychological factors well beyond the control of reason. He may even make inexplicable gestures of love and solidarity for the person he is supposed to hate, just as Velchaninov will help to slake the thirst of his would-be killer. Love and hatred are not easily defined or circumscribed. "It was from hatred that he loved me," says Velchaninov of Trusotsky, "[and] that's the strongest of all loves" (461).

Part 4

The Short Stories

The writing of short stories gave Dostoevsky an opportunity both to supplement his income and to publicize some favorite ideas without incurring the difficulties inseparable from the publication of serialized novels, which had not only to pass censorship but to be written in such a way as to sustain the reader's interest from one issue to the next. The greater concision and intensity of the short stories convey a direct, immediate impression of Dostoevsky's personality, his voice, and his feeling for the St. Petersburg milieu in which the action is usually laid.

Though Dostoevsky even here does not entirely refrain from editorial comment and analysis, his short stories derive their effectiveness primarily from his realistic and supple use of dialogue, a feature that ensures their liveliness and readability and would make them readily producible as one-act plays. The slight, uncomplicated actions are framed amid the ordinary circumstances of Russian life, and each tale focuses upon a character whose existence is illuminated by a particular incident, vision, or dream.

Clearly, Dostoevsky's primary intention is not so much to narrate a striking external occurrence as to allow the reader to eavesdrop on the intimate secrets of a character and come to a growing understanding of his nature, the quality of his life, and the situation in which he is entangled. The unity for which the author strove in each of his short stories owes less to the working out of a dramatic complication than to the revelation of the characters' inner selves.

14

Pre-Siberian Stories

Ten of Dostoevsky's short stories were written during the two or three years that preceded his arrest in 1849, while six more followed his Siberian exile. Highly varied in detail, the pre-Siberian stories resemble the long tale of *The Double* in that they tend to occupy a middle ground between reality and fantasy. Facing thus in both directions as they live out their grotesque existences, the characters grope for ways of escaping from the sordid reality of a hostile social environment or an oppressive bureaucratic order. They outdo themselves in inventing fanciful defense bulwarks or images of a brighter world. But the more they dream and soar in airy realms, the more they lose themselves in wild illusions and the more their personalities take on the qualities of the "fantastic."

This trait is already apparent in *Mr. Prokharchin* (1846), the earliest of Dostoevsky's "escape" stories, in which social commentary is interwoven with psychological analysis. It tells of an elderly, impoverished, and mentally limited government clerk called Semyon Ivanovich Prokharchin who rents a dark, humble corner in a boardinghouse patronized by several younger colleagues. Parsimonious and niggardly in the extreme, Mr. Prokharchin goes without socks and underwear to save on laundry bills, and limits himself to half or less of the standard boardinghouse diet.

Although his quiet demeanor makes him a favorite of his landlady, she does observe "something fantastical" about him. Sometimes, the reader is told, he "completely forgot himself, and sitting in his seat with his mouth open and his pen in the air, as though frozen or petrified, looked more like the shadow of a rational being than that rational being itself" (11). Such a man could hardly be popular with his fellow boarders, and the latter in fact take a malicious pleasure in playing upon his fearfulness and insecurity, joking about the locked trunk under his bed, and circulating vague rumors about the impending elimination of his job. These insinuations strike panic into the soul of Mr. Prokharchin, who lives in constant fear of failure and is anguished by his lack of the "necessary egoism" to survive in a hostile environment.

Devastated by a rebuke from his official supervisor, Mr. Prokharchin inexplicably disappears for several days — to the dismay of the landlady and the other boarders — eventually reappearing in the arms of a night cabman who declares his passenger to be "off his head." Twitching convulsively and blinking in bewilderment at the boarders gathered around his bed, Prokharchin begs them not to leave him in want. The boarders, touched by the true spirit of Russian fraternity, suspend their persecution and even take up a collection for his benefit.

In his delirium, Prokharchin has a series of macabre dreams that feature past misdemeanors and are described by Dostoevsky in tones of mingled horror and black humor. Bloodcurdling shrieks are heard at dead of night as the sick man attempts to fight off two real, flesh-and-blood assailants who suspect a fortune may be hidden in or under his bed. By the time the other lodgers have reached the scene, Mr. Prokharchin is lying dead on the floor, while the landlady has already rummaged in his boots and laid hold of his little trunk.

The authorities arrive, and the trunk is opened and found to contain nothing of value; but the mattress, which has aroused suspicion because of its weight, proves to contain innumerable small packets of rubles and kopecks. As the slitting and slashing of the mattress continue, the stuffing flies, the heaps of coins and notes grow larger, and the disordered scene reaches a pitch of frenzy. "Only Semyon Ivanovich preserved his composure, lying calmly...and seeming to have no foreboding of his ruin" (34).

With the search completed and Mr. Prokharchin's small hoard turned over to the authorities, the boarders linger to study the face of the dead man. He seems to want to communicate with the landlady. "I am dead; there's no need of fuss now...but I say what if I'm not dead, what if I get up?...What would happen then?" Macabre references to the return of the dead occur often in Dostoevsky's works and dreams. Here, they give an unexpected twist to the age-old tale of the miser who dies of neglect and inanition on a bed filled with his own treasure.

An even earlier short story, *A Novel in Nine Letters*, had been written by Dostoevsky in a single night in 1845 for Nekrasov's proposed satirical almanac, *The Scoffer*. That publication, however, was quashed by the censorship, and Dostoevsky's story consequently remained unpublished until the inaugural number of *The Contemporary* appeared in 1847. In the meantime, Dostoevsky wrote Mikhail in 1845, "My novel was read to our whole circle at Turgenev's... and it produced a furor" (*Letters*, I, 118). Belinsky, the critic and Dostoevsky's early supporter, on the other hand, complained of the same story that he could "hardly get through it."[1]

Though clever enough in itself, *A Novel in Nine Letters* has little in common with Dostoevsky's more mature work. A comic anecdote in the farcical, tit-for-tat tradition of "the trickster tricked," it takes the form of a correspondence between two Petersburg men-about-town, both young, both married, and both involved, socially and perhaps financially, with a wealthy young man from the provinces whom they evidently hope to relieve of some of his riches. While the detailed relationships among the characters can only be guessed at, it is evident that one of the young men — who are as alike as Tweedledum and Tweedledee — is trying to arrange a meeting with his confederate while the other evades him with farfetched excuses, ranging from the death of an aunt to his wife's illness and his baby's teething. In the denouement, the two men exchange purloined letters showing that each of their wives has had an illicit love affair with the young provincial they had planned to dupe.

Slight as it is, the story provides an amusing contrast to Dostoevsky's more serious efforts. Felicitous details, such as those surrounding a loaned copy of *Don Quixote* and a lost pair of galoshes, help bring the period to vivid life.

A very different kind of story is *The Landlady* (1847), a long, mysterious tale suffused with an eerie, supernatural atmosphere akin to that which produced the horror film, *The Exorcist*. On a less fanciful plane, it may also be taken as an illustration of the dangers arising from too much introspection and too little interaction with one's fellows. "The more spirit and inner content we have in ourselves, the better is our corner in life," Dostoevsky wrote Mikhail while composing this story early in 1847. "Of course, the dissonance and disequilibrium that society presents to us are terrible. *The external* must be balanced with *the internal*. Otherwise, with the absence of external phenomena, the internal will gain too dangerous an influence. Nerves and fantasy will occupy too much space in a being" (*Letters*, I, 148).

"Nerves and fantasy" unquestionably occupied too much space in Vasily Mikhailovich Ordynov, the reclusive, scholarly young protagonist of *The Landlady*. Vasily has dreamed of discovering a new and unknown world, of formulating a "philosophical system." His passion for philosophy has "consumed his youth, marred his rest at nights with its slow, intoxicating poison, [and] robbed him of wholesome food and of fresh air which never penetrated to his stifling corner" (61). But Ordynov falls under a different kind of spell when he one day glimpses a beautiful young woman who is weeping in church and is then led away by a severe-looking older man. From that moment, the would-be philosopher is racked with mental pain that alternates with sweet anguish and yearning.

Following the mysterious couple to their domicile, the young hero manages, despite the old man's mistrustful air, to sublet a tiny room in the couple's cramped apartment. As he is shown into his new quarters, he stumbles over a heap of firewood, loses consciousness, and on reviving opens his eyes to the divine vision that has bewitched him. Katerina, his new "landlady," her face drenched in tears, has been seeing to his comfort and bends over him in a gentle, motherly attitude of infinite compassion. Moved to the core of his being, the young man is on the verge of serious illness and soon lies in delirium while Katerina nurses him, caresses his feverish lips with a long, burning kiss, and extracts his promise that on his recovery they will live together "as brother and sister."

Ordynov's strange new existence unfolds in a series of hallucinating dreams and broken, enigmatic images, alternately filling him with deep lethargy and supreme ecstasy. Katerina's caresses stir childhood recollections of his mother's sweetness, yet even in his moments of joy he is dimly aware of the menacing presence of the old man. The reader will not overlook the parallel with Dostoevsky's childhood love for his mother and fear of his own father.

The old man, too, appears to suffer from some strange illness, and Ordynov notices that he too comes in for a share of Katerina's ineffable tenderness. Impetuously, the young man at one point rushes into the couple's room and narrowly misses being shot by his sick host, who, gun in hand, falls to the floor in an epileptic seizure. Neighbors tell Ordynov that the old man, Ilya Murin, is a once wealthy, now ruined capitalist from the Volga region who had fallen into despondency and at different times attempted both homicide and suicide. Endowed with the gift of second sight, he has become a mystic who devotes himself to penance and religious readings and exercises great influence over those who seek his counsel.

To judge from Katerina's confused ramblings, the old man is holding her in a state of mental and moral servitude, tormenting her with accusations of incest and frightening her with the specter of eternal

damnation. Among other things, he has told her that she is under
her mother's curse as a murderess; that he himself was once her
mother's lover, and that she is his illegitimate daughter. What Katerina claims to know for certain is that on the night when her father
was killed and her mother left behind on her deathbed, she herself, as Murin's shameless slave, absconded with him and has since
remained inescapably in his power.

Blind fury surges in the soul of Ordynov, who sees the old man as a
mortal foe against whom he must defend both Katerina and himself.
But Katerina's increasingly strange behavior convinces him that her
psyche has been irretrievably distorted and that she is, in fact, insane.
A session with the old man, whose credibility seems scarcely greater
than Katerina's, nevertheless confirms this dismaying hypothesis.
Katerina's "sick brain," Murin explains, continually leads her into
the sin of lust — she "always wants a sweetheart"; but he, Murin,
loves her despite her insanity and will relinquish her to no one.

Heeding the mystic's advice to leave before harm befalls him,
the devastated Ordynov hastily evacuates and removes to a remote
neighborhood where he again falls ill. His creative capacities exhausted, his mind becomes obsessed with mysticism, fatalism, and
belief in occult powers. Destroyed by a malevolent external force,
the would-be philosopher is seen lying on the church pavement as
though unconscious and praying for hours at a stretch.

In his delirium, Ordynov imagines that Katerina is innocent of
crime, that her reason is sound, and that the truth has been system-
atically twisted to her detriment. It was only her naïveté, he reasons,
that enabled Murin to flatter the inclinations of her heart, so that
her "free soul had been clipped of its wings till it was incapable . . . of
resistance or of free movement towards free life" (141). It was Katerina's "weak heart," the young man concludes, that had blinded
her to reality and mysteriously subjected her to Murin's power.

But any lingering hope that she might still be rescued from Murin's
clutches is blasted by the news that the old man and his "wife" have
already left St. Petersburg and returned to their provincial homeland.

Belinsky, Russia's leading critic, liked *The Landlady* no better
than *A Novel in Nine Letters*. Impervious to the story's mysterious
fascination, he looked in vain for a "single simple or living word
or expression." Everything, to him, was "farfetched, exaggerated,
stilted, spurious and false."[2] Later critics, more alert to Dostoevsky's symbolism, have paid more attention to its two outstanding
character types, "the dreamer" and the "weak heart." Ordynov,
a dreamer *par excellence,* is intelligent and noble-minded but es-

tranged from reality and powerless to liberate his own or Katerina's human personality.

Katerina herself, subdued by moral and emotional imprisonment, fails to react against Murin's enslavement of her soul; indeed, like not a few of Dostoevsky's characters, she admits to an unhealthy enjoyment of her own sorrow and sinfulness. She does not deny that she derives a masochistic pleasure from self-laceration and self-punishment. She is less grieved at having become Murin's slave, she tells Ordynov, than at her enjoyment of her own degradation: "My shame and disgrace are dear to me.... It is dear to my greedy heart to remember my sorrow as though it were joy and happiness" (111). Dostoevsky here seems to be reversing Dante's famous claim that there is "no greater grief than to remember days / Of joy, when misery is at hand" (*Hell,* canto 5, 1:118).

Another character who suffers from a "weak heart" — in other words, from too much modesty and too little assertiveness — is the central figure in the story actually entitled *A Weak Heart* (1848), one of six published by Dostoevsky during the creative year that preceded his arrest and imprisonment. Reminiscent in some ways of the Parisian artists' life then taking literary form in Henri Murger's *Scènes de la vie de Bohème,* it tells of two young government clerks who live together in St. Petersburg and share their modest resources in an exuberant spirit of brotherly affection.

One of the two friends, Vasya Shumkov, a man of lowly origins and slightly lame, is described as a "kind, softhearted fellow, but weak, unpardonably weak [and] a dreamer" (199). His very docility and mildness, set off by ebullient good humor and eagerness for knowledge and self-improvement, make him a natural candidate for victimization by St. Petersburg's ruthless power machine. His friend Arkady Ivanovich Nefdevich, or Arkasha, tries hard but unsuccessfully to protect him from the consequences of his gentleness and naïveté.

The action takes place during a New Year's holiday in the course of which Vasya progresses from delirious happiness over his impending marriage to despair and ruin due to his inability to complete a copying assignment given him by his office superior. Dressed for New Year's Eve in his best trousers and a clean shirt front, Vasya unexpectedly informs his incredulous friend that he is engaged to be married. Disdaining to discuss ways and means — though he has no regular salary, and Lizanka, the bride-to-be, is admittedly very poor — he assures the sympathetic Arkasha that all will be well and that all three of them will in the future live together in mutual affection.

Hurrying off to visit the bride and her family, the two friends stop to buy Lizanka a lovely cap decorated with ribbons, ruches, and lace. A radiant Lizanka greets them at the door, "breathlessly, with her heart throbbing like a captured bird's, flushing and turning as red as a cherry, a fruit which she wonderfully resembled" (182). She, too, enthusiastically agrees that the three of them shall live together, and Arkady's instant attraction to the young girl enhances their mutual delight.

The only cloud on the horizon is that Vasya has neglected to complete his copying assignment, due immediately after the holiday. Heroically, he determines to make up for lost time by skipping the holiday festivities and working around the clock until the job is done. A prey to deep and disturbing guilt feelings, he rejects the idea of asking for an extension of time, preferring to work himself to the point of collapse. The job, in reality, is of no great importance, yet Vasya magnifies his failure to complete it as an unpardonable lapse. "Vasya felt guilty *in his own eyes*," Dostoevsky explains, "felt he was ungrateful to destiny...was crushed, overwhelmed by happiness and thought himself unworthy of it" — whereas "in fact, he was simply trying to find an excuse to go off his head" (204).

That, indeed, is the consequence of Vasya's superhuman effort. Working day and night as though in a trance, he eventually is overcome by fatigue and falls into a deep sleep. Arkady, too, dozes in his chair and has a strange, agitated dream in which Vasya appears to him as a lifeless corpse. Awakening, he is horrified to see that his friend is still working but has forgotten the ink and is moving a dry pen over the paper, turning over a series of perfectly blank pages. Vasya has lost his mind. "Why kill [Lizanka]?" he cries. "How is she to blame? The sin is mine, the sin is mine!"

Vasya now imagines that he is being conscripted into the army, a real threat at that period for persons of inferior social status. In the climactic scene, he stands before his office superior, head high, stiffly erect, his feet together and his hands held rigidly at his sides. A pale and pitiful "recruit," he pleads with the "officer": "I have a physical defect and am small and weak, and I am not fit for military service, Your Excellency." To the superior's inquiry what has brought him to this pass, friend Arkady replies, "Gratitude." Having tasted of happiness for the first time in his life, Arkady implies, Vasya was unable to bear its weight and transferred his sense of guilt to the neglected copying job.

A carriage and warders arrive from the hospital where the pathetic young clerk must now be taken. As the two friends embrace for the last time, Vasya thrusts into Arkady's hand a tiny packet containing a lock of Lizanka's black hair, a symbol of the happiness that has driven him mad.

Still another marriage that fails to take place, this time because of an April Fools' joke that backfired, is the subject of *Polzunkov* (1848), a comparatively brief, semihumorous story originally entitled *The Buffoon*. Its protagonist is a down-at-heels ex-government clerk, Osip Mikhailovich Polzunkov by name, who ekes out a precarious existence by clowning and making himself ridiculous and then appealing to his amused acquaintances for financial support in the form of "loans." This curious, self-abasing personage, who allegedly will commit any vile act "just to please the next person," is alternately described by Dostoevsky as "a most honest and noble man" and as "a comic martyr."

Climbing onto a chair at a social gathering one evening, Polzunkov undertakes to entertain the guests by telling them the tragicomic tale of why he never married. His long and involved story is repeatedly interrupted by sardonic comments from his listeners, who beg him to speak more simply and succinctly — perhaps an indirect acknowledgment by Dostoevsky of his own tendency to verboseness.

Polzunkov's story centers on an admittedly disreputable action in which he had accepted a large sum of money from his official superior, one Fedosey Nikolaevich, in return for the surrender of certain papers that would have seriously compromised the latter. In appreciation of this gesture, he is made much of by Fedosey and his family and even becomes engaged to Fedosey's daughter, who, it is hinted, has herself been compromised by her past association with a certain cavalry officer. Polzunkov has mixed feelings about the sudden change in his prospects as he sits down to tea with his future family. "I, too, had a samovar in my chest boiling inside me while my legs turned to ice," he recalls.

The following day being the first of April, Polzunkov determines to play a joke on his future father-in-law by handing in his own resignation, a step that will theoretically leave him free to give evidence against his superior. Fedosey is stunned by this action on the part of the man he had singled out to save the family's honor. When Polzunkov playfully calls out, "April Fool," his superior embraces him with relief and evidences his appreciation by giving Polzunkov the huge task of straightening out the disordered affairs of the office.

But Polzunkov's apparently glittering prospects are doomed to remain unrealized. The tables are turned when Fedosey, who now pretends to be mortally ill, summons Polzunkov to his bedside and tells him that he urgently needs to borrow back the "hush money" paid to his future son-in-law in order to cover a deficit at the office before it is discovered by a government auditor. The gullible Polzunkov obligingly returns the entire sum, minus fifty rubles he has already spent, and provides a receipt for the latter amount as a supposed advance on his salary.

Then, on the very next morning, Polzunkov receives notice that his bogus "resignation" has been accepted! In consternation he rushes off to Fedosey Nikolaevich, who now laughs at the idea that the resignation could have been meant as a joke. Such jokes, he points out, could easily result in banishment to Siberia. The marriage project, too, evaporates now that Fedosey has retrieved the hush money. To cap Polzunkov's misery, the caged blackbird he had presented to his fiancée — perhaps forgetting that the blackbird is a traditional symbol for a simpleton — is unceremoniously returned to him with a note that reads simply, "April Fool!"

When Polzunkov later met Fedosey Nikolaevich on the street, he tells his audience, he attempted to denounce him to his face but, as he ruefully admits, "I wasn't able to utter a word, gentlemen!" Over and above Polzunkov's personal debasement, the reader is aware of Dostoevsky's distaste for the mores of Russia's bureaucratic jungle, in which some of Polzunkov's own listeners were doubtless carrying on a similar struggle for survival. Polzunkov — whose name means "crawling" — may perhaps be seen as a sort of horizontal "double," crawling on the ground while a mirror on his back reflects the fellow creatures who bear their own share in the sins of the world.

The story entitled *An Honest Thief* is a later amalgam of two sketches originally published in *Notes of the Fatherland* in 1848 as *The Pensioner* and *An Honest Thief: From the Diary of an Unknown.* This moving and unpretentious little reminiscence is focused upon the power of human weakness — in this case, the craving for alcohol — and the pathetic effort of one of its victims to atone for his own shortcomings.

The nominal narrator is one of Dostoevsky's typical middle-aged bureaucrats, living in modest circumstances and cared for by a single female servant, the taciturn but strong-minded Agrafena. On her recommendation, he rents a corner of his kitchen as a lodging for a certain Astafy Ivanovich, an old soldier who is a tailor by trade and requires nothing but a bed and a "living space" on the windowsill. The theft of the bureaucrat's overcoat by an unknown intruder affords the new lodger a pretext to narrate his own experience of an earlier theft and of the perpetrator's repentance.

He himself, Astafy Ivanovich explains, had at one time been the reluctant host and patron of a destitute drunkard named Emelyan Ilyich, a man who originally came to him for a meal and remained to batten on the charity of his by no means affluent host. Ill fitted for any kind of work, incapable even of threading a needle for his benefactor, Emelyan had been a good-hearted, inoffensive creature to whom people were all too ready to offer another drink in the hope of mitigating his habitual misery.

Astafy himself, he confesses, had become much attached to his "Emelyanushka," to whom he felt linked by a bond of solidarity — or at least compassion — that forbade him to evict his troublesome guest. But when a pair of riding breeches he was making for a noble client disappeared from his trunk, Astafy's anger knew no bounds and he bitterly accused Emelyan of the theft. Emelyan, deeply wounded and tearfully denying the charge, had remained mute for three days and had then disappeared, to his host's extreme alarm. On his reappearance some days later in a half-dead condition, the relieved Astafy had given him a prodigal's welcome, nursed, consoled him, even provided him with liquor. Ill with fever, heartbreak, and remorse, and now on his deathbed, the repentant Emelyan admitted to the theft of the breeches and, to compensate his benefactor for all his good deeds, bequeathed to him his only possession, a worthless, ragged coat that might possibly bring a few kopecks in the secondhand market.

In spite of the exaggerated sentimentality with which Dostoevsky portrays the degraded but grateful drunkard and his generous, long-suffering host, the little story vividly illustrates the writer's conviction that the truth is bound to prevail and that the innate qualities of Russia's common people will lead them in the paths of righteousness. This faith in the inherent virtues of the Russian people, united in human solidarity through their traditional Christian faith, is of course the core of Dostoevsky's later teaching as a novelist and spiritual guide.

Equally slight in form, though weighty with psychological meaning, is *A Christmas Tree and a Wedding* (1848). The story plays on three of Dostoevsky's most characteristic themes and their associated character types: the rapacious, ruthless male who holds a position of power; the ingenuous young girl who is his victim; and the poor, socially inferior but sensitive young boy whom he persecutes and humiliates.

A children's ball is taking place at New Year's in the home of a distinguished upper-class family. The children play with — or break — their expensive toys around the Christmas tree while the adult guests pursue their banal intrigues or relapse into deadly boredom. One guest devotes the entire evening to smoothing his side-whiskers; another, to reckoning up the accumulating value of the handsome dowry earmarked for one of the little girl guests.

This exquisite child, the eleven-year-old daughter of a wealthy financier, has withdrawn from the rough-and-tumble around the Christmas tree and made friends with the bashful young son of a woman who serves as governess in the host's family. Despite his inferior social rank, this lad had desperately wanted to join in the theater game the wealthy children were playing, and he had not been above "practicing a little servility" in the hope of breaking down the rigid caste barriers maintained by his lilliputian contemporaries. But his efforts to humble himself for the edification of his social superiors had earned him nothing but a sound beating by another boy.

The unaffected sympathy and incipient friendship between the two sensitive children is rudely broken in upon by the vulgar Julian Mastakovich, the greedy guest who is already laying plans to snare the young girl's fortune. Roughly shoving the boy aside, he pats the little girl on her cheek, flattering and kissing her in a way that foreshadows the child-abuse theme so often met with in Dostoevsky's later works. Other guests arrive to find both children on the verge of tears; but Mastakovich, who has not relinquished his designs on the little girl's dowry, continues his sadistic pursuit of the boy and roughly brushes off his host's request for help in finding the lad a berth.

A brief epilogue gives us a glimpse of the wedding, five years later, of the lecherous, potbellied, fifty-year-old Mastakovich and the sixteen-year-old heiress who first attracted his notice at the children's party. There is something almost obscene in this incongruous match, and the bride, pale and sad though radiantly beautiful, wears a distracted expression while her eyes betray the signs of recent tears. Beneath her sadness, a bystander still notes a semblance of childlike innocence as she seems to utter a silent, fervent prayer for mercy.

This troubling little story offers further evidence of Dostoevsky's deep concern with the vulnerability and impressionability of children and with the plight of society's less fortunate members, those he would later call the "insulted and injured." But it also reminds one that the privilege of wealth, as in the young bride's case, is not always an advantage.[3]

Each June, the inhabitants of St. Petersburg's northerly latitudes experience the long hours of eerie, unreal daylight that provide the title, and something of the feverish atmosphere, of the fifth of Dostoevsky's short stories from the year 1848. The action of *White Nights,* a touchingly sentimental tale that may contain an autobiographical element,[4] unfolds in the course of four of these June nights during which the narrator — a timorous, lonely clerk, "a dreamer with little real life" — emerges from the cobwebs of his squalid chamber to roam the capital's nocturnal streets, soaring in the airy realms of romantic illusion and enjoying one moment of true bliss before falling back into the hopeless banality of his everyday existence.

Night One. An evening ramble amid the rustic sights and sounds of the city's environs imbues the solitary dreamer with an unaccountable sense of exaltation. "Such was the impact of nature upon me, a semi-invalid city dweller who'd almost suffocated within the city walls, that I felt almost as if I'd found myself in Italy" (11). In this susceptible condition he returns to the city and is much affected by the sight of a young girl who leans against the railing of the Neva embankment and quietly weeps as she gazes into the murky water.

When another man accosts her, the twenty-six-year-old narrator puts the intruder to flight and offers the young lady his arm, confessing at the same time that he is "quite unused to being with women" and in fact has never had any close acquaintance: "I've only gone around dreaming that one day I might meet ... the ideal woman. ... I can dream up whole novels. ... " "I thought you were crying, and I couldn't bear it," he adds. " ... My heart shrank. ... Why shouldn't I be entitled to grieve with you? ... is it a sin for me to feel brotherly compassion for your sorrow?" (16).

Like Katerina of *The Landlady,* the girl seems willing and even eager to accept the young man's "brotherly" attentions, although she has a reason for insisting that he not fall in love with her as he seems about to do.

Night Two. In a duet that reminds one of Rodolfo and Mimi in the opera *La Bohème,* the two young people exchange the stories of their lives. The romantic dreamer explains in heroic accents that he is not a real human being at all, but a sort of intermediary creature, installed in a remote corner of the earth and shrinking from the light of day. "Couldn't you please speak less beautifully?" the puzzled girl interrupts. "You sound as though you were reading aloud from a book."

But the young man, once launched, is incapable of stemming the flow. His "Goddess of Fantasy" has spun a golden web around him, marvelous patterns unfold before his eyes, and, in Dostoevsky's words, "fancy becomes like a flame itself, flashing and flaring.... How naturally the dreamer's world of fantasy springs up!... He almost believes that his dream life is no figment of the imagination, no self-deception, no delusion, but something real, actual, existing" (25, 27). Soaring on the wings of fantasy, the narrator-dreamer deluges the girl with literary, poetic, and musical meanderings until, finally, "My dramatic exclamations over, I fell dramatically silent," allowing her to tell her own story.

"Nastenka," seventeen years old, is an orphan who lives with her blind grandmother, a rather severe woman who has been wont to curb her grandchild's wanderings by pinning Nastenka's dress to her own. To eke out her meager pension, the old lady had some time ago taken in a lodger, a diffident but kind young man with whom Nastenka had naturally fallen in love. He had escorted the two ladies to the opera and loaned them volumes of Walter Scott and Pushkin for Nastenka to read to her grandmother.

On leaving St. Petersburg, the lodger had promised to return in a year's time to the very spot where the dreamer had first caught sight of Nastenka; and he had pledged that if the girl still loved him, they would build a happy life together. But the year has now passed, and her elusive admirer, though he has returned to the capital, has failed to keep the promised rendezvous. The distraught Nastenka has been able to find no better course than to write him a letter, which the naive if well-intentioned dreamer enthusiastically undertakes to deliver for her.

Night Three. Nastenka and her new friend stand in the drizzling rain awaiting the appearance of the errant admirer. Dostoevsky thoroughly understands the psychology of the apparently jilted maiden who seeks relief from her fear and frustration in an exaggerated show of affection for a surrogate: "Strangely, she doubled the attention she showered on me, as if she wanted instinctively to give me something she feared she wouldn't get" (44). Although Nastenka admittedly continues to love her earlier friend, she acknowledges the superiority of the noble and selfless dreamer and insists that even after her marriage they will live together in intimate association, since she loves him almost as much as her (hoped-for) future husband. In opening up this prospect, the childlike Nastenka reveals herself as another of Dostoevsky's numerous "bigamous" characters who find no difficulty in loving two persons at once.

Night Four. The now familiar couple disconsolately await the arrival of the cruel deserter, who has failed either to appear or to acknowledge the letter of his distraught fiancée. Unable to keep his own love a secret any longer, the dreamer shyly but ardently declares his passion, and Nastenka's reply affords him a real "moment of bliss," for it appears that she loves him in the same way he loves her. Dostoevsky excels in the description of her momentary reversal of feeling. Perhaps her love for the cruel deserter was nothing but a delusion? Perhaps it had all begun as a childish adventure? Perhaps she had wanted only to "unpin" herself from her grandmother?

Nastenka, in any case, is now ready to offer true love to the dreamer — but, at this climactic moment, the long-awaited pretender suddenly appears. Instinctively loyal to her first love, Nastenka tears herself from the dreamer's embrace, rushes to his rival, flings herself into his arms, then quickly runs back to the dreamer to give him a passionate kiss. Returning again to her intended, she catches his hand and hurries away with him.

The Next Morning. Racked with fever and pain, the dreamer awakens to another dreary, rainy day. From Nastenka arrives a letter of apology and gratitude. "Oh God," she writes, "if only it were possible to love both of you at the same time! Ah, if only you could be him!" Bitterly disillusioned and aware that solitude has again enveloped him, the dreamer can still utter a fervent prayer for the happiness of her who had given him "a moment of bliss . . . enough for a whole lifetime."

Another Man's Wife; or, The Husband under the Bed: An Extraordinary Adventure (1848) represents Dostoevsky's most determined effort at farce comedy in the French bedroom style. Like *An Honest Thief,* it is a composite of two short sketches — *Another Man's Wife (A Street Scene)* and *A Jealous Husband (An Extraordinary Occurrence)* — which were separately published in 1848 and combined in 1860 under the present title. Its unifying figure is a jealous husband, the well-bred but distraught Ivan Andreevich, who spends his time in futile pursuit of his frivolous wife, Glafira Petrovna.

The story opens on a St. Petersburg evening that finds two men pacing separately in front of an apartment building, both apparently waiting for a lady to emerge. The older man, dressed in a fur coat, is the high-ranking and distinguished Ivan Andreevich; the younger one is the well-off Ivan Ilyich Tvorogov, dressed in a cape with a

beaver collar in which he buries his nose by way of showing that
he is annoyed by the other's presence. Eventually the two agree to
divide the sidewalk in such a way as to ensure that the lady cannot
escape them when she comes out.

But the lady fails to appear, and at eight o'clock the two decide
to join forces and enter the building together. They climb the dark
stairs to the third-floor apartment of a certain Mr. Bobinizin, where
Ivan Andreevich fearfully expects to find his wife in flagrante delicto. Listening outside Bobinizin's door, the two men carry on an
amusing dialogue of mixed identities, which is interrupted when the
door opens from within. The timid Ivan Andreevich hastily conceals
himself, but Tvorogov waits on the landing to face Mr. Bobinizin
and Glafira Petrovna — for it is indeed she.

As Bobinizin goes down to summon a sleigh, Tvorogov seizes the
opportunity to remind Glafira that she has also made a commitment
to him! She protests that Bobinizin is actually her husband; but just
then her real husband, Ivan Andreevich, emerges from his hiding
place. Adroitly concocting a spur-of-the-moment explanation for
her presence in the apartment, Glafira expresses heartfelt gratitude
to Mr. Tvorogov for having succored her when her sleigh over-
turned — a purely imaginary event. Tvorogov is unable to protest
as Ivan Andreevich thanks him for his gallantry.

Bobinizin now returns, and to him Glafira repeats the story of her
rescue and of her relief that her husband has now arrived. Introducing Bobinizin as "a friend," she hints that they will meet again
on the morrow at the Karpovs' masked ball. But Bobinizin, apparently in no mood for a fresh intrigue, moodily drives off in the sleigh
he had hired for himself and Glafira. She in turn departs with Ivan
Andreevich, leaving the young man in the beaver-collared cape be-
wildered, frustrated, and stupefied by the woman's extraordinary
resourcefulness.

If Dostoevsky's readers were confused by all this byplay, worse
mystification awaited them in the second part of the story. On the
next evening, Ivan Andreevich attends the Italian Opera, where
he has become accustomed to sleep for an hour or two since his
tormenting jealousy has allowed him little sleep at home. In the
second-tier boxes he catches sight of his wife Glafira, who had earlier
told him she would not attend the opera. She is now in the company of her relatives and an unknown man who, naturally, arouses
the suspicions of a husband increasingly tormented by the young
woman's duplicity.

Dostoevsky here inserts some satirical remarks about the behavior of Russian audiences at the opera, where a bored public diverts itself by watching the programs that flutter down from the galleries. Onto Ivan Andreevich's partly bald head there now falls not a program but a perfumed billet-doux, apparently dropped accidentally by its writer. It contains an urgent summons to a tryst immediately after the performance on the third floor of the apartment building at a certain nearby address. Although Ivan Andreevich does not recognize the handwriting, in his fevered state he instantly ascribes the note to his wife's hand. "Jealousy," writes Dostoevsky, "is the most exclusive passion of all the passions in the world" (400).

With the final curtain, Ivan Andreevich rushes off to the indicated address, again prepared to seize his wife in flagrante delicto. As he enters the building, an elegantly dressed young man is already bounding up the stairs to the third floor! Ivan Andreevich reaches the landing just before the door is closed, and just as another carriage arrives with an elderly, coughing passenger who eventually turns out to be the rightful occupant of the third-floor apartment.

Entering this strange flat "with all the solemnity of an offended husband," Ivan Andreevich penetrates to the bedroom and finds himself face-to-face with a beautiful young lady, one whose terror at the intrusion is evidently compounded by the approaching steps of her husband. The lady turns whiter than her dressing gown; the heavy tread of the coughing husband comes closer; the door of the bedroom begins to open; and Andrey Andreevich, who is himself an offended husband but is quite incapable of facing another one, slips under the bed!

But that convenient refuge is already occupied by another man, apparently the same Tvorogov who had shared Ivan Andreevich's adventure of the previous evening. Some diverting pages describe the two men's jockeying for position in the limited space under the bed, a counterpart of the story's opening sidewalk scene. The coughing husband, who is rather deaf, mistakes their whispered conversation for the hissing of cats, and there follows a hilarious — if totally unbelievable — quadripartite conversation between the properly married couple above and the two intruders below.

Eventually realizing that they have come to the wrong floor, the two men under the bed are drawn closer by a spirit of human solidarity and vow that they will stay together through thick and thin; but when the coughing husband lifts the blanket to look for the hissing cats, the younger man quickly slips out on the other side of the bed and disappears. Ivan Andreevich, who has inadvertently smothered the lady's lapdog in attempting to quiet it, is left to be

discovered by the husband and to explain his presence as best he
can in a lengthy discussion that is obviously intended to represent
the height of comedy.

Returning eventually to his wife Glafira, whom he bitterly blames
for the entire misunderstanding, Ivan Andreevich learns that his
spouse had actually left the opera early and is now in her room,
nursing a toothache and angrily awaiting an explanation of his
own eccentric behavior. So all his exertions had been in vain. The
conclusion of the story is simple: "Jealousy is an unpardonable
passion... it's even a calamity!"

As an amusing game of mistaken identities in the vaudeville tradition, *Another Man's Wife* does offer some food for thought, both
about jealousy and about the inability of some people to speak
plainly and openly. Not without sympathetic understanding is Dostoevsky's portrait of the luckless Ivan Andreevich, gnawed by doubt
and suspicion and betraying at every moment his inexperience and
ineptitude in dealing with such a situation. The exigencies of comedy
require all the characters to avoid acting in a straightforward manner or clarifying the ambiguous, compromising situations in which
they find themselves.

Albert Camus later treated the same theme in a negative, tragic
way in his well-known play, *The Misunderstanding,* in which the
final calamity would have been averted if only the victim of the
"misunderstanding" had adopted the sincerity and frankness Camus himself advocated. Dostoevsky gives us the same message
humoristically in the guise of a French bedroom farce.

The last of Dostoevsky's pre-Siberian stories, *A Little Hero* (1849,
published 1857), was written in prison while its apprehensive author awaited the consequences of his arrest. Its form is that of a
fictional memoir, a mature man's recollection of the period of his
life when, as an eleven-year-old boy, he awakened to the mysteries
of love. The delicacy and sensitivity with which Dostoevsky depicts
the youngster's fascinated, troubled feelings reminds one of Cheru-
bino's experience in Mozart's opera, *The Marriage of Figaro.* As in
that work, the scene of *A Little Hero* is a luxurious country estate,
situated in this case not far from Moscow, while the large cast of
characters affords revealing insights into the attitudes and manners
of the Russian ruling class of the day.

As an unsupervised guest at a huge, ongoing house party, the
"little hero" finds himself in contact with two women, radically
different in appearance and character, whose behavior evokes an in-

tense and dangerous curiosity and sense of adventure. One of them is a blonde, blue-eyed, capricious beauty to whom he refers as his "blonde divinity" or "the madcap." She finds a perverse amusement in teasing and tormenting the boy, who is embarrassed by her attentions but gazes entranced at her "marvelous, fascinating shoulders, plump and white as milk."

The other woman — a cousin of the blonde lady — is Mme. M., gentle, timid, beautiful, and melancholy figure whose large, sad eyes betray the cruel tyranny of a brutal husband. With her the boy falls head over heels in love. He and she are thrown together at a rehearsal for a medieval *tableau vivant* entitled "The Lady of the Castle and the Page";[5] and she subsequently invites her *cavalier servente,* as her husband sarcastically calls him, to walk with her in the copse — though only to divert attention from an intrigue in which she is involved in another quarter.

The boy's discomfiture at the continued teasing carried on by his blonde persecutress reaches a peak when the mischievous creature subjects him to general ridicule by publicly pointing him out as the sworn foe and natural rival of Mme. M.'s husband. Mortified and close to tears, the boy indignantly accuses his temptress of telling wicked lies. An opportunity of avenging his humiliation occurs when his "madcap," not content with the misery she has already caused, publicly challenges him to mount a fiery, unbroken stallion that none of the other guests has dared to ride.

A rush of vengeful hatred floods the boy's heart; images of tournaments, paladins, heroes, lovely ladies, clashing swords, and shouting crowds whirl in his giddy brain. Forgetting danger, he succeeds in mounting the wild creature that "dashes off like a hurricane," filling the boy's exultant heart with knight-errantly pride and pleasure. Other guests head off the galloping steed before real harm can occur. "My knightly exploits," the narrator wryly recalls, "were all over in an instant or it would have gone badly with the knight."

Belatedly smitten with some compunction, the blonde divinity now showers attention and affection on the little hero; but it is the Madonna-like Mme. M. who still holds his heart in thrall. Next day, to his astonishment, he catches sight of this inamorata in the company of a mounted gentleman who hastily hands her a sealed envelope, kisses her fervently, and swiftly departs. Returning pensively homeward, Mme. M. inadvertently drops the envelope. The little hero retrieves it, but finds himself in agonizing uncertainty as to how to return it without revealing that he has witnessed the entire scene. Mme. M.'s discomposure on realizing her loss redoubles his anxiety. Escorting the anxious lady into the garden, he eventually decides to return the letter to her in a bouquet of freshly gathered flowers.

Dostoevsky's account of the making of this bouquet is one of his most charming pages:

> I picked... dog-rose and wild jasmine.... I knew that not far off there was a field of rye.... I ran there for cornflowers; I mixed them with tall ears of rye, picking out the finest and most golden. Close by I came upon a perfect nest of forget-me-nots.... Farther away in the meadow there were dark blue campanulas and wild pinks, and I ran down to the very edge of the river to get yellow water lilies.... Going for an instant into the wood to get some bright green fan-shaped leaves of the maple to put around the nosegay, I happened to come across a whole family of pansies, close to which... the fragrant scent of violets betrayed the little flower hiding in the thick lush grass and still glistening with drops of dew. The nosegay was complete. (395–96)

Still engrossed in her reflections, Mme. M. graciously accepts the bouquet, only to lay it aside without noticing the concealed envelope. But a deus ex machina appears in the form a big golden bee brought by a kindly breeze. Mme. M. waves the bee away with the nosegay and, to her intense relief and joy, the letter falls out from among the flowers. The little hero, who by now is tactfully feigning sleep, is rewarded by a swift, burning kiss that scalds his lips. The lady then drops her handkerchief over his eyes in token of her thanks for his devotion and his respect for her secret.

"Quivering like a blade of grass, [I] gave myself up to the first consciousness and revelation of my heart, the first vague glimpse of my nature. My childhood was over from that moment," the narrator recalls. Two hours later, Mme. M. left for Moscow with her husband, and the little hero never saw her again.

Unshadowed as it is by the grim experiences Dostoevsky was passing through at the time it was written, this delicate and charming piece tells the reader a great deal about the author's interest in the varied manifestations of feminine personality. Two completely different types of women — who, however, as in *Netochka Nezvanova,* appear to be closely bound to one another — awaken the boy to consciousness and stir his latent erotic sensibility.

To Dostoevsky, some women are fiery, tyrannical, and born to dominate while others appear as gentle, submissive, conscientious sisters of mercy. What is it, he wonders, that can bestow such opposite dispositions on two women of the same age and social rank, one treacherous and wounding, the other a gentle, serene, and lovable Madonna? It is worth noting that Dostoevsky had not yet made the acquaintance of either Polina Suslova or Anna Snitkina, two opposite character types who would later provide a living example of the antinomies he described so delicately and tactfully in *A Little Hero.*

If one is to seek a common theme amid the rich diversity of Dostoevsky's pre-Siberian stories, it may be found in the travail inflicted upon the defenseless individual by a callously indifferent bureaucratic and social order. These stories are emphatically not propaganda pieces in support of a particular ideology; yet almost all of them are concerned with the human consequences flowing from the oppressively hierarchical organization of Russian government and society.

Downtrodden clerks whose state of mind is already morbid, like Mr. Prokharchin or like Golyadkin in *The Double,* are gripped by powerful delusions, or, like Polzunkov, degrade and humiliate themselves by voluntarily playing the fool. In the extreme case, they take refuge in sheer insanity, again like Golyadkin or like Vasya in *A Weak Heart.* It may be recalled that Dostoevsky had written to Mikhail that "nerves and fantasy occupy too much space in [these beings]."

Nor are the victims of St. Petersburg's crushing environment limited to the official bureaucracy. Defenseless women and children are sacrificed to unscrupulous, brutal males like Julian Mastakovich in *A Christmas Tree and a Wedding,* Mme. M.'s husband in *A Little Hero,* or, perhaps, the sinister Murin in *The Landlady.* Dostoevsky's downtrodden characters and romantic dreamers seek escape from reality in amorous liaisons or in illusions that may help sustain their barren existence, like the narrator of *White Nights* whose moment of bliss must suffice for an entire lifetime.

Although the action of Dostoevsky's pre-Siberian stories is comparatively slight, they abound in brilliant evocations of particular scenes, special moments, and states of mind that afford innumerable comic and tragic glimpses into the souls of the writer's contemporaries. They also reflect an evolution in Dostoevsky's philosophical outlook even before the trauma of his arrest and imprisonment. Society, he seems to suggest at times, cannot alone be held responsible for human misery; some blame must also attach to the weaknesses and failures of the individuals themselves — an insight that paves the way for Dostoevsky's later doctrine of self-purification.[6]

At the same time, Dostoevsky displays unshakable faith in the fine and noble qualities of the Russian soul, in the love, brotherhood, and human solidarity that inspire his "good" drunkards, his "sisters of mercy" who lovingly nurse their "enemies," and his pairs of loyal and loving friends. To Russians in general he ascribes almost the characteristics of a chosen people, the people on whom he will later confer preeminence over the exponents of European materialism and "progress." More of this exaltation of "Russian" as opposed to "European" values will be apparent in the half-dozen post-Siberian stories in which the reader will also encounter a new severity in the chastisement of those Russian attitudes and practices that fail to measure up to Dostoevsky's high standards.

15

Post-Siberian Stories

The stories from the years that followed Dostoevsky's Siberian exile naturally display a greater maturity of outlook and a surer mastery of literary technique than did his earlier efforts. Ranging in subject matter from slapstick comedy to the grisly and the macabre, they achieve in one or two instances a depth of insight and a purity of emotional expression that ranks them with the author's greatest novels.

The protagonist of *A Nasty Tale* (1862), the first of the post-Siberian stories (also called *An Unpleasant Predicament*), is a self-important, fatuous upper civil servant who prides himself on what he mistakenly considers his progressive, humanitarian outlook. The theme is the unbridgeable gulf between this ideal self-image and the real man who emerges in shame and humiliation from a cruelly comic ordeal that mercilessly exposes the hollowness of his pretensions.

Actual State Councillor Ivan Ilyich Pralinsky, forty-three years old but of considerably younger appearance, is tall, handsome, well-mannered, elegantly dressed, with an aristocratic education and dreams of marrying a wealthy, perhaps even noble lady. He is, however, plagued by a keen perception of the two sides of his own personality, in which abject weakness, which sometimes plunges him into the depths of self-abasement, contends with dizzying flights of vanity, when he assures himself that he will be remembered as a great Russian statesman. By spouting predictions about Russia's coming regeneration through the efforts of "the people," he has gained a fashionable reputation as a "desperate liberal."

On his way home one evening from a dinner at which he has imbibed considerable amounts of champagne, the already tipsy Pralinsky hears music coming from a rickety house where, he learns, one of his own subordinates named Pseldonimov is just celebrating his wedding. Though uninvited, the state councillor magnanimously

decides to look in on the party. His reasons are the opposite of those
of Mr. Golyadkin in *The Double,* who aspires to climb higher on
the social ladder that Pralinsky, in this instance, will be descending.
"I will turn [this] into my subordinate's happiest day, and a wild
gesture into something normal, patriarchal, moral and exalted," he
tells himself (196).

Mentally rehearsing a dramatic entrance that will attenuate his
awesome authority and put the guests at their ease, Pralinsky walks
boldly up to the house, plumping one foot, galosh and all, into the
dish of galantine that has been put out on the doorstep to set. Re-
pressing an impulse to retreat, he enters the house but is taken aback
by the signs of abashed astonishment on the faces of those present.
As "the open space between [Pralinsky] and the guests [grows]
gradually bigger and bigger," the goggle-eyed host and bridegroom
eventually regains his wits, makes a servile bow, and invites His
Excellency to be seated.

The embarrassed guests continue to view with hostility this big-
wig who has burst in to spoil their festivities. The bridegroom
grows more somber, and Pralinsky himself begins to realize that
his magnanimous gesture has fallen flat. Eventually, however, a
magical change takes place. "The rumor, whisper, realization...
began to circulate by some mysterious means, that the guest was
apparently...somewhat under the influence" (210). Relieved, the
company ceases to notice the intruder and returns to its merry-
making.

Pralinsky, by now beginning to feel quite inebriated, is resolved
to cut his experiment short; but instead of taking leave as intended,
he somehow finds himself sitting in the place of honor at the supper
table. Here he vigorously attacks the herring and vodka that serve
as hors d'oeuvres to the "middle-class" meal of galantine, tongue
with potatoes, cutlets with green peas, and blancmange, all duly
moistened with beer, vodka, and sherry. Swallowing a large glass
of "people's" vodka — which he has never drunk before, since he
belongs to the champagne class — His Excellency feels "as though
he were flying downhill, flying, flying, and that he must stop, catch
hold of something, but could not possibly do it."

Though he had entered the house with a sense of "stretching out
his arms to embrace the whole of humanity and all his underlings"
(215), Pralinsky by now hates and curses the assembled company,
all of whom, he now realizes, hate him for having foisted himself
on their celebration. Still planning his long overdue escape, he is
determined that he will first clarify the "moral intention" of his

unannounced visit. He must convince these people that as a true progressive he is ready to condescend humanely to even the lowest of God's creatures.

But the "psychological moment" for his departure still eludes him, and the drunken Pralinsky vacillates more and more between a courageous will to conquer and an agonizing fear of "What will people say?... How will it end? What will happen tomorrow?" As he attempts to spout his progressive clichés, he finds that his tongue will not obey him and that saliva is spurting out of his mouth, spraying the cheek of the person next to him — who is deferentially sitting "like a wet hen" and fears to wipe it off until Pralinsky, in a scene of outright slapstick, himself takes a napkin to wipe his neighbor's face.

Then there is a squabble with a young radical journalist who accuses His Excellency of being a reactionary. These political overtones, however, are less interesting to the contemporary reader than the stunning contrast between the state councillor's still-inviolable authority and the submissiveness of the pitiful bridegroom. That unfortunate feels compelled to turn out of the house the friend and legitimate guest who has insulted the powerful bureaucrat.

Having thus far preserved his own supremacy, Pralinsky sinks down in his chair as though unconscious. Putting both arms on the table, he lets his head drop straight into the plate of blancmange. Moments later, in a last attempt to flee, he lurches, trips, falls flat on the floor, and there lies quite still and begins to snore. Where to put the sleeping Excellency without disturbing his slumber? The only available bed is the bridal couch, draped in its quilted pink satin coverlet, with its four pink calico pillows in muslin cases trimmed with white frills, under a baldachin of muslin curtains hanging from a gilt ring.

The indignation of the bride on finding Pralinsky in the nuptial bed may be imagined. Further "nasty" happenings accent this night of horrors. The makeshift bed prepared for the bride and groom in the other room collapses, and the offended bride shrieks her rage while the ineffectual groom reflects upon the need to secure a transfer out of Pralinsky's office. While depicting Pralinsky himself as a pompous fool, Dostoevsky makes no attempt to idealize or glamorize the subordinate characters, who are as grotesquely stupid and unattractive as can well be imagined.

The one exception is the bridegroom's mother, a peasant woman from the provinces who surely deserves inclusion among Dostoevsky's selfless, pitying "sisters of mercy." This generous and courageous woman, in a gesture of solidarity with the "enemy," which reminds one of *The Eternal Husband* and *An Honest Thief*, personally undresses the sick and loathsome Pralinsky and nurses him like her own son through a night that is made hideous by his recurrent paroxysms. Sleepless, she lies on the floor beside him on a rug, covered only with her old fur coat.

Before dawn, His Excellency stealthily departs and returns home, where he remains for a week in humiliated seclusion during which he seriously considers becoming a monk. Morally rather than physically ill, he suffers redoubled "attacks of conscience" over what he calls his *"existence manquée."* But on finally deciding to return to his office, he is agreeably surprised to find that no one is whispering behind his back, that no malignant smiles appear on the faces of his subordinates. Informed of Pseldonimov's request to be transferred to another department, he is deeply relieved but quite fails to grasp Pseldonimov's delicacy in not having publicized his misadventure. "Tell Pseldonimov that I wish him no harm," he pompously declares. "...I am ready to forget all that has happened."

Pralinsky does, however, blush bright red under a belated attack from his own conscience. "He felt ashamed and oppressed as he had never done in the most unbearable moments of his eight-day illness [and sank] helplessly into his chair." These are the concluding words of this "nasty tale" about a man who finally glimpsed himself in the light of harsh reality and finally perceived that, in the Russian society of his day, the presence of a high-ranking bureaucrat in the midst of "the people" he claimed to love could only be interpreted as an act of callous condescension.

The cold complacency of the high-ranking Russian bureaucrat again draws Dostoevsky's mockery in his unfinished satirical tale of *The Crocodile* (1865). Its relentless ridicule of the fashionable "Westernizing" ideas of the period was widely regarded at the time as a belated attack on the doctrines of Nikolay Chernyshevsky, author of the radical novel, *What Is to Be Done?* (1863), who had by then been publicly degraded and exiled to Siberia. Later research has shown, however, that Dostoevsky's barbs were directed primarily at the Westernizing radicals of the *Russian Word*, the advocates of what to Dostoevsky were "inhuman" capitalistic doctrines aimed at accelerating Russia's economic development and thus hastening its progress toward socialism.[1] A century and a quarter later, Dostoevsky's story was to gain new piquancy from the attempts by a later government to reverse course and move from socialism back to capitalism.

As always, Dostoevsky's satire has a freshness and trenchancy

that has outlived its immediate targets. The story of *The Crocodile*
is that of a man who is swallowed by one of these tropical beasts at
a St. Petersburg exposition, yet survives in the creature's belly and
remains in touch with the outside world. What most impresses the
reader is the equanimity and cold-blooded selfishness with which the
victim, his wife, and all those involved accept this strange occurrence
and try to turn it to their individual advantage.

Most of the action unfolds in St. Petersburg's Arcade, a place
for public exhibits and lectures. A satiric note is sounded at the
very beginning when the crocodile's victim-to-be — Ivan Matveich,
a liberal-minded bureaucrat on the eve of a trip to western Europe —
decides to view the beast that is on display there in order to gain
familiarity with the "aborigines" whose land he is about to visit.
Accompanied by his wife and the close friend who will act as narrator, Ivan Matveich finds the crocodile (personified as a "foreigner")
lying lethargically in his tub, debilitated by Russia's inhospitable
climate. The animal's German owner prods the reptile with a stick
for the edification of the viewers; but when Ivan Matveich boldly
tickles the animal's snout with his glove, he is promptly seized and
swallowed by the carnivorous vertebrate. For a moment, Ivan's despairing face reappears, only to drop its eyeglasses and then vanish
again — a comical sight at which the narrator, for all his goodwill,
cannot help laughing.

The German owner, indifferent to the fate of the bureaucrat and
concerned only with safeguarding his own property, is joined by his
"Mutter" in loudly demanding payment for damages. The victim's
own wife, the diminutive, flirtatious Elena Ivanovna, screams and
shouts *"vsporot"* (cut), meaning that someone should open the reptile's belly to release her husband. Unfortunately, her cry reverberates
through the Arcade as *"vysporot"* (flog). Infuriated by such cruelty — though seemingly indifferent to the fate of the bureaucrat —
a member of the "progressive intelligentsia" admonishes the hysterical lady, reminding her that whipping and flogging are frowned on
in contemporary Russia as a relic of barbarism.

The voice of Ivan Matveich himself is now heard from inside the
crocodile. Apparently unhurt, though worried about his superiors'
reaction to his failure to go abroad as scheduled, he reveals that he
is quite comfortably settled in the animal's belly and has no serious
complaint except that his host seems to be "definitely lacking in humor." The German owner, elated by a development that promises
to enhance the public interest in his show, makes plans to double
his entrance fee; and, to his delight, Ivan Matveich himself signi-

fies his approval of this application of the (inhuman) "principles of economics."

Encouraged by Ivan's collaboration, the German also escalates his claim for damages from three to four and then to five thousand rubles, and Ivan begs the narrator to visit their mutual friend, the bureaucrat Timofey Semyonovich, in an attempt to raise the ransom money. As the narrator and the victim's wife leave the scene — the latter feeling "something like a widow" — the German owner warns that on their return they will have to pay another entrance fee.

Dostoevsky here advises his readers that he is going to switch from a "not so elevated" tone to a more natural one; and indeed the rest of the tale flows more quickly — though ending, unfortunately, before the reader's curiosity is satisfied.

The narrator's visit to Timofey Semyonovich turns out to be a complete failure, for this elderly pedant summarily dismisses any idea of providing aid for the progressive Ivan Matveich. Apparently hoping that the latter's imprisonment may favor his own intimacy with the victim's wife, Timofey Semyonovich also supports the German owner's claims to compensation. Invoking the sacredness of private property and the same inhuman "principles of economics" the reader has already encountered, he too seems wholly indifferent to the fate of his fellow bureaucrat and only interested in its social and economic implications.

In developing this theme, Timofey Semyonovich subjects the narrator to a lengthy discourse about the supposed desirability of selling Russia's communal land to foreign investors, permitting free operation of the laws of supply and demand, and creating conditions for the establishment of a large middle class and a hardworking proletariat. The "extraordinary occurrence" that has befallen their friend Ivan Matveich, he explains, will make it possible to attract other crocodiles from abroad and enable each owner to accumulate capital that will redound to the benefit of the Russian economy; whereas the slitting of the crocodile's belly in order to release its victim would only discourage the inflow of foreign capital. Ivan Matveich, he concludes, must stay where he is for the sake of the fatherland!

Returning empty-handed to the Arcade, the narrator finds the German exulting over the prospect of increased gate receipts, while Ivan Matveich himself is planning a brilliant career as "an example of greatness and humility in the face of destiny." Using the crocodile's belly as his pulpit, he will preach "humanity." Truth and light will shine from the darkness of the belly; and the path to paradise will be illumined by this great man's thought. With exaggerated generosity, Ivan even suggests that his wife and the narrator should join him in the crocodile's roomy interior. The narrator wonders whether his friend has become delirious. The wife, when informed of her husband's idea, callously protests that her hat and crinoline could not possibly pass the creature's jaws.

The closing section of *The Crocodile* describes some inaccurate reports of the affair that have appeared in the Russian press. Replete with amusing parodies and predictable jokes and puns, the newspaper accounts reveal a total lack of humane feeling toward Ivan Matveich but voice unbounded sympathy for the crocodile that has swallowed him.

Whatever may be thought of *The Crocodile* as a work of literary art, it is surely one of Dostoevsky's most scathing indictments of humanity's inhumanity. No one but the narrator seems to feel any sympathy for the victim, and even he bursts out laughing at his friend's vanishing act. The wife's initial hysteria soon subsides, and not much time elapses before she is inquiring about the possibilities of divorce and pondering the attractions of a certain swarthy young gentleman.

In contrast to *A Nasty Tale,* the reader is left in ignorance of the way in which Dostoevsky intended to end his story. One is at liberty to speculate about whether and in what way Ivan Matveich would be liberated from the crocodile, and whether or not he would be called upon to face the kind of humiliation and defeat that had befallen the self-important Pralinsky in the earlier story.

Perhaps most important among the shorter narratives of Dostoevsky's maturity are three "fantastic tales" that appeared in *The Diary of a Writer* during the years 1873 to 1877: *Bobok, A Gentle Creature,* and *The Dream of a Ridiculous Man.* The earliest of these creations, the one that bears the mysterious title of *Bobok* (1873), is still another scathing satire on contemporary ethics and morals, this one in the form of a "cemetery dream" — a vision of death in somewhat the style of the medieval *danse macabre* or *Totentanz.* Its use of the fantastic and unbelievable as a means of emphasizing the author's satirical point recalls the technique already employed in *The Crocodile.*

The story's rather lengthy introduction, evocative in some ways of Dostoevsky's own life as a man of letters, presents a struggling, cynical, somewhat bibulous writer who will serve as narrator and is himself a critic of the contemporary outlook. A portrait of this

Ivan Ivanovich, the reader is told, had been exhibited in public. "Go and look at that face, so unhealthy, so close to insanity," the critics had written. "How can people be so blunt in print?" the narrator asks. "Nowadays humor and good style are disappearing and abuse is accepted in place of wit. I'm not offended: I'm not enough of a literary man to go out of my mind" (165). Recalling the rejection both of his own novel and of any number of articles he has written for the press, the narrator reveals that he survives by translations from the French and by writing advertising copy.

Ivan Ivanovich is somewhat worried about his own sanity. Admitting that his character seems to be changing, he reveals that he suffers from headache and has a feeling as though someone close by were constantly uttering the irrational syllables "bobok, bobok, bobok," a sound reminiscent of the Russian word for a little bean in a pod.

The narrator's problem comes to a head — and the real story begins — when he accompanies the funeral procession of a distant relative to a foul-smelling cemetery where a row of corpses is awaiting burial. Relaxing on a tombstone after the ceremony, he becomes lost in reflection and suddenly hears sepulchral voices issuing from the graves around him. The grave on which he is sitting, he discovers, belongs to a major general apparently engaged in conversation — banal in substance, but meticulous in its respect for social distinctions — with a court councillor, a society lady, and a shopkeeper in nearby graves.

Comments about the stench of rotting flesh, interspersed with tidbits of political and social gossip, are bandied about in this incongruous and macabre dialogue of the dead. In explanation of this curious phenomenon, one speaker cites the opinion of a deceased philosopher-scientist, Platon Nikolayevich by name, who maintains that conscious life continues by force of inertia for some months after physical death. This philosopher, although his body is by now almost completely decomposed, is still occasionally heard to utter "a word or two...about some little bean: 'Bobok, bobok.' " The prevailing stench, according to the same authority, is actually the "moral stink of the soul" during the brief period of grace that is allotted to the dead for the reconsideration of their faults.

A rather different use of this interval is proposed by the recently deceased Baron Kinevich, a cynical swindler who suggests that the existence of the dead be reorganized on more rational principles. His recommendation to his dead neighbors is to unite in shedding all sense of shame and devoting the available time to living out their vices without hypocrisy. An engineer booms agreement, and the ladies coyly assent to Kinevich's call for "unashamed truth! let's strip ourselves naked!" A fearsome hullabaloo ensues as the corpses, becoming coarse and shameless, fling insults and profanities at one another. Only one dissenting voice is heard. "Verily my soul is passing through its forty days of torment" moans a dignified and pious tradesman — the only corpse, Dostoevsky implies, that has kept its links with the people and the faith.

Suddenly the narrator sneezes. In an instant, everything becomes "as silent as the grave.... A real silence of the tomb settled over everything." In vain does Ivan Ivanovich wait for the corpses to resume talking. "I can't suppose they were afraid of being reported to the police.... I can't help coming to the conclusion that they must have some secret unknown to mortals, that they are careful to conceal from every mortal" (180–81). Determined to return to the cemetery and visit other classes of graves as well, Ivan Ivanovich hopes he may stumble on something more reassuring than the prospect of a future that holds nothing but "bobok."

The blend of comic and grotesque in Dostoevsky's surreal dialogue enhances his scathing denunciation of public and private morality in the Russia of the early 1870s. "And so this is the contemporary corpse!" the narrator ruefully exclaims. All of the horror Dostoevsky finds in the souls of the living is concentrated in this *danse macabre* in the public cemetery, replete with repugnant details and poignant imagery.[2] Little do these noisy cadavers know, the novelist seems to say, that if they would just decompose in silence, repentance, and self-purification, they might be worthier of God's mercy.

The Boy at Christ's Christmas-Tree Party, which appeared in the January 1876 issue of *The Diary of a Writer,* has been compared with Hans Christian Andersen's *The Little Match Girl.*[3] Dostoevsky's pity for the poor and downtrodden finds ample scope in this brief account of the last hours of a little homeless boy — one of innumerable such children, the author assures the reader — who freezes to death on Christmas Eve but is warmed and comforted, reunited with his mother, and introduced to other congenial children at a splendid Christmas party offered by the Lord Jesus himself.

A more substantial story, which appeared in *The Diary of a Writer* in November 1876, is *A Gentle Creature,* sometimes called *A Gentle Spirit* or *A Gentle Girl.* Subtitled "A Fantastic Tale," it is cast in the form of an internal monologue that is formally reminiscent of *Notes from Underground*. The fevered reflections of a bereaved husband in the aftermath of his young wife's suicide present a historical overview of their tormented relations during the brief period of their association.

Pacing back and forth before the table on which his wife's body has been laid, the middle-aged pawnbroker recalls his first encounters with the fair, slender, gentle young girl who had come to borrow money on her pitiful, almost worthless possessions — a trashy little locket and silver-gilt earrings, or the remnants of an old hareskin jacket. Invariably she had accepted his meager allowance without argument or protest; but when he one day ventured a joke about the worthlessness of an item she had brought him, she flushed with resentment and her eyes blazed as she picked up her "rags" and left the shop.

The pawnbroker is a gentleman by birth, an ex-lieutenant in a brilliant regiment. His interest in the young girl increases when she brings him an icon of the Madonna and, in response to a reference to his own past difficulties, suggests that he is now "revenging [himself] on the world." Moved to investigate her identity, he learns that she is an orphan living with two disreputable aunts who keep her in cruel subjection. Making up his mind to claim this gentle creature in honest matrimony, the pawnbroker exults in the power he will be able to exercise over her. His first gesture as her "deliverer" will be to "save" her from the clutches of a fat shopkeeper who "had ill-treated two wives and now...was looking for a third."

The pawnbroker is forty-one while his bride is only sixteen, and he intends to take full advantage of his superiority in age, rank, and fortune. Admitting to himself that "the feeling of inequality was very sweet," he sternly demands submission and expects her to stand in deference to his "past sufferings." Later, in words that recall the underground man's treatment of the prostitute Liza, he will reveal that his attempts at domination were rooted in his own insecurities: "In my eyes, she was so conquered, so humiliated, so crushed, that sometimes I felt agonies of pity for her, though sometimes the thought of her humiliation was actually pleasing to me. The thought of our inequality pleased me" (576).

This unbalanced approach to matrimony proved anything but a success. Both parties were soon maintaining total silence in each other's company. The gentle and trusting wife began to observe her husband stealthily, eyeing him with wordless contempt. As her loathing increased, she grew more independent, defiant, and rebellious, to a point where he could call her "the insufferable tyrant and torture of [his] soul" (561). His objection to her free-and-easy manner of lending pawnshop funds caused her to leap up, tremble, and "stamp her foot at [him with] the frenzy of a wild animal."

From a lieutenant in her husband's former regiment, she learns the pawnbroker's ignominious story. At one time, she is told, he had been forced to resign from the military because he was afraid to fight a duel (an allegation he later denies in part), and for three years he roamed the streets of St. Petersburg like a tramp, begging for coppers and spending his nights in billiard rooms. These disclosures happen to be overheard by the pawnbroker himself, who has followed his wife to the rendezvous and is pleasantly surprised by her correct behavior. Indignantly rejecting the lieutenant's amorous advances, she emerges victorious in what her husband will describe as a verbal duel "between a noble, lofty woman and a worldly, corrupt, dense man with a crawling soul" (566).

That the pawnbroker does not lack physical courage is demonstrated when he awakens in the night and keeps his composure on finding that his wife is holding a gun to his head. Although her failure to pull the trigger gives him a sense of victory, he realizes nevertheless that the marriage bond is now broken and that a life-and-death struggle between the two spouses has begun. Like so many Dostoevsky characters, the young wife at this point falls a prey to "brain fever," while her husband, in a typically Dostoevskian routine involving the nursing of an "enemy," lavishes money and attentions upon her in the hope of restoring her to health.

By now he has come to a better understanding of his "gentle creature," and dreams of a brighter future together. "That is what is wrong," he reflects, "that I am a dreamer: I had enough material for my dreams" — for he had long dreamed of retiring to the Crimea — "and about her, I thought she could *wait*" (575). Now, at the sound of her soft singing, "as though the song itself were sick," he kisses her feet in delirium and rapture, groveling for her physical affection as Dostoevsky himself had groveled at the feet of Polina Suslova. But the gentle creature, amazed and alarmed that he should still be seeking her love, becomes hysterical with fright. "And the husband wants love!" the narrator bitterly recalls. "Oh, the delusion! Oh, my blindness!"

In an unexpected reverse reaction, the gentle creature now goes to her husband with clasped hands, blames herself as a criminal, expresses gratitude for his generosity, and vows to remain his faithful, respectful wife. Leaping up and embracing her madly, kissing her face and lips "like a husband for the first time after a long separation," the pawnbroker rushes out to secure passports for the trip abroad that he has planned in the hope of speeding her convalescence. Returning two hours later, he learns that the young woman has just leaped to her death, clasping her icon to her bosom.

What was the motive of the gentle creature's suicide? Frightened and seemingly repelled by her husband's love, uncertain whether to accept it or not, unable to confide in her husband, unable to love him or to honor her promise to be a faithful, respectful wife, she had preferred to die. Her honesty had bidden her to love him altogether, not halfway as she might have loved the fat shopkeeper. Constrained by social and economic circumstances to humble herself and accept a marriage that would at least assure her survival, she was simply too honest and too just, both with herself and with her husband, to break those bonds that kept her from gaining freedom and independence. Too chaste, too pure, too honest a wife to consent to any compromise, the heroine of this admirable and moving story — whom the reader sees only through the eyes of her husband — has made a clear-sighted, conscious choice to sacrifice her own life.

Realizing all at once his irreparable loss, restlessly roaming the two-room flat, the husband sees solace neither in society nor in religion. "What do I care for your customs, your morals, your life, your state, your faith!" he cries in despair. "Oh, blind force! Oh, Nature! Men are alone on earth." Too late, he is ready to accept even his wife's scorn: "Ah, let her, let her despise me all her life even, only let her be living" (587). His last thought is for himself: "When they take her away tomorrow, what will become of me?"

The gentle creature's escape through suicide reverses the image of Liza's action in *Notes from Underground.* Unlike the pawnbroker's wife, the prostitute *was* able to love the antihero of that work, yet walked irrevocably away from him because of *his* lack of honesty.[4] Both women gain the upper hand vis-à-vis the males who have sought to dominate them; while both men, the pawnbroker and the underground man, have occasion to learn the truth of Lamartine's famous line: "Un seul être vous manque et tout est dépeuplé!" (The absence of one being depopulates the universe!)

The Dream of a Ridiculous Man (1877), another "fantastic story" in five parts, is more a parable than a conventional short story. It tells of how one human being came to appreciate the inadequacy of a secular, science-based outlook and to rely instead upon the promptings of the heart in a vision of universal love.

The story's narrator, he informs us, had always been considered "a ridiculous man" because his highly individual viewpoint so markedly set him apart from his fellows. Within the past year, however, he has achieved an insight so precious that he no longer resents their incomprehension and laughter, hard as it is to be "the only one to know the truth."

It appears that this "ridiculous man" had grown up a classic solipsist, one who believed that the world and its people had no existence outside of himself — "that all the world and all the people are nothing but me" (210) — and, consequently, that nothing that happened in the world made any real difference. So convinced was he of the validity of this supposedly "rational" insight that he had even bought a revolver in preparation for committing suicide at an appropriate moment.

His disillusionment and subsequent enlightenment occurred on a dismal, rainy November night when a glimpse of a single star, seen through a gap in the clouds, seemed to him a sign that the moment for self-destruction had come. Before returning to his lodging, however, he had a curious encounter with a little girl, shivering with cold and hunger and obviously in some sort of trouble, whom he brutally drove away instead of responding to her plea for assistance. Somewhat ashamed of his own behavior, he then returned to his lodging, took out his revolver, and would have shot himself then and there, "had it not been for that little girl." The fact that he was able to feel a belated pity and shame in connection with this unfortunate child suggested to him that there must have been a flaw in his philosophical assumptions; and this idea is enough to stay his hand at the critical moment.

The "ridiculous man" then falls asleep and, in his dream, sees himself point the revolver at himself — not, however, at his head but at his heart. Hurriedly he pulls the trigger, and in due course is placed in a closed coffin and buried in the earth. He does not lose consciousness, however, and the coffin is presently opened by a dark, mysterious creature that bears a human resemblance but fills him with "a deep aversion."

Hurtling together through space, the pair eventually arrive at a planet that resembles the earth in its physical attributes but, unlike the earth, is inhabited by a race of beings who enjoy the blessings of supreme happiness and mutual love. Some such notion, recalling the legends of humanity's golden age, had sometimes captured the narrator's fancy while still alive on earth. At such moments, he had been unable to contemplate a sunset without tears, nor to nourish hatred for his fellow creatures without loving them at the same time.

The happy, innocent inhabitants of this favored planet receive the new arrival with cordial hospitality and attempt to erase from his features all traces of suffering, an experience unknown to them. "On our old earth," the man marvels, "we can truly love only with suffering and through suffering. We don't know how to love otherwise" (215). He notices with bewilderment that his new acquaintances, instead of an abstract, rational, scientific understanding of nature, hold communion with and possess a direct, tangible knowledge of the entire universe.

"Being a modern Russian believer in progress," the visitor sarcastically observes, "I couldn't see how they could know so much when there was no indication that they had any knowledge of the achievements of our modern science. But I soon realized that their knowledge fed upon different revelations than ours and that their aspirations were quite different" (216). These happy people obviously loved one another sincerely and, though they built no temples, clearly believed in a higher spiritual force and in eternal life.

Having duly celebrated the idyllic existence of these denizens of "an earth unstained by the Fall," the narrator proceeds to reveal the horrible consequences of his own visit. For that entire, innocent, blissful population came to be totally corrupted by his mere presence among them. Falling from the state of grace, they became alienated from one another, loved themselves more than their neighbors, and began to display marks of suffering on their own faces. Like the germ of a sinister plague that devastates whole kingdoms, the man from earth contaminated the planet with a knowledge of sin, evil, and pain. Its inhabitants, learning to rely upon science, wisdom, and the instinct of self-preservation, soon found themselves enmeshed in the same historical processes that, on earth, had favored the (to Dostoevsky) deplorable advances of democracy and socialism.

Stricken with a sense of guilt and anxious to free himself from this moral burden, the dreamer seeks martyrdom at the hands of the population he has corrupted; but they only jeer at him and warn that he will be confined to a lunatic asylum if he persists in such folly. The shock of rejection awakens the "ridiculous man" from his slumber, and he perceives that his space experience was only a dream. Yet his feelings of love for those pure people of the sinless planet remain, and he thirsts to live as Christ lived, preaching love for all and especially for those who mock him.

Having once seen the truth, the "ridiculous man" no longer can believe that wickedness is the normal state of humankind. Now no less a "madman" than Christ himself, he is convinced that earth's sick society can be cured of its ills. The old maxim, "Love others as you love yourself," though repeated ad infinitum, has still not taken root, he realizes; yet he is sure that "if everyone wanted it, everything could be arranged immediately" (226).

In its championship of the heart against the head, of love against science and reason, *The Dream of a Ridiculous Man* can be seen as an epitome of Dostoevsky's philosophical and moral system — a system in which acceptance of personal guilt offers freedom from the alienation produced by psychological solipsism.[5] Contrasting with the "internal monologue" of *A Gentle Creature,* one critic classifies this last of Dostoevsky's short stories as "an internal religious dialogue," a dialogue in which the writer gropes for — and finds — a positive answer such as could only come from "a glimpse of the Absolute."[6]

Part 5

Theater, Memoirs, and Journalism

16

Theater; *House of the Dead; Winter Notes on Summer Impressions;* and *The Diary of a Writer*

Although Dostoevsky's worldwide reputation rests mainly on his novels, one should not underestimate the importance of his semi-fictionalized memoirs or the journalistic ventures in which he gave expression to his views on literary, social, and political matters. He was the author of two autobiographical works, the celebrated account of his experiences in the Siberian prison camp, and the highly subjective record of his first travels in western Europe. Both were published in one of the monthly periodicals to which he also contributed innumerable articles on contemporary affairs.

The drama, too, was an important element in Dostoevsky's artistic personality, despite the absence of dramatic works from the catalog of his completed writings. He himself began to try his hand at dramatic composition while still a student at the Academy of Military Engineers. The haunted atmosphere of the Mikhailovsky Palace contributed to the gestation of two historical dramas, now lost — *Boris Godunov,* based on Pushkin's tragedy of the same name, and *Mary Stuart,* an echo of Schiller's celebrated poetic drama. In addition, Dostoevsky refers in an 1844 letter to Mikhail to a "completed drama" called *The Jew Yankel;* later scholarship suggests that it utilized characters and themes from Shakespeare's *Measure for Measure* and Gogol's *Taras Bulba.*[1]

Dostoevsky continued in later years to attach great importance to the drama, both written and unwritten, as a creative art form that derives its essence from the actor's mimetic talent and the psychological interplay between actor and audience. He deeply admired the actor-serf Mikhail Shchepkin, in whom he saw the product of a felicitous conjunction between civilized society and the Russian soil. "You of course know the *Notes of the Actor Shchepkin*," he wrote to Mikhail in 1864.

Shchepkin was a serf almost to the age of thirty. But meanwhile he has been part of civilized society nearly since childhood, without ceasing to be of the soil. We write about joining the soil. Therefore, from that point of view we should draw attention to Shchepkin as a living example. Secondly, the joining up with civilization, that is, with us, occurred in the serf Shchepkin exclusively thanks to the direct power of art (the theater). There is the question of art, too, and even that of its material and social utility.... An article from this point of view would turn out to be very interesting." (*Letters*, II, 96)

Dostoevsky's second wife is authority for the statement, made in conversation with Konstantin Stanislavsky, the founder and director of the Moscow Art Theater, that the short novel entitled *The Village of Stepanchikovo and Its Inhabitants* was originally conceived as a play. The novelist himself, as previously noted, informed a friend that he had "started a comedy...as a joke" but had later "abandoned the form of the comedy" in order to write "a comic novel." Like Dostoevsky's other works of fiction, *The Village of Stepanchikovo* reveals his mastery of dramatic dialogue, and it is not surprising that Stanislavsky was able to adapt it for the stage in 1891, directing the ensemble and himself playing the part of the submissive Colonel Rostanev.[2]

Dostoevsky, like Charles Dickens, also enjoyed exercising his own mimetic talent, and he is said to have faultlessly performed the role of the postmaster Shpekin in Gogol's *The Inspector General* in a benefit performance at St. Petersburg in 1860 in which Turgenev appeared as one of the local merchants.

To Dostoevsky, the theater was an art form capable of enthralling its audience, freeing its members from their inhibitions, and enabling them to give themselves wholeheartedly to the enjoyment of the moment. Well aware of the social potency of this theatrical alchemy, he tells in *House of the Dead* of how even coarse and brutal convicts could be temporarily transformed into cheerful, satisfied, even happy individuals through the magic of the stage. It can even be argued that the novelist anticipated modern theories about the therapeutic value of theater, music, and painting in the treatment of physical ailments and the reinforcement of the immunogenic system. His supreme testimony to the psychological and social power of the theater occurs in *House of the Dead*, a work of inexhaustible significance to which we now turn.

House of the Dead (1850–62)

The thinly veiled account of Dostoevsky's prison experiences that appeared in 1861 under the striking title, *Notes from the House of the Dead,* usually contracted to *House of the Dead,* is unique in world literature. The writer's first mention of this seminal work occurs in a letter of October 9, 1859, in which he begs his brother Mikhail to give the manuscript to an "educated censor" lest its publication be banned by a less perceptive official. "These *Notes from the House of the Dead* have taken on a full and definite plan in my head now," he writes. " ... My person will disappear. These are the notes of an unknown person: but I vouch for their interest. ... There will be serious and gloomy and humorous things, and popular speech with the special convict coloring ... and the depiction of personalities *unheard of* in literature, and touching things" (*Letters,* I, 390).

Written as the fictional memoir of a man condemned to ten years' penal servitude for the murder of his wife, *House of the Dead* affords the reader frightening insights into the physical and moral aspects of Dostoevsky's own experience as a man fettered, deprived of human and civil rights, condemned to a subhuman existence amid filth and vermin, in a ponderous and suffocating atmosphere whose monotony is scarcely broken save by incidents of the most appalling cruelty.

Borrowing the low-keyed, dispassionate style of an objective, factual report, the book derives its somewhat rambling organization from the movement of the author's mind as it roves backward and forward over his personal experiences, his observations of particular individuals among the motley crowd of his associates, and his conclusions about the prison population and humanity in general.

Nothing is more striking than the sense of menace and isolation experienced by this educated member of the nobility on finding himself suddenly plunged into the midst of common criminals who regard him with suspicion and hatred and from whom he cannot possibly distance himself. "I could never have conceived," he writes, "how terrible and agonizing it would be not once ... to be alone. At work to be constantly under guard, in the barracks to be with two hundred other convicts, and ... never once to be alone!" (30).

What human situations brought about the crimes for which these men are imprisoned, he wonders. May not the peasants among them have actually sought for confinement as an escape from the even more prisonlike existence they endure as downtrodden outcasts of society? And how is he to conduct himself in this unpredictable assemblage of desperate individuals who seem bent on confronting him with the severest moral and physical difficulties? "[The convicts] are coarse people, irritable and spiteful," he later wrote. "Their hatred of the nobility exceeds all bounds, and therefore they greeted us nobles with hostility and with malicious joy over our woe. They would have eaten us up if they had been allowed to.... If we could in any way save ourselves from grief then it was through indifference, moral superiority, which they couldn't help but understand and respect, and through resistance to their will" (*Letters,* I, 186–87).

Dostoevsky did gradually come to realize that this threatening horde comprised an infinite diversity of separate individuals, among whom not all were hostile while a few were positively friendly. Yet all of them showed the degrading effects of prison life: "If they hadn't been depraved before they came to prison, they became so here. They had all been gathered here against their wills; they were all strangers to one another" (33). Whatever measures are taken to subjugate them, "it is impossible to convert a living man into a corpse: he retains his feelings, his thirst for vengeance and life, his passions and his desire to satisfy them" (78).

The convicts are obedient and submissive up to a point, Dostoevsky observes, but there is a limit to their endurance. Often a man will suffer in patience for years but then suddenly erupt over some trifle:

This sudden outburst... is nothing more than an anguished, convulsive manifestation of the man's personality, his instinctive anguish and... his desire to declare himself and his humiliated personality, ... which sometimes ends in anger, in frenzied rage, in insanity, fits, convulsions. So, perhaps, a man who has been buried alive in his coffin and who has woken up in it hammers on its lid and struggles to throw it open, although of course his reason tells him that all his efforts will be in vain (110).[3]

It would be better, Dostoevsky asserts, never to let a prisoner reach this point of mental stress and convulsive reaction. "But," he rhetorically concludes, "how can this be done?"

Always curious about human motivations, Dostoevsky makes no attempt to approach the convicts, but does not reject their advances to him either. A show of familiarity designed to seek their favor might be interpreted as cowardice and bring only contempt; while aloofness and disdain would only aggravate their hatred. This agonizing dilemma is poignantly resolved in a scene in which he finds a surrogate for human companionship in the warm, joyful response of the prison dog, the faithful Sharik.

Dostoevsky's attempts to classify the prisoners cannot succeed amid the infinite diversity of character prevailing even in this grim setting. The only general truth he can enunciate is that "no man can live without some goal to aspire towards. If he loses his goal, his hope, the resultant anguish will frequently turn him into a monster" (305). One conspicuous characteristic, however, is common to all the members of this strange family, and that is their haughtiness and arrogance. No slightest trace of repentance, no realization of the seriousness of their crimes is visible in the behavior of these parricides, infanticides, and arsonists. They are out-of-scale, frightening incarnations of all-powerful evil. Yet at the same time, even the strongest and most individualistic personalities attempt to accommodate themselves to the "general tone" of the prison and are preoccupied with questions of good form in regard to their outward behavior. Even the most obsessively vain convicts inevitably are brought to heel; they grow resigned and accept the prison's rules.

Who can fathom the depths of these lost hearts, Dostoevsky wonders, and read the secrets hidden from the whole world? As his warmhearted understanding and pity for the criminals asserts itself, he examines with sympathetic insight the contradictions in their nature, which may equally well result in outbursts of animal violence or in sudden manifestations of warmth. Through his vigorous reevaluation of the prevailing preconceptions and prejudices, he reintegrates these outcasts into the human fold.

The rigors of prison and forced labor, Dostoevsky is convinced, serve only to promote hatred, a thirst for forbidden pleasures, and a terrible frivolity. Reflecting on the inequality of the punishments imposed for the same crime, and on the impossibility of comparing criminals and their acts, he emphasizes the differing effects of punishment on different individuals. Can the same punishment be felt in equal measure by an educated man with a sensitive conscience and by one who never reflects on his own crime but simply considers himself in the right and society in the wrong? The problem is insoluble, Dostoevsky finds. As for himself, he feels compelled to live out the threefold process of sin, repentance, and redemption, admitting his guilt and bearing his punishment without vindictiveness.

Among the "first impressions" to which he devotes several of his earlier chapters, Dostoevsky evokes the figure of one Gazin, a fearsome individual who has a deeply disturbing effect on all his fellows. He sees the violent and monstrous Gazin as a huge, outsized spider. He also conjures up the image of A——v, a revolting specimen of human immorality, repulsiveness, and shameless depravity, a glaring example of what the physical side of man can produce if unrestrained by any inner norm or set of laws. "I was horrified by [his] terrible vileness and baseness. . . . I thought that everything in this place was equally vile and base. But I was mistaken: I was judging all the men by A——v" (107).

That not all the men were like A——v is Dostoevsky's amazing discovery, for he comes to realize that some have in them a spark of humanity and even a touch of the divine! He senses that the Russian people yearn for Christ in their hearts, and it is at this point that he ceases to look upon the convicts as monsters and begins to perceive that there is an element of the transgressor not only in the condemned criminals but in every human being, himself included. He summons up childhood memories of Lenten rituals in which the devout peasants seemed to him to pray differently from the landowners — humbly and fervently, even prostrating themselves as though admitting their lowly station. Now it is *his* turn to stand in the back of the church, in self-effacement and in fetters. Now he can understand that there is a common denominator uniting all the convicts including himself.

No less horrendous than the prisoner A——v is the hated major in charge of administering the camp and exercising almost unlimited power over the two hundred souls who make up Dostoevsky's little world. A frightening man of spite and caprice, the major regards the convicts as his natural enemies. In bitterly satirical terms, he is portrayed by Dostoevsky as an "executor of the law," a loathsome, narrow-minded, shortsighted individual full of harshness and arrogance. In his first letter to Mikhail after his release from prison, Feodor describes and identifies this despicable creature:

[Omsk Deputy Commandant Krivtsov] is a scoundrel the likes of which are few, a petty barbarian, quarrelsome, a drunkard, everything repellent that one can possibly imagine. . . . He promised to have us flogged at the first opportunity. He had already been deputy commandant for two years and was responsible for the most horrible injustices. . . . He always came riding in drunk (I never saw him sober), would pick on a sober prisoner and flog him on the pretext that the latter was drunk as a cobbler. At other times while visiting at night, he'd do the same thing for someone's not sleeping on his right side, for someone's crying out in his sleep or hallucinating at night, for whatever idea came into his drunken head. (*Letters,* I, 186)

Dostoevsky has plenty of scathing comments about officers who rise from the lower ranks and acquire exaggerated notions of their power, importance, and impunity. Unbridled despots to their subordinates, they are always servile toward their superiors. It is just this type of officer who drives the most obedient men beyond the bounds of patience: "Everyone, whoever he is and however lowly the circumstances into which he has been pushed, demands, albeit instinctively and unconsciously, that respect be shown for his human dignity; ... no brands, no fetters will ever be able to make him forget that he is a human being. *Human* treatment may even render human a man in whom the image of God has long grown tarnished. . . . A few kind words — and the convicts experienced something approaching a moral resurrection" (145).

Observing the conduct of prisoners awaiting corporal punishment — from which he himself was apparently exempted as a member of the nobility — Dostoevsky notes: "A 'desperate' man ... often longs for [his] punishment, longs to be *dealt with,* because in the end his affected *desperation* has become too much for him to bear" (140). The book is replete with detailed descriptions of the brutal flogging of convicts and the sadistic behavior of those responsible for inflicting corporal punishment. But it also has its lighter, more entertaining pages as Dostoevsky describes the behavior of the convicts at work and at play — for they had their hours of rest and recreation and displayed an infinite resourcefulness in devising means of combating the prevalent boredom.

There are also touching passages like the story of Aley, a young Tartar who befriends the writer in the midst of the general hostility surrounding him. Aley has a handsome, open, intelligent face that immediately draws the author's heart, and the encounter is described as "one of the best I experienced in all my life." Aley's nature is so inherently beautiful and so richly endowed by God that its alteration for the worse can be ruled out as an impossibility. His inner soul is revealed in an exchange of knowledge: Aley teaches Dostoevsky many new things about the Caucasus, and Dostoevsky teaches the young Muslim the Russian language from the New Testament, the only book he is allowed to keep in prison. Studying with fervor and enthusiasm, Aley gains a thorough knowledge of literary Russian in three weeks' time, to Dostoevsky's great delight; and in two months he has learned to write the language perfectly. His thanks to his teacher, who has done more for him than his own mother and father, are moving indeed: "You've made me into a man, God will reward you and I will never forget you."

Contrasting with the vivid Aley is the nondescript figure of Sushilov, an abject creature who invents a thousand duties to be performed for Dostoevsky's benefit: "He was neither tall nor short, handsome nor ugly, stupid nor clever, young nor old. . . . It was impossible to say anything very definite about him" (99). Sushilov is derided by the other convicts because he has "swapped himself" on the march to Siberia — that is, has exchanged his identity and relatively light punishment for a red shirt and one silver ruble offered by another prisoner who had been condemned to the heaviest penal labor. Unlike Aley, Sushilov is utterly servile, downtrodden by nature, and, one must believe, incapable of aspiring to greater knowledge and learning.

A section of *House of the Dead* examines the absence of what may be called a sense of reality in prison life. A free man is carried along in the whirl of real life, living, acting, and hoping for fortune, success, and all good things. The convict, on the other hand, is unable to accept his fate as part of real life or as something positive and final. "No convict feels *at home* in prison, but rather as if he were on a visit there. He contemplates twenty years as though they were two, and is quite certain that when he leaves prison at the age of fifty-five he will be the same strapping fellow he is now at thirty-five" (128). His very survival hinges on the preservation of his mental balance amid the constant psychological unease and nervous tension prevailing in the closed atmosphere of the barracks. Purposeful work is the best preservative against mental breakdown; Dostoevsky's own physical labor — baking and pounding of alabaster, rotating a lathe in the workshop, and shoveling snow — though utterly exhausting, improved both his physical constitution and his spirits.

The arrival of Christmas — a holiday recognized by law as one of the three days in the year when prisoners could not be sent out to work — brings with it an unconscious feeling of reintegration with the outside world as the prisoners join in respectful observance of the holy festival. It also brings us to two of the high points in Dostoevsky's narrative, his celebrated account of the communal pre-Christmas bath and his description of the amateur theatricals organized by the prisoners in celebration of the holidays.

Four days before the Christmas festivities, the convicts are taken to one of the two public bathhouses in the penal colony for an exceptional preholiday cleansing. The intense dramatic power, the theatrical effectiveness of Dostoevsky's description of the soaking, scouring, and steaming of the men in the communal bath is universally recognized and has even been compared to Michelangelo's celebrated fresco depicting the Last Judgment. A crowd of almost two hundred convicts, crammed inside a dirty, dilapidated public establishment, undress in the cold antechamber and labor to undo the leather straps around the legs of their underwear, just below the iron rings of the fetters. The reader sees a veritable chaos of writhing men attempting to disentangle themselves from their garments. Each convict is given a small tubful of hot water that he carries into the bath — a small, steamy room into which are squeezed as many human bodies as is physically possible.

Once all the places on the wall bench have been occupied, the remaining men are forced to stand or squat on the filthy floor, which is coated with a thick layer of sticky, sooty grime. The convicts huddled on the floor splash themselves from their tubs, while those standing in their midst allow the dirty water streaming off their bodies to fall straight onto the shaven heads and scalded red bodies of those below. About fifty men lash themselves with birchen switches into a state of monstrous ecstasy; more steam is created until the temperature rises infernally, while the men clamor and cackle to the accompaniment of their rattling chains as they steam themselves into virtual oblivion. Some become entangled in the chains of others and fall into the hot grime, cursing and dragging their mates in the tangle. To the prevailing cacophony is added a searing visual impression: the convicts' backs, covered with welts raised by whips and staves, seem to have been freshly lacerated. "Through the cloud of steam one caught a glimpse of mercilessly beaten backs, shaven heads, doubled up arms and legs" (156) over which dirty water streams incessantly.

The dramatic horror of the bathhouse does not, however, prevent Dostoevsky from lightening the hellish vision with a touch of humor. His strange prison acquaintance, Petrov, insists on washing Dostoevsky's "footsies," supporting him all the while "as if [he] were made of porcelain." There is no servility in Petrov's use of this childish diminutive, Dostoevsky observes; it is simply that the powerful and fearless convict, who has killed a colonel for striking him, regards his fellow prisoner as a child with plenty of book learning but no understanding of life's elementary realities.

Contrasting with this glimpse of Pandemonium is Dostoevsky's almost lyrical account of the actual Christmas observances, an occasion marked in equal measure by religious reverence, food and drink, and the uplifting experience of the amateur theatricals. A simple religious ceremony takes place in the military barracks, where a priest places a cross and holy water on a small table, covered with a clean towel, on which stand an icon and a lighted lamp. After praying and singing the liturgy before the icon, the priest stands facing the convicts as they devoutly come forward one by one to kiss the cross. Walking around the entire barracks, he sprinkles the inmates with holy water before they reverently escort him from the prison.

After the religious ceremony, the festivities unfold in a dramatic crescendo: a lull, an initial show of decorum and friendliness, as gifts of food and drink are shared; and then an explosion of drunken rowdiness. The volume of shouting and fighting reaches a peak, then gradually subsides in a diminuendo of reeking stupor, depression, and final hopelessness as the presence of Christ, so vivid a short time before, fades from consciousness.

The prisoners' spirits revive after sleeping off their debauch and awakening to the prospect of the barrack-room theatricals. Dostoevsky describes the evening's entertainment in terms that testify to his belief in the alchemy and curative power of the theatrical experience. The improvised theater in the bare military barracks is vividly described. Most striking is the enormous stage curtain, stretched across the entire width of the barracks and consisting of bits of old cloth sewn together with pieces of paper begged from the various prison offices. Trees, arbors, ponds, and stars have been painted on the curtain in oil colors. "The effect was overwhelming. A luxury such as this was enough to gladden the hearts of even the most sullen and starchy convicts." Lighting was supplied by a few tallow candles cut in pieces. The convict audience remained standing throughout the performance, although a few chairs and kitchen benches were provided for those who were expected to contribute most to the collection plate. Dostoevsky himself was accorded a privileged place because he was regarded as a connoisseur and judge, familiar with theaters rather different from this one.

The program for the evening featured a popular vaudeville skit, *Filatka and Miroshka,* about two rivals for the hand of a "Lady Bountiful," followed by an unpublished traditional piece called *Kedril the Glutton* that concluded with a pantomime to music. Dostoevsky praises the skill and talent of the peasant performers, the authenticity of their acting, their dignity and professional sense, and the excellence of their presentation. One of the convict actors, Baklushin, a born comic and mime, actually strikes him as superior to any other performer he had seen in the role of Filatka: "I have seen *Filatka* performed several times on the stages of the Moscow and Petersburg theaters, and I can positively say that in each city the actor who played Filatka was not as good as Baklushin. Compared with him they came across as *paysans* [i.e., artificially] and not as authentic peasants" (*House of the Dead,* 194).

Impressed by Baklushin's uncanny acting talent, yet recognizing that the show could never have been thought up by the convicts themselves, Dostoevsky reflects on the origins of his country's popular dramatic art. The private theaters of landowners and Moscow nobles, staffed by serf-actors, had, he tells the reader, traditionally presented plays that had never appeared in print but had probably been kept alive in handed-down copies written out by the landowners' servants. The continuity of tradition, acting techniques, and specific concepts in works passed on from generation to generation is described in terms that recall the Italian commedia dell'arte. Soldiers, factory workers, artisans, and shopkeepers, as well as the servants in the large landowners' houses in villages and provincial towns, had kept the traditions alive. And, characteristically, the convict actors improvise continuously so that the show varies slightly from one performance to another but is always basically successful (186–87).

Turning on the first evening to look at the throng of prisoners standing behind him, all eager for the curtain to "rise," Dostoevsky was struck by the look of childlike joy and good-natured contentment in these faces that usually expressed only gloom and sullenness. During the performance, the eyes of these hard-hearted men sparkled with a light that faded as soon as the Christmas celebrations ended. For the rest of the year, in lieu of prison stage shows the convicts would resort to a less artistic but no less authentic form of entertainment in the guise of cursing and tongue-lashing — permitted pastimes in the "House of the Dead," where the "dialectician of the curse" was held in great esteem and applauded "almost like a actor."

Three chapters in *House of the Dead* are dedicated to the prison hospital, to which the ailing writer had himself been taken after the Christmas celebrations. Though located outside the fortress, the military hospital is an unsanitary, reeking haven of vermin and filth. Its oppressive air is contaminated and stinks of the night pail that remains in the ward all night long. With scathing severity, Dostoevsky denounces the senseless cruelty of the hospital regulation that prohibits the use of the corridor toilet during the night, as well as the still more monstrous cruelty that keeps a dying convict in fetters up to his last breath.

Springtime makes the prisoners even more aware of their unenviable lot: "Unsettling even to a man in fetters, [the springtime] aroused in him indefinite desires and aspirations, a vague melancholy. A man seems to pine for freedom even more in the sun's bright rays than he does on a wet day in winter or autumn" (270). All of the convicts dream of escape, and one in a hundred actually attempts it; for this is the time when, with the first skylark, drifters unable to resist the call of the wild begin their vagrancy all over Russia and Siberia. It is the season when "God's people escape from prison and take to the forests." But Dostoevsky is not one of those who will try to escape. His passionate desire for resurrection, for renewal, strengthen his will to wait and hope. He draws up a mental plan for his future and pledges himself to adhere to it.

Finally, his term of imprisonment runs out. His fetters are struck off, and the convicts gruffly bid him good-bye. "Freedom, a new life, resurrection from the dead.... What a glorious moment!" — such are the closing words of the book. It is the moment when, in the words of one commentator, "with freedom, the divine gift of personality is restored to the hero."[4]

Dostoevsky's prison experience was of course the central turning point in the development of his social and spiritual outlook. It did not weaken his belief in the superior merits of the old Russian aristocracy, to which, in *A Raw Youth,* he would later attribute "forms of honor and duty which have never existed anywhere in Russia except in the nobility" (*A Raw Youth,* 604). At the same time, his encounter with the common people of Russia bred a sense of spiritual unity with them, of direct participation in their lot. He felt himself a convict just like the others, even though he could not inwardly share their habits, notions, opinions, and customs.

The prison world reproduced to some extent the inequalities prevailing in free society, as well as the peculiarities and potentialities of free individuals; but it also intensified the common characteristics found in all humans. For lack of other distractions and especially of reading matter, Dostoevsky concentrated intently on the existential aspects of prison life. Study of these taciturn convicts, so compressed in time and space, revealed to him that the parameters of so-called truth are ambiguous and contradictory; that candor and astuteness, goodness and savagery can exist concomitantly in a single individual.

This discovery of the irreducibility of humankind to any neat pattern was immeasurably important in the development of Dostoevsky's thought. Released from his early bondage to socialist ideology in its naively utopian form, he was at last in a position to formulate a new ideology based on reevaluation of Russian tradition and orthodoxy, firm adherence to the values and even the very substance of the Russian land.

Two philosophic truths may be said to emerge with special clarity from *House of the Dead.* One of them is that human beings cannot be cut down to one size, to one particular pattern, because such attempts are always defeated by incidents of individual self-assertion. The other truth, equally opposed to the "progressive" and positivistic thought of his day, is that the human soul cannot be regarded as a tabula rasa, a piece of wax from which the general, universal man can be molded irrespective of his national character and native soil.

These same perceptions underlie another work derived from Dostoevsky's personal experience, *Winter Notes on Summer Impressions*. In it he reasserts his view that orderly, well-defined and solidly based relationships among men, and between man and society, can be established only through the Russian principle of commonality.

Winter Notes on Summer Impressions (1863)

Dostoevsky's account of his visit to western Europe in 1862 is autobiography of a completely different sort. This curious travel diary is concerned not with monuments and galleries, but with plainclothes police spies in his French railway coach and with mothers introducing their twelve-year-old daughters "into the business" in London's Haymarket. Cast in the form of a series of philosophical and historical "essays" on national mores and economic systems, *Winter Notes on Summer Impressions* unfolds as a continuous dialogue with Dostoevsky's readers, whom he addresses as "my friends" or "gentlemen," and whose pardon he repeatedly begs for straying from his subject or narrating seemingly "superfluous" anecdotes.

The true nature of this highly polemical work is that of a continuing diatribe against the alleged vices of Western society. A month in Paris and eight days in London, far from dispelling Dostoevsky's original anti-European prejudices, confirmed and strengthened his belief that the materialistic civilization of the West, far from offering an answer to Russia's problems, was a vital threat to Russian values, to the integrity of the Russian soul.

Dostoevsky ridicules those jaded Russian tourists who expected to find a comforting refuge in Europe.

They all go about with guidebooks and greedily throw themselves on every city to look at the curiosities ... as if it were an obligation ... to the fatherland; they do not miss a single three-windowed palace if it is mentioned in the guidebook, not a single burgermeister's home, remarkably similar to the most ordinary Moscow or Petersburg home; they gape at a side of beef by Rubens and believe that it is the Three Graces because that is what the guidebook has ordered them to believe; they dash to the Sistine

Madonna and stand before her in blank expectation: something will happen any second, someone will slip out from under the floor and dispel their meaningless melancholy and weariness. And they leave amazed that nothing has happened. (25–26)

Nothing has happened, of course, because for Dostoevsky western Europe is the last place to look for a miracle that would dispel the sadness, anxiety, and restless melancholy that cloud the faces of his fellow Russians abroad. Europeans, in his view, are so morally stultified, so depraved, their selfishness is so ingrained, and feelings of love, altruism, and fraternity are so lacking in their composition that they positively take evil for good and remain oblivious to the poverty, suffering, and stagnation of the masses in their own societies.

Russians alone aspire instinctively to brotherhood, according to Dostoevsky, and they are the only people who, despite a good dose of moral delinquency in their present makeup, will be able to achieve the goal of universal fraternity and love. Communal interaction, the renunciation of self-interest by the individual and by society, are concepts understood only by Russians. The goal of human aspiration, he feels, is a state of reciprocity in which the individual and the community each desire only the other's welfare; and the closest approach to that ideal situation, he asserts, will be achieved through the Russian peasant's instinct for brotherhood and the mysterious "chemical bond between the human spirit and its native soil" (9).

In consequence, Dostoevsky insisted, the utopian socialist ideologues who sought to construct in Europe a world based on brotherly love were wholly off in their reckoning. The very nature of Western man, animated as he is by principles of reason, benefit, individual profit, and selfishness, precludes the building of acceptable political institutions on European soil. "In order to make a rabbit stew," he argues in a homely peasant metaphor, "one must first of all have a rabbit. But [in Europe] there is no rabbit, that is, no nature capable of brotherhood" (50–51).

Carried along by his own Russophilia, Dostoevsky decries his countrymen's want of appreciation for their own fatherland. " 'Le Russe est sceptique et moqueur' [the Russian is a skeptic and a scoffer], the Frenchmen say of us and it is true. We are more cynical; we hold what is our own less dear; we do not even like what is our own, or at least we do not respect it..., failing to understand what it is. We devote ourselves to European interests and to the general interests of humanity and belong to no nation" (69). Having himself rallied to the Slavophile camp, Dostoevsky denounces those Russian "Westernizers" with whom he had previously been allied: "I think Belinsky himself [who disdained everything Russian] was secretly a Slavophile.... I remember that back then — fifteen years ago, when I knew Belinsky — I remember that the whole circle from that period bowed before the West... with a reverence that approached oddity" (7).

Ever since Peter the Great's time, Dostoevsky avers, educated Russians have held ambivalent attitudes toward European culture as successive waves of European influence have impelled them to "bow before the West." The influence of European thought has been essentially destructive, he maintains, because admiration for the West has produced an anomalous attitude in which a sense of inferiority is at odds with a need for independence.

The origins of this fateful Russian-European relationship are sketched in a chapter artfully entitled "And a Completely Superfluous One," in which the figure of Gvozdilov, an eighteenth-century Russian dramatic character, serves as a horrible example of the kind of "progress" achieved through corruption by European ways.

Now even Gvozdilov himself maintains his skill when it comes to nailing [his wife to the wall to beat her], observes propriety, becomes a French bourgeois, and... will begin defending with the Scriptures the necessity of buying and selling Negroes, as in the Southern states of North America.... His wife has not been the "pretty, pretty young woman" she once was. She has aged, her face sunken and pale, furrowed with wrinkles and suffering. But when her husband... lay sick... she did not leave his bedside and spent sleepless nights over him, comforting him and weeping hot tears over him.... Long live the Russian woman, for there is nothing better in our Russian world than her boundless, forgiving love.... [Gvozdilov] cannot manage without her; he is calculating, a bourgeois, and when he beats her now it is only in his drunkenness.... Well, this is progress. (21)

Three interrelated elements stand out in this passage: recognition of the basic delinquency of Russian drunkards; ridicule of the Russian "progressive" corrupted by Western manners; and celebration of the innate love and dedication of Russian womanhood.

"Who among all of us Russians (that is, those who at least read the journals) does not know Europe twice as well as he knows Russia?" Dostoevsky asks sarcastically (1). "We now despise our people and native origins so deeply that we treat them with... disgust...; but, as you wish, that is progress." It is as one of these Russians, who "reads the journals" and has been taught to look on Europe with mental respect, that Dostoevsky himself is traveling to see the dying civilization of the "land of holy wonders." "Lord, what kind of Russians are we?" he asks. " ... Why does Europe create such a powerful, magical, alluring impression on us ... ? You see, all, decidedly almost all, the development, science, art, civil consciousness, and humanity we have — all of it, all I say, comes from that land of holy wonders!" (8–9).

Long before his departure for Europe, Dostoevsky had been persuaded that the death of the West was a reality because it had lost its spiritual bond of unity. An entire chapter of *Winter Notes* is dedicated to "Baal," that god of ancient Mediterranean civilizations whose cult — characterized, according to its detractors, by gross sensuality and licentiousness — sometimes demanded human sacrifices. "And so I am in Paris," begins the "Baal" chapter,

[and] I have formed a definition of Paris, attached an epithet to it.... Namely: this is the most moral and most voluptuous city in the whole world. What order! What prudence, what well defined and solidly established relationships; how secure and sharply delineated everything is; how content everyone is; how they struggle to convince themselves that they are content.... They have struggled to the point where they have actually convinced themselves that they are content ... and ... they have stopped at that. The road goes no further.... What comfort, what conveniences of every kind for those who have a right to conveniences and, again, what order. (35–36)

A few pages later, he mockingly exclaims: "When, Lord, will I accustom myself to order?"

The French bourgeoisie, Dostoevsky explains in a chapter entitled "Bribri and Ma Biche," openly proclaims that "money is the highest virtue and human obligation," and that the accumulation of as many objects as possible is the "primary code of morality." The French "land of holy wonders" had been enjoying a period of economic boom under Napoleon III's Second Empire, which had brought enormous prosperity to the *grande bourgeoisie*. But, Dostoevsky warns, the bourgeois "has paid a terrible price for his prosperity, and fears everything precisely because he has attained everything." Socialism, he reassures his readers, "is quite possible, but only in places other than France"; for "when you have attained everything, it becomes painful to lose *everything*. And from this, my friends, it directly follows that he who fears most is the one who prospers most" (52).

With scathing irony, Dostoevsky charges that the French love eloquence for the sake of eloquence, for "with eloquence one can do a great deal with a Frenchman." Whenever a bourgeois wants to deceive his wife, the writer asserts, he invariably calls her *ma biche* (my doe). Conversely, the loving wife calls her husband *bribri* (sweet little bird), to the great satisfaction of his own spirit and that of the "national majority." *Ma biche* and *bribri* are treated as symbolic figures, acting out the idiosyncrasies of bourgeois capitalism and the social-legal antics of French society. "Of course, there are such social relationships everywhere," Dostoevsky concludes, "but ... here it is all more national. Here is the wellspring and embryo of that bourgeois social form which now reigns all over the world as an eternal imitation of a great nation" (67).

After Paris, London. Here, "the same desperate struggle to maintain the status quo out of despair, to tear from oneself all desires and hopes, to curse one's future, and to bow down to Baal" (36). In this vast, swarming city he sees the extremes of poverty and wealth: "sparkling expensive clothes and ... rags ... gathered all together."

Beneath a glittering surface, Dostoevsky instantly perceives the underlying corruption born of the Industrial Revolution. Political liberty, he tells the reader, is an illusion, since it offers no guarantees against material misery.

Liberty. What liberty? Equal liberty for everyone to do anything he wants within the limits of the law. When may you do anything you want to? When you have millions. Does liberty give each person a million? The person without a million is not the one who does anything he wants to but the one with whom they do anything they want. And what follows from this? It follows that besides liberty there is still equality, namely equality before the law. Regarding this equality before the law, it may only be said that, in the manner in which it is now applied, every Frenchman can and must take it as a personal insult. What remains of the formula? Brotherhood — [which] continues to form the chief stumbling block for the West (48).

Not even religion is true religion in the West, according to Dostoevsky. Catholic priests help the poor only to seek their conversion, while Anglicanism does not pretend to be anything but the religion of the wealthy.

Catholic propaganda ... is subtle and calculating. The Catholic priest himself will track down and force his way into the poor family of some worker. He will find, for example, a sick man lying in a pile of straw on a damp floor, surrounded by children crazed with hunger and cold and by a hungry and often drunk wife. He will feed and clothe all of them ... and end up by converting them all to Catholicism. ... Anglican priests and bishops

are proud and wealthy, live in rich parishes, and grow fat with their consciences completely at peace.... It is a religion of the rich and wears no
mask.... [T]he rich Englishmen and all the golden calves in general are extremely religious, dismally, morosely, and peculiarly so.... The same proud
and dismal spirit... regally hovers over the gigantic city.... Baal does not
conceal from himself... the savage, suspicious, and disturbing phenomena
of life. (42)

Ignoring for the moment the flagrant weaknesses of Russia's own
economic and social condition, Dostoevsky seems unaware of the
difficulty Tolstoy perceived in "becoming brothers, even for a day."
Dostoevsky seems genuinely to have believed that the Russian soil
was destined to produce humanity's new leader, one who would inspire humankind with the lofty social and moral principles needed
to build a new world order. But within this future all-embracing
brotherhood, he still insists upon the right of every individual to
withhold his assent to "order" if it means the renunciation of personal freedom. Even at the cost of starvation, he is convinced, the
human being will renounce material goods in favor of his freedom.
One must forever remain free to rise up against any system that
denies the free exercise of one's will. As in *House of the Dead,* Dostoevsky is convinced that conflict must arise between the individual
and the group, between the single human being and the rational,
egoistic anthill society that demands the surrender of freedom.

From this point of view, *Winter Notes on Summer Impressions*
may be seen not only as a natural sequel to *House of the Dead* but
also as the forerunner of *Notes from Underground,*[5] the work that
immediately followed it. Still another despairing, divided character,
similar to the underground man of that work, will be Ivan Karamazov in *The Brothers Karamazov.* The outlook that found expression
in *Winter Notes* profoundly influenced Dostoevsky's later writings
as well. As the translator of this seminal work has pointed out, "On
the surface it is a dialogue between what is Russian and what is
European... but underneath there is the struggle between truth and
lie, spirit and mammon, life and death."[6]

The Diary of a Writer (1873, 1876–77, 1880–81)

The ideas put forward in *Winter Notes on Summer Impressions*
reappear in a somewhat mellowed guise in *The Diary of a Writer,*
the series of essays and stories Dostoevsky contributed to the periodical press in the years that followed his return from abroad. In their
collected form, these minor works are an invaluable companion to

Dostoevsky's later writings and an important aid in the interpretation of more than one of his novels. Certain pages of *The Devils,*
A Raw Youth, and *The Idiot* share a common thematic treatment
with articles in the *Diary,* and this interdependence becomes even
more marked with *The Brothers Karamazov.*

For this greatest of his novels, Dostoevsky felt a need to know
"reality" in its smallest details, to immerse himself in the minutiae
of his period, to study the problems of the new generation and the
contemporary Russian family. *The Diary of a Writer* provided an
ideal means of establishing this contact with reality. In addition, it
afforded him a kind of spiritual retreat, a pause for reflection, and
even an aid to the working out of plot and character types. Thus, for
example, the *Diary* article relating the story of Agrafena, an idiot girl
on the Dostoevskys' country estate of Darovoe, later finds a place
as the episode of "Stinking Lizaveta" in *The Brothers Karamazov.*[7]

A glance at two or three items from the riches of the *Diary* for
1873, when it was being published as a supplement to *The Citizen,*
may convey some notion of Dostoevsky's creative and journalistic
artistry. *Vlas,* for instance, takes its title from a poem by Nekrasov
about a "godless" peasant who had experienced a religious conversion during an illness and had since wandered over hill and dale,
a white-headed penitent in sackcloth, collecting money to build a
church. Dostoevsky tells of another Vlas, also a Russian penitent,
who had frivolously accepted a challenge to defile the holy sacra-
ment and now, repentant and on his knees, drags himself over long
distances to seek salvation under the spiritual guidance of a famous
monk.

Vlas's original transgression is described in half a page of dialogue.
Dared by a fellow villager, he receives communion but, instead of
swallowing the host, takes it to a vegetable patch, sets it up on a
pole, and fires his gun at it. But in taking aim to shoot, he has had a
vision of the crucified Christ and falls to the ground in a dead faint.

The remaining ten and one-half pages of the feuilleton are taken
up with a minute psychological analysis of the two protagonists, the
"Russian Mephistopheles" who challenged Vlas, and Vlas himself,
the characteristic Russian type who was willing to deny Christ out
of contempt for himself and his traditions. Beneath Vlas's peasant
bravado, Dostoevsky intimates, there lay a diabolical urge to self-
destruction, a reflection of the Russian's basic spiritual need to suffer
and even to enjoy suffering. As in *The Eternal Husband,* the author
sees both victim and persecutor as linked in a reciprocal hatred that
is dissolved in their mutual need of one another. The apparition of

Christ, Dostoevsky concludes, came from the peasant's own soul; and it will be the penitent Vlases of contemporary Russia who, in the service of Christ, will point out a new path and new solutions for problems that may currently seem insoluble. "Light and salvation will shine from below" (57), he writes in reaffirming his belief that true liberty, true equality, true understanding and love are possible only in and through Christ.

In another of the *Diary* articles of 1873, Dostoevsky responds to an attack by the editors of the *Russian World* on his use of the notorious Nechaev affair in writing *The Devils*. Nechaev's followers among contemporary Russian youth, Dostoevsky asserts, are not essentially different from the young adherents of Petrashevsky, the socialist thinker with whom he himself had been associated in the 1840s. Such followership will always exist, the writer maintains, and may occur among all types of young people, not only the do-nothings but even the studious, not just the "fanatic idiots" but also clever, intelligent, educated youth.

Drawing on personal experience to emphasize his point, Dostoevsky reminds his critics that, when he faced the firing squad in 1849, he found himself in the company of educated and well-motivated convicts. Not only are all young people potential revolutionaries, he insists, but he himself in his youth might even have joined forces with Nechaev; for ideas and ideals are highly contagious, and "grand causes" exert a powerful attraction. His own book, *The Devils,* Dostoevsky points out, had shown the variety of motivations through which even pure-hearted individuals may be moved to commit monstrous crimes.

Tragically, the novelist continues, in Russia and indeed everywhere, the most vile and abominable acts can be committed by honest, ingenuous young people who are tormented by the doubts and incertitudes of their era. They become followers of Nechaev because they are not protected against nefarious influences (i.e., Westernizers and atheists). Contemporary youth is defenseless; the old Russian society is rapidly being undermined; Christ has been repudiated; and Russia imitates Europe. A fog of false ideas has obscured the vision of young people and their parents as well. As one means of dispelling the uncertainties and "outlandishness" of Russian social life, Dostoevsky suggests that his readers be "less insensitive" and "unashamed...to tell the truth."

Also deserving notice among the *Diary* entries of 1873 is an article entitled "Apropos of the Exhibit" — ostensibly a review of an exhibition of Russian paintings in Vienna, but actually another commentary on the contrasts between Russians and Europeans. Russian literature and art, Dostoevsky asserts, are generally inaccessible to the comprehension of Westerners. Even in the best translations of Gogol into French, Gogol's humor literally disappears; Pushkin's works lose half their substance in translation, since whatever is characteristically Russian in them is unknowable to Europeans, who do not understand the Russian nature. Russians, on the other hand, Dostoevsky asserts, understand Dickens just as well as the English, and love his work as well as his compatriots, because the Russian has a special gift for learning European languages and penetrating into the soul of European peoples. For Russians, Europe is a second fatherland, and whereas Europeans live for themselves, Russians live for the whole world. This special gift with which nature has endowed the Russian, Dostoevsky assures the reader, promises much for the future when many assignments will be given the new world heroes!

These remarks are merely the prelude to Dostoevsky's critical observations on Russian landscape and historical painting — which, he says, may be understandable to Europeans but does not represent the branch of art in which the contemporary Russian truly excels: namely, genre. There follows a fine analysis of the facial expressions in a small genre painting of Vladimir Makovsky (1839–1920) depicting a canary trilling to a group of enthralled listeners. Dostoevsky reads significance into every detail of the picture and even supplies dialogue for its human figures! In this painting, he discerns all that Viennese observers would certainly fail to see, all that is typically Russian — above all, a love for all humanity.

Dostoevsky's lively commentary concludes with an exhortation to Russian genre painters to show greater independence from schools, tendencies, and public opinion. They must freely respond to their natural need to paint those images that rise spontaneously from within the soul. Strive, he admonishes, for what Dickens achieved in his art: the ideal. Genre is the art that represents fluid reality as personally lived by the artist and seen with his own eyes. Dickens, who is nothing but a genre painter, "never saw Pickwick with his own eyes," but depicted him in the multiple reality he had observed, created the character, and presented him as the result of his observations. So Pickwick is real, even though Dickens grasped only the ideal of his reality. "And so [the artist] must give greater freedom to his idea and not fear that which is ideal" (111).

Realizing belatedly that he has quite forgotten to speak about the exhibition in Vienna, Dostoevsky concludes his penetrating commentary with the ironical question, "What kind of a reporter am I anyway?"

The second *The Diary of a Writer,* which appeared in 1876–77 as an independent monthly under Dostoevsky's editorship, was more rewarding financially and, in addition, provided the writer with a new platform from which to reiterate many of the same ideas he had expounded in *Time, Epoch,* and the earlier *Diary* of 1873. As one of nineteenth-century Russia's important ideological media, this second *Diary* helped create the aura that surrounded Dostoevsky at the time of his speech at the unveiling of Moscow's Pushkin monument.

The publication of this second *Diary* coincided also with a major Near Eastern crisis fueled by Turkish atrocities in the Balkans and, in Russia, by the rising tide of nationalist and Pan-Slavic feeling that ultimately found vent in the Russo-Turkish war of 1877–78. Writing in an atmosphere of inflamed nationalism, an atmosphere that he himself was doing much to foment, Dostoevsky sharpened and refined his concept of Russia's historic destiny as the savior and unifier of a degenerate Europe. Again condemning the European intellectual for his alleged materialism and denial of Christ, Dostoevsky portrays the Russian as the perfect cosmopolitan who will lead Europe to salvation in the kingdom of God. This historic Russian mission, Dostoevsky once again asserts, flows directly from the unique qualities of the "Russian soul," in which are blended the virtues of the Russian intellectual on the one hand and the Russian peasant on the other. Each of these elements, according to Dostoevsky, has something to teach and something to learn from the other; and the "Russian soul," the product of their interaction, is something that for Dostoevsky has by now become synonymous with Christ's truth.

It has been convincingly pointed out[8] that in the process of putting forward these somewhat mystical views, Dostoevsky was reinterpreting his experience in the Siberian prison camp, an experience he now endowed with novel overtones appropriate to the ideological requirements of the new era. Previous accounts of his prison years, in *House of the Dead* and elsewhere, had said nothing of the rediscovery of Christ's truth, or of Christ himself, through fraternal union with the people in their common misfortune. A reader of *House of the Dead* might well gain the impression that his Siberian prison was the very last place for the nobleman and intellectual to correct his bookish knowledge of the people and to discover Christ's truth in the Russian soul.

In reality, it is only in *The Diary of a Writer* that one finds the full development of Dostoevsky's concept of the Russian soul, of Russia's messianic mission as leader of the Slavic peoples and the predestined savior of Europe. These notions, as put forward by Dostoevsky in the 1870s, were thoroughly in tune with the official ideology of a country involved in a crusade for the liberation of oppressed Christian and Slavic peoples. One need not conclude that Dostoevsky was cynically tailoring his views to conform to the official line. It does seem clear, however, that his attitude was changing as time passed and events appeared to validate his conservative and nationalistic outlook.

Less open to possible misunderstanding are those *Diary* entries that helped to focus public attention on the so-called woman question, the problem of women's place in Russian life. Just as he contrasts the noble Russian with the soulless European, Dostoevsky distinguishes sharply between the corrupting influence of profit, cynicism, and materialism on the Russian male and the idealism of the Russian woman in her self-abnegation, dedication, and spirit of service. Noting the undeniable respect the Russian woman has achieved over the past twenty years through her active desire to share in the common task, Dostoevsky presents her as an essential element in the anticipated national renewal.

By way of illustration, the writer tells in his June 1876 article (II, 5) of a young woman who had sought his encouragement in her decision to leave her family and studies in order to help nurse the wounded in Serbia. The article was reprinted almost in full in a current woman's magazine, whose editors expressed appreciation of Dostoevsky's reflections, particularly his championship of higher education as a way of accommodating the modern woman's need to be active and participate in building the nation. Only the seriousness and fascination of higher learning, according to Dostoevsky, can meet the contemporary woman's aspirations, answer her questions, strengthen her mind, and guide her thoughts. He is confident that higher education for women, with all its correlative rights, will in itself permit Russia to take a giant stride ahead of Europe in the achievement of humanity's rebirth.

In the same issue of *The Diary* (I, 1, 2) Dostoevsky pays homage to George Sand, the recently deceased French novelist. Women the world over, he declares, should put on mourning in honor of "one of the highest representatives of womanhood." Though no longer in sympathy with Sand's socialistic ideas, he credits her with cherishing one of Christianity's fundamental notions, the recognition of

individual personality and of human freedom, with the responsibility this implies. He likens the young nursing volunteer in Serbia
to some of the heroines of Sand's early period: pure, proud young
women eager for self-sacrifice and the opportunity of doing good
to others.

The originality and apparent sincerity of the 1876–77 *Diary*
gained Dostoevsky the approval of a wide readership. If it voiced
many paradoxical thoughts, it also offered innumerable profound,
just, and clear ideas, expressed in a heartfelt and convincing manner.
It must be admitted that Dostoevsky lacked time to decant his material and that it sometimes remained cloudy. André Gide went so
far as to pronounce the theoretical and critical articles "mediocre"
and to assert that Dostoevsky's political predictions and social theories were propounded "most maladroitly."[9] Another critic asserts
that the so-called dialogues with the reader often tend to degenerate
into overlong monologues, while the snowball effect of Dostoevsky's style, in which words tumble and accumulate at a dizzying
rate, sometimes takes the breath away from both the writer-orator
and his reader-listener.[10] No one has ever blamed Dostoevsky for a
want of verbal dynamism.

Part 6

The Zenith

The Brothers Karamazov (1879–80)

The greatest of Dostoevsky's masterpieces was published at a time when the author's fame in Russia was already at its zenith. Readers of *The Brothers Karamazov* immediately recognized that Dostoevsky had produced a work of genius that far transcended his stated purpose of performing a "civic duty" through the defeat of "anarchism." At a time when the novelist professed to see "no moral ideas left" in the Russian state, when he viewed the Russian socialists as "conscious Jesuits and liars who do not admit that their ideal is...the coercion of the human conscience and the reduction of mankind to the level of cattle,"[1] Dostoevsky had felt impelled to shape the final stage of his political thought in a sweeping vision and vindication of the Russian Orthodox Church.

The Brothers Karamazov is, however, less a work of ecclesiastical apologetics than a glorification of the Slavophile ideal of "living Christianity" — of a religion rooted in freedom, love, and fullness of heart rather than in institutional formulas and practices. Into his exaltation of Russian Orthodoxy, Dostoevsky weaves his characters' agonizing search for faith and for God; his own observations of the baffling interpenetration of good and evil; terrible struggles of personal love and hatred; and, of course, his deep concern about the perceived destructiveness of Russian socialism, whose adherents he sees as following "the devil's advice" rather than "the teachings of Christ."

In *The Devils,* Dostoevsky had portrayed two generations in conflict. In *The Brothers Karamazov,* he returns to the radical heirs of the liberalism of the 1840s, who have now achieved dominance in "contemporary educated Russia." This is the turbulent Russia of the late 1870s and early 1880s, when "universal disorder," as Dostoevsky wrote in his notes, "reigns everywhere in society, in its affairs,...in the disintegration of family life." Such is the ominous backdrop of this novel of character that, once again, is built around a crime motif, but that emphasizes the sociopsychological ramifications of the crime and the attendant guilt feelings rather than limiting itself to the conventional search for the perpetrator and his motivations.

With burning imagination and a deepened awareness of the complicated springs of human action, Dostoevsky tells of a parricide that, though technically the crime of a single individual, was committed in spirit, will, or deed by each of four brothers, all of whom share in the moral guilt and, in addition, may be seen collectively as a spiritual composite of the author himself.

Considering the brothers in an ascending order of culpability, the youngest of the four, the pure, saintly, and mystical Alyosha, comes before the reader as no more than a subconscious wrongdoer who has secretly wished his disgusting father out of the way. The sensual, violent eldest brother, Dmitry, armed with a half-formed resolve and even a suitable weapon, seems fully capable of the deed but stops short of actually committing it. Ivan, the middle brother, a cerebral intriguer and perhaps even a would-be parricide, more or less deliberately opens the door for the real murderer, their epileptic, bastard half brother Smerdyakov. He it is who supplies not only the cold-blooded calculation but the aggressive physical force and the crude but effective weapon that are needed to do away with the unpleasant old man. But the blood from Smerdyakov's stained hands spills over into the soul of his innocent brother Dmitry, who is actually convicted of the crime, in a symbolic baptism that will at least partially placate the furies who pursue the Karamazov family.

In a brief introductory note, Dostoevsky states that the novel is to be regarded as a "biography of my hero, Alexey Fyodorovich Karamazov [Alyosha] . . . not by any means a great man [but] remarkable as far as I am concerned . . . a strange, almost eccentric sort of man." Realizing that the subject matter of his novel is far too rich and varied to be subsumed under any simple unitary formula, the author admits that he really has "two novels on [his] hands," and that the second and main novel would be "unintelligible" without the first.

This first or introductory novel, as it may be called, sketches a background of some thirteen years of Karamazov family history in the provincial Russian town of Skotoprigonyevsk (Pigsty) — "alas, that was the name of our little town" (IV, 11, II); while the "second" novel will tell of the activity of the hero and of other events occurring "in our own day."

Alexey, identified by Dostoevsky as his "hero" and known to all by the diminutive name of "Alyosha," is the third and youngest legitimate son of a depraved landowner, Feodor Pavlovich Karamazov, who, in the course of two marriages, has successively become the father of Dmitry (Mitya), Ivan, and Alyosha. The reader's attention is first directed, however, to Dmitry, the eldest son and only child of the first marriage. After his first wife's desertion, the reader is told, the derelict father "completely forgot about [Mitya's] existence," and the three-year-old child was actually brought up by the faithful family servant, Grigory Kutuzov, and his wife.

Responsibility for Mitya's education was later assumed by a maternal uncle, "a European *par excellence*, and towards the end of his life a liberal of the forties and fifties [who] had known both Proudhon and Bakunin personally." But this uncle, who had settled permanently in Paris, also "forgot all about the child," as Dostoevsky sarcastically reports, "especially when the February Revolution [of 1848] broke out" (I, 1, II). After a turbulent boyhood and youth, Mitya had abandoned secondary school in favor of a military college, where he had led a riotous life and run constantly into debt.

Short of funds and believing himself entitled to certain property left him by his mother, the twenty-eight-year-old Mitya has now returned to Skotoprigonyevsk in order to clarify the matter with his father. But the two are antagonistic from the first. Feodor Pavlovich considers his son "thoughtless, violent, passionate, impatient, dissipated"; while Mitya, stunned at the discovery that he has been shorn of his property rights, suspects his disreputable father of deliberate prevarication and fraud.

Old Karamazov's second wife, the mother of Ivan and Alyosha, had been a "meek, inoffensive, gentle creature" who was cruelly victimized by her loathsome husband. Although she died when Alyosha was only four years old, it was from her that the boy had gained his first decisive religious impressions, and he cherished lasting memories of her — "just as though she were standing alive before me," as he said. Grigory, the honest and incorruptible servant, had served as a surrogate father to Ivan and Alyosha, since they too had been completely "forgotten" by Karamazov and were shunted from one benefactress or benefactor to another during their early years.

Ivan, the second brother, is described as having been a "glum" but by no means timid schoolboy. With an exceptional capacity for learning, he had brilliantly completed his university studies and published some articles in leading newspapers, which gained him a reputation in literary circles. One of his publications, dealing with the widely debated question of ecclesiastical courts, was applauded by churchmen and atheists alike. "The Church," Ivan had written, "ought to contain the whole State...and ought...to be set up as the direct and chief aim of Christian society.... Every State on earth must eventually be transformed into a Church... renouncing those of its aims which are incompatible with the principles of the Church" (I, 2, V). A copy of this article had even found its way into the local monastery of Skotoprigonyevsk, where its twenty-four-year-old author has come to take up residence in his disreputable father's house.

A year before the arrival of the two elder brothers, the twenty-year-old Alyosha, a "precocious lover of humanity," had interrupted his own studies in response to a mysterious "call" and had attached himself to the town monastery, where he was now preparing to take his vows. This most retiring and meditative of the Karamazovs, the reader is told, had chosen the monastic way of life because "it alone appealed powerfully to his imagination and showed him ... the ideal way of an escape for his soul struggling to emerge from the darkness of worldly wickedness to the light of love" (I, 1, IV).

Linking himself indissolubly with the monastery's famous elder, Father Zossima — a wise man with a "special quality of soul," who preaches love as the path to the expiation of sin — Alyosha has been seeking to gain wisdom and a full measure of inward spirituality. A religion of the heart, stressing direct contact with divinity rather than ritual and dogma, is central to the teaching of the elder Zossima, one of Dostoevsky's most notable religious figures.

"What, then, is an elder?" Dostoevsky asks, and provides this answer:

An elder is a man who takes your soul and your will into his soul and will. Having chosen your elder, you renounce your will and yield it to him in complete submission and complete self-abnegation. This novitiate, this terrible discipline is accepted voluntarily by the man who consecrates himself to this life in the hope that after a long novitiate he will attain to such a degree of self-mastery and self-conquest that at last he will, after a life of obedience, achieve complete freedom, that is to say, freedom from himself, and so escape the fate of those who have lived their whole lives without finding themselves in themselves. (I, 1, V)

Although the ailing, sixty-five-year-old Zossima comes of a family of landowners, his philosophy springs from a concept of the master as servant to his own servants, of equality as the basis of spiritual dignity. For years people have been flocking to hear Zossima's preachings, to beg his advice and healing words. Ascribing to him powers of clairvoyance and prophecy, his followers see in him a guardian of wisdom and a divine force. One frequent visitor is a sentimental society woman, Mrs. Khokhlakov, who seeks a miracle of healing for her fourteen-year-old daughter Lise, a victim of temporary paralysis in both legs.

So many were the secret sorrows the elder had absorbed over the years that he was able to discern the sources of grief and torment on the faces of outright strangers even before they had uttered a word. Alyosha, fully believing in his teacher's spiritual powers and leadership on the path of renewal for all, confidently awaits the day when truth will finally be established on earth by his master and teacher.

A fourth, illegitimate son had also been engendered by the licentious Feodor Pavlovich Karamazov. The mother was the town's mute idiot, Lizaveta Smerdyashchaya ("Stinking Lizaveta"), a pathetic wanderer nourished on bread and water whom Karamazov, still in mourning for his first wife, had raped one night "for laughs" in the presence of his drunken cronies (I, 3, II). This child, too, who was given the surname Smerdyakov, was brought up by the faithful Grigory, in whose cottage he continued to live while serving as cook and servant to his brutal progenitor.

The now aged and bloated Karamazov is a repulsive figure, especially in the eyes of his oldest son, Dmitry. His face, Dostoevsky tells the reader, bears unmistakable traces of his life of dissipation. "In addition to the long fleshy bags under his little eyes, which were always insolent, suspicious, and sardonic, in addition to the multitude of deep wrinkles on his fat little face, there hung under his sharp chin a large Adam's apple, fleshy and longish like a little purse, which gave him a sort of revoltingly sensual appearance. Add to that a long, cruel, and sensual mouth with full lips, between which could be seen stumps of black and almost decayed teeth" (I, 1, IV).

When the disagreement over Dmitry's inheritance had reached a crisis, this repellent little man had jokingly suggested that the family seek the mediation of Father Zossima. A gathering of the ill-assorted Karamazovs does in fact take place in the monk's cell, where the father bitterly denounces his eldest son — not only for having allegedly defrauded him but also for having compromised "a most honorable young girl" while, at the same time, running after another young woman to whom the elder Karamazov refers as the town's "siren."

Father and son, the reader learns, are actually rivals for the favors of this "siren," the voluptuous Grushenka; whereas the "most honorable young girl" whom Dmitry has allegedly "compromised" is the beautiful, imperious Katerina Verkhovtsev, the daughter of a lieutenant colonel who had earlier been Mitya's commanding officer.

Katerina, a proud girl of high moral principles who again is partially modeled on Polina Suslova, had placed herself in a most awkward position in attempting to save her father from the consequences of a reprehensible action involving the diversion of public funds to private speculation. Desperately in need of cash to make up the deficiency, she had appealed to Dmitry Karamazov for a loan, notwithstanding her expectation that he would use the opportunity to demand sexual favors. But Dmitry, for once behaving like a gentleman, had advanced the money, bowing deeply and respectfully but asking no quid pro quo. Moved by profound gratitude, Katerina had gone down on her knees at Dmitry's feet, her head touching the floor in an act of self-abasement that had provided him with what Dostoevsky calls "a moment of ecstasy."

Three months later, Dmitry and Katerina had become engaged. In her wounded pride, she had convinced herself that she actually loved him — perhaps the only way she could escape the terrible shame she felt at having accepted the money. "I am madly in love with you," she had written Dmitry from Moscow. "I don't care if you don't love me...only be my husband." Dmitry, in response, had sent her his brother Ivan, who happened to be in Moscow at the time, and the inevitable had promptly occurred as Ivan and Katerina fell in love with one another. Katerina nevertheless continued to persuade herself that she loved only Dmitry, although that fickle person had meanwhile extricated himself from the unwelcome engagement and begun to pay his addresses to the seductive Grushenka. "As soon as I began visiting Grushenka," he tells his young brother Alyosha, "I ceased to be engaged to Katerina. I've ceased to be an honest man" (I, 3, V).

Now, as the family argument in Zossima's cell approaches its climax, Dmitry, looking at his father with indescribable contempt, growls in a hollow voice, "Why does such a man live?" His father's retort foreshadows events to come: "Listen, listen, monks, to the parricide!" The scandalous scene ends on a shocking yet baffling note as Zossima, the elder, actually prostrates himself at the feet of Dmitry in what is later explained as an acknowledgment of the sufferings in store for this eldest of the Karamazov brothers. Dmitry, thunderstruck, covers his face with his hands and rushes out of the cell (I, 2, VI).

Aware that his own death is imminent, Zossima advises Alyosha to remain close to his two brothers, telling him at the same time that he must leave the monastery since he is destined to do "great service in the world." For the moment, however, Alyosha's "service" is limited to acting as liaison among the members of his family and between Katerina, Dmitry, and Grushenka. In the course of this activity, he makes some new acquaintances when he happens to be caught in a stone-throwing fight among some schoolboys, one of whom viciously seizes and bites his hand when he attempts to intervene. On Alyosha's gentle reproof, the boy bursts into tears and runs from the scene (II, 4, III).

Alyosha's inquiries reveal that this boy, Ilyusha Snegiryov by name, is the son of a retired, impoverished, and alcoholic captain whom the inebriated Dmitry had recently humiliated by dragging him through the streets by his beard, the young boy meanwhile running behind, sobbing and shouting, "Forgive my Daddy, forgive my Daddy!" The experience had taught Ilyusha a terrible lesson of "truth and justice," his father tells Alyosha when the latter pays him a sympathetic call. "That truth entered him and crushed him forever," says the captain. Alyosha realizes that it was the boy's love for his father that prompted the attack on himself as the brother of the captain's insulter.

After this very human story, Dostoevsky launches into the fifth book of *The Brothers Karamazov*, which is entitled "Pro and Contra" and is charged with such weighty matter that the author considered it the culmination of the entire novel. It is here that Ivan Karamazov, opening himself unreservedly to Alyosha as the two dine privately together at a tavern, sets forth his fundamental beliefs and recites his now well-known philosophical "poem" on the subject of the Grand Inquisitor.

Affectionately terming Alyosha "a little fellow [with] a firm hold on life," Ivan expresses a fondness that Alyosha fully reciprocates, even though his brother remains a "riddle" to him. But Alyosha is understandably disturbed when Ivan begins to expound the thesis that love for one's neighbors and, in particular, "Christ's love for men is ... a miracle that is impossible on earth." To love a human being, according to Ivan, "it's necessary that he be hidden, for as soon as he shows his face, love is gone.... Theoretically it is still possible to love one's neighbors ... from a distance, but at close quarters almost never." " ... Honorable beggars," Ivan adds on a startlingly modern note, "should never show themselves in the streets, but ask for charity through newspapers" (II, 5, IV).

In another manifestation of the frenzied Karamazov thirst for life, Ivan tells of his desire to travel to western Europe, simply to fall on his knees before the tombstones of great men who struggled for truth and science. "I'm only going to a graveyard," he says, "but...precious are the dead who lie there....Every stone over them speaks of such ardent life in the past, of such a passionate faith in their achievements, their truth, their struggles, and their science, that I know beforehand that I shall fall on the ground and kiss those stones and weep over them" (II, 5, III).

Acknowledging that the earth is saturated with human tears "from its crust to its center," Ivan asserts that everyone must suffer in order to "buy eternal harmony." He does, however, make a significant exception in that he adamantly refuses to accept the suffering of innocent children. "If the suffering of children go to make up the sum of sufferings which is necessary for the purchase of truth, then I say...that the entire truth is not worth such a price" (II, 5, IV).

So far as the existence of God is concerned, Ivan is consumed in the furnace of doubt. "I have a Euclidean, an earthly mind," he explains, "and so how can I be expected to solve problems which are not of this world....And so I accept God, and I accept him not only without reluctance, but...I accept his divine wisdom and his purpose — which are completely beyond comprehension. I believe in the underlying order and meaning of life....I refuse to accept this world of God's, and though I know that it exists, I absolutely refuse to admit its existence....It is not God that I do not accept," he concludes, "but the world he has created....I've brought my argument down to my despair" (II, 5, III).

In such phrases, Ivan denies what he sees as God's unjust world with all its purposeless suffering. He refutes not God himself, but the meaning of his creation; and from the absurdity of the suffering of the innocent, he deduces the absurdity of all historic reality. Alyosha can do no more than drop his eyes and murmur, "This is rebellion." Christ, he suggests, forgave everyone and everything, "because he gave his innocent blood for all and for everything." Ivan, by way of retort, invites Alyosha to hear his "poem" about Christ — the celebrated legend of the Grand Inquisitor, into which Dostoevsky has woven the social and metaphysical themes of his own childhood and militant youth (II, 5, V).

In this vision, which alone would guarantee the status of *The Brothers Karamazov* in world literature, Christ returns to the earth he left so many centuries earlier. He has decided to show himself to the suffering, miserable, sinful people of Seville, who love him "naively." His appearance, however, coincides with the worst moment of the notorious Inquisition. Only the day before, nearly one hundred heretics had been burned at the stake in a "magnificent auto-da-fé" for the greater glory of God.

Wearing a smile of infinite compassion, Christ moves through the crowds, his eyes radiating "Light, Enlightenment, and Power." But as he is performing a miracle, a ninety-year-old cardinal — the Grand Inquisitor — passes by the cathedral, his hollow eyes burning with sinister brilliance. Indicating Christ to the guards, he orders him seized. The crowd bows down as one person before the Grand Inquisitor, whose power over them is so great and whom they are so accustomed to obey. Blessing them in silence, the Grand Inquisitor passes on. His intention is to condemn Christ and have him burned as a heretic; and he is sure that the people who today were kissing Christ's feet will tomorrow be heaping up coals at his stake.

During the night, the Grand Inquisitor visits Christ in his prison cell and arraigns him in a lengthy monologue. Why, he asks, did the prisoner reappear on earth without being called? Having once been relegated to the past, the visitor asserts, he no longer had the right to add anything to what he had said in the days of old — an indirect criticism of what Dostoevsky saw as the muzzling by the Roman Catholic Church of Christ's own freedom of speech as well as that of humankind.

Ivan, at this point in his recital, interrupts himself to offer some further clarification. "This is the most fundamental feature of Roman Catholicism, in my opinion," he says. "... 'Everything' the [Grand Inquisitor] tells [Christ], 'has been handed over by you to the Pope and, therefore, everything now is in the Pope's hands, and there's no need for you to come at all now — at any rate, do not interfere for the time being.' " If he is to avoid being seen as a destroyer of the established order, and consequently burned as a heretic, Christ must remain within the limits prescribed by the ecclesiastical hierarchy as represented by the Pope and his Inquisitor.

Christ, the Grand Inquisitor continues in what is seen by many as the most significant part of his recital, brought to humankind the "terrible gift" of freedom, a gift it was unworthy to shoulder, and had then left the earth in the throes of confusion and suffering — for, says the old man, "nothing has ever been more unendurable to man and to human society than freedom!" It was to redress the balance of this disarranged world, in which weak humanity cowers under the weight of freedom and responsibility, that the Roman Catholic Church had sponsored a terrestrial order based on *"miracle, mystery, and authority"* — so that now, the Grand Inquisitor claims, humans rejoice at being once more led like sheep, the "terrible gift" having been lifted from their hearts.

The Grand Inquisitor further accuses Christ of having failed to "unite all in a common harmonious, and incontestable anthill" — Dostoevsky's sardonic metaphor for socialism. Mankind, he asserts, "has always striven to organize itself into a world state. Who [he asks] is to wield dominion over men if not those who have taken possession of their consciences and in whose hands is their bread?" To Christ's power and philosophy founded on freedom and love, the Grand Inquisitor opposes the insidious forces of the State, which he himself represents and in which, moreover, he arrogates to himself a sovereign authority over good and evil.

"We shall permit [humans] to sin," the Grand Inquisitor asserts,

...for they are weak and helpless, and they will love us...for allowing them to sin. We shall tell them that every sin can be expiated, if committed with our permission; that we allow them to sin because we love them all and as for the punishment for their sins — oh well, we shall take it upon ourselves....We shall allow or forbid them to live with their wives and mistresses, to have or not have children...and they will be glad to believe in our decision, because it will relieve them of their...terrible torments of coming to a free decision themselves.

Throughout the Grand Inquisitor's harangue, Christ remains silent. Then, for all answer, he kisses the old man's pale lips. Tremulously, the Grand Inquisitor opens the cell door, inviting Christ to leave and never to return — a clear implication that the Roman Catholic Church wishes to dissociate itself from the real, living Christ. Christ goes out into the darkness alone, while the Grand Inquisitor remains. "The kiss glows in his heart, but the old man sticks to his idea," Ivan dryly concludes. He too, Ivan implies, sticks to his idea and, in concert with the Inquisitor, arrogates to himself the right to sanction evil.

Alyosha, having heard Ivan out, utters a cry of distress and sympathy at the "hell" his brother carries "in his heart and his head." Is this why he has decided to leave his town and perhaps his country — to escape an anguish he cannot endure? Ivan, however, protests that "there is a force that can endure all!...a Karamazov one — the force of the Karamazov baseness." He himself, he intimates, will continue to "wallow in vice" and "stifle [his] soul in corruption" — after which he will "escape it," inasmuch as God is dead and "*à la* Karamazov...everything is permitted" (II, 5, V).

A refutation of Ivan's dismaying doctrines is the central concern of Dostoevsky's book six, which is dedicated to the life, discourses, and sermons of Father Zossima. Here a quite different atmosphere prevails; one critic, in fact, has remarked that the elder's preachings sound like "pious platitudes" as compared with Ivan's more convincing "blasphemies."[2] Titled "The Russian Monk," this book recapitulates episodes of Zossima's wild youth as well as his later life of conversions, monks, and monasteries. In its pages are evoked those very confrontations between God and Satan, between good and evil, which had tormented Dostoevsky throughout his own life.

In contrast to Ivan's pessimism, the seraphic Zossima proffers an optimistic doctrine based on the spiritualizing role of suffering. For him, the "spontaneous" religion of the Russian people derives directly from the will of God and embodies the salvation of the nation. "The people will meet the atheist and overcome him, and Russia will be one and orthodox," Zossima declares. "This people is a Godbearer" (II, 6, III).

Prominent among the highlights of Zossima's life, in which is developed an ethic of human relations purged of the evil of social differentiation, is the story of his brother Markel. Originally an intolerant, egocentric atheist, Markel had died at seventeen of galloping consumption. Before his death he had undergone a spiritual transformation through fasting and church attendance; and it was from him that Zossima had learned the words, "Let me be the servant of my servants."

Zossima himself had experienced a spiritual transformation whose origins went back to a church reading of the Book of Job when he was eight years old. This experience had so upset the well-established equilibrium between good and evil in his own mind that he had felt no qualms about spending his youth in "drunkenness, debauchery and daredevilry." As a young army officer, he had formed an attachment to a beautiful young girl; but he had still persisted in his licentious bachelor life, and had been much taken aback when the girl married a rich landowner. Zossima had promptly found an occasion to "insult" his successful rival and provoke a duel; but other events of an almost miraculous nature had intervened to change the course of his entire life.

On the day before the scheduled combat, Zossima, in an ugly, ferocious mood, had slapped the face of his servant, Afanasy, so hard that it became covered with blood. As he contemplated the beauties of nature at dawn on the following morning, Zossima was filled with shame and remorse. "That was what a man had been brought to," he thought; "that was a man beating a fellow man!

What a horrible crime!... [Why should] another man, a man like
me created in God's image...wait on me?" Throwing himself at
Afanasy's feet, dressed in full uniform, his forehead touching the
ground, Zossima begged his servant's forgiveness.

The absurdity of the impending duel was now clear to Zossima.
After apologies to his opponent — whom he allowed to fire his first
shot — he flung his pistol into the wood and announced his intention
of entering a monastery once he had obtained his discharge from
the army. In answer to the indignant protests of those present, he
proffered this advice: "Gentlemen...look around you at God's gifts:
the clear sky, the pure air, the tender grass, the birds. Nature is
beautiful and without sin, and we, we alone, are godless and foolish
and we don't understand that life is paradise, for we have only to
want to understand and it will at once come in all its beauty and we
shall embrace and weep" (II, 6, II).

The death of Father Zossima will mark a turning point in the life
of Alyosha, his young disciple. The novice and others sustain a violent shock when the body of this highly just man and "great saint"
begins to decompose within twenty-four hours of his death, emit-
ting an "odor of corruption" quite at odds with the hagiographic
tradition that holds that bodily preservation and the emission of
sweet fragrance are marks of special holiness.[3] Alyosha's dismay at
this event inspires a sinful revolt against the God who has permitted the natural law of decomposition to violate what Alyosha calls
a "higher justice." "Where was Providence and its finger?" cries
the distraught young man. "Why did it hide its finger at the most
critical moment...and seem anxious itself to submit to the blind,
dumb, and pitiless laws of nature?"

So shaken is the young man by this antimiracle that his face loses
its habitually meek expression, and to an associate, the seminarist
Rakitin, he utters negations lifted straight from his brother Ivan's
credo: "I haven't taken up arms against God....I simply 'don't accept his world'" (III, 7, II). Gloatingly, the materialistic Rakitin feeds
the incipient rebel on sausage and vodka and enlists his company
on a visit to the siren Grushenka.

Expecting to meet a wicked, abandoned woman, Alyosha is surprised to find in Grushenka a truly loving sister, a treasure who
"restores [his] soul." Grushenka, on her side, confesses that Alyosha is the first man to move her heart. To illustrate the mystery
of love as she understands it, she relates a tale in which the giving
of an onion represents a good deed — a simple story that serves
to free Alyosha from his tormenting doubts and negative impulses.

On his return to the monastery, "there was no weeping, gnawing, poignant compassion in his heart as [before]. . . . His mind and heart were [now] full of gladness" (III, 7, IV).

Alyosha dozes off while one of the monks is reading aloud the New Testament story of the marriage feast at Cana in Galilee (John 2:1–12). In his dream, Father Zossima appears in the company of Christ — not, however, the Grand Inquisitor's Christ, who had sought to give humans their freedom, but rather a loving, pitying Christ who unobtrusively heeds his mother's request to assist the unhappy host at the wedding party when his wine runs out. Zossima, in his dream, gives Alyosha to understand that it is time to begin his missionary work in the world. Awakening with a cry of rapture, the young man runs out of the monastery into the mysteries of the night. The beauty of his vision of nature redoubles his faith in God and fills him with love for all creation. Prostrating himself, he covers the earth with his kisses and tears of joy.

Thus, on the very night when old Karamazov was being murdered, his son Alyosha, who "had fallen upon the earth a weak youth . . . rose from it a resolute fighter for the rest of his life" (III, 7, IV). Three days later, Alyosha finally left the monastery in accordance with his elder's bidding to "sojourn in the world."

On the night of the murder, the elder Karamazov had been waiting at home in the belief that Grushenka was finally yielding to his importunities and was about to pay him a long-denied visit. Alone with the rats whose company helped to relieve his boredom, he waited in uneasy suspense, suspecting that his son Dmitry was also on the watch and might be lying in wait to intercept her. Dmitry is in fact on the premises, armed with a heavy brass pestle picked up earlier, and now taps on his father's window frame to give the signal (which he has learned from Smerdyakov) that "Grushenka is here."

Old Karamazov immediately comes to the window, expecting to greet his desired mistress-to-be. The sight of the lustful old man arouses in Dmitry an instantaneous desire to kill his father outright, and he draws the improvised weapon from his pocket. But just at that moment he is clutched from behind by the old servant, Grigory, and thus it is Grigory rather than Karamazov who is struck on the head by the brass pestle. Alarmed by the blood profusely inundating Grigory's face and forehead, the confused Dmitry tries desperately to wipe it off with his clean white handkerchief. No longer capable of rational thought, he then vaults the fence and runs off to Grushenka's house.

As this night of horrors unfolds, Dmitry learns that Grushenka has meanwhile eloped with her first love, a rather nondescript Polish officer who has come to claim her after five years' absence. Dmitry, following the couple in hot pursuit to the nearby town that is their destination, takes command of the situation by organizing a sumptuous banquet with abundant supplies of food and liquor and even a group of entertainers. Elbowing the Pole aside, he reclaims Grushenka's affection and plunges into a delirious orgy — which, however, is shortly interrupted by the police, already on the trail of the "monster and parricide" against whom, they say, his "old father's blood cries out."

Although the reader knows Dmitry to be at least technically innocent, he is now formally charged with the murder of his father, who has been found dead on the floor of his room with his skull fractured — supposedly by the same weapon that had previously struck Grigory. An envelope addressed by Karamazov to Grushenka, and believed to have contained money, has been found ripped open and empty. To the authorities it seems self-evident that Dmitry has killed his father, has taken the money, and is now spending it on a drunken revel.

Dmitry, at first not understanding the evidence against him, looks wildly at the people in the room. Then he suddenly rises, flings up his hands, and cries in a loud voice, "I'm not guilty! I'm not guilty of that murder! I'm not guilty of my father's murder. I meant to kill him, but I'm not guilty. It wasn't me!" (III, 9, III).

The chapters Dostoevsky devotes to the interrogation of the suspect and other witnesses are obviously intended as a satire on those self-important "preliminary investigators" who pride themselves on their supposed ability to apprehend the inner workings of the human soul. To them, the evidence points ineluctably to Dmitry's guilt. Dmitry himself, on the other hand, now realizes that the parricide can only have been his half brother Smerdyakov, the only person who knew where Karamazov had hidden the envelope with the money for Grushenka.

It was in fact the unprepossessing Smerdyakov who had planned and carried out the murder. Smerdyakov had not, however, acted in total independence, for he had believed that his half brother Ivan was tacitly in league with him and that, from a philosophic standpoint, he was covered by Ivan's doctrine that "all was permitted" to the two of them. Accordingly, Smerdyakov had arranged to carry out the crime at a time when Ivan would be of town, an absence of which Ivan had told him in advance and which he rightly interpreted as an implied authorization to act. After cracking Karamazov's skull with a heavy iron paperweight — rather than the brass pestle that had injured Grigory — Smerdyakov had concealed his own role by deliberately falling down the cellar stairs in a feigned epileptic fit. The fall had left him in a prolonged state of unconsciousness that made him unavailable for interrogation.

Dmitry, faced with what seems an open-and-shut case against him, continues to plead his innocence even as he accepts his public disgrace. "I want to suffer and be cleansed by my suffering," he says. "I accept my punishment not because I killed him, but because I wanted to kill him and, perhaps, would, in fact, have killed him" (III, 9, IX). By the day before the trial, Alyosha, too, has become convinced of Dmitry's innocence and Smerdyakov's guilt; but Ivan, filled with contempt for Dmitry and indignant at Katerina's seemingly unextinguished love for his hated brother, holds firmly to the idea that Dmitry really is the parricide. In spite of this belief, Ivan plans to organize and finance Dmitry's escape from his jailers — because, he thinks, "at heart, I, too, am just such a murderer" (IV, 11, VII).

Ivan's sense of personal guilt is deepened by the behavior of Smerdyakov, who, on recovering consciousness, insinuates to him that it was indeed he, Ivan, who had put him up to the crime. "Only with you, sir," he says. "I killed him with your help, sir. Your brother's quite innocent, sir.... It's you who's the rightful murderer." Although Ivan intends to denounce Smerdyakov when the case comes to trial, he has already accepted his feelings of personal responsibility; and he who, of all the brothers, seemed most indifferent to considerations of human accountability is now filled with "a sort of gladness.... He felt a sort of unbounded determination; an end to the vacillations which had tormented him so much all these last few weeks!" (IV, 11, VIII).

Ivan's moral rebirth begins with his succoring of a peasant whom he had earlier knocked down and left lying unconscious, probably to freeze to death. But Ivan is already experiencing the first symptoms of the "brain fever" that often overtakes Dostoevsky's overwrought characters at crucial moments. On the evening before the trial, he suffers a frightening hallucination as a spot on his sofa transforms itself in his imagination into a polished, affable "gentleman caller" who turns out to be none other than the devil himself.

Earlier in the novel, Ivan had confided to Alyosha his notion of this malign spirit: "I can't help thinking that if the devil doesn't exist and, therefore, man has created him, he has created him in his own image and likeness" (II, 5, IV). The devil now standing before him is, Ivan is convinced, his own secret soul — "a lie... my illness... a phantom.... You are my hallucination," he tells the visitor. "You're the embodiment of myself, but only of one side of me — of my thoughts and feelings, but only the most vile and stupid."

In a tone of mocking superiority, the cynical, persuasive devil engages Ivan in a conversation obviously designed to sow doubts in his half-crazed mind about the existence of God and Satan, the blurring of good and evil, and the authenticity of the "new man" to whom, allegedly, "everything is permitted" and who supposedly "has a right to carry on as he pleases in accordance with the new principles." Caught in a fierce, agonizing debate, horrified by his feverish vision, Ivan applies cold compresses in hope of obtaining relief from his alter ego's merciless "hammering on my brain like an excruciating nightmare."

Realizing that his night visitor personifies the evil side of himself — the satanic pride that denies belief in God and that he would like to expurgate from his chaotic soul — Ivan is immeasurably relieved by the arrival of his youngest brother as the new day begins. Far from being the bearer of good news, however, Alyosha brings the shocking intelligence that Smerdyakov has just hanged himself — an action that, among other things, precludes his appearance at the coming trial. Alyosha fears that the frenzied Ivan, too, may be seized by despair and tempted by suicide, but Ivan firmly disabuses him before falling into a state of unconsciousness.

In a section tellingly entitled "A Miscarriage of Justice," Dostoevsky recapitulates the events of Dmitry's trial in a way that shows his skepticism about the workings of Russia's new court system and the innovation of trial by jury. Ivan appears and testifies — unconvincingly — that it was Smerdyakov, not Dmitry, who killed their father; and he then goes on to accuse himself as well: "He murdered him, and I told him to do it." "Who doesn't wish his father dead?" Ivan adds, to the consternation of the shocked court.

To the presiding judge's question whether he is in his right mind, Ivan's devastating retort encompasses the entire courtroom. "Yes," he says, "I'm afraid that's the trouble that I'm in my right mind — and in the same vile mind as yourself and all these — ugly faces!.... My father has been murdered and they pretend to be horrified... the liars! They all wish their fathers dead.... If there had been no murder of a father, they'd all have... gone home in a bad temper.... Circuses! 'Bread and circuses!' " (IV, 12, V).

But neither Ivan's testimony nor that of Dmitry's other intimates, including Katerina Ivanovna and Grushenka, prevent the young man's conviction on circumstantial evidence. In answer to the prosecutor's demand that the blood of the father — allegedly shed by Dmitry "with the base motive of robbery" — be avenged, the counsel for the defense begs the court to show mercy. In an impassioned if somewhat artificial speech, he tells the jury that the Russian court "does not exist for punishment only, but also for the salvation of a ruined man." Dmitry, however, is duly found guilty and sentenced to penal servitude in Siberia.

In the epilogue to this gigantic novel, Ivan has devised a plan to enable Dmitry to escape when the prisoner convoy reaches its third stopover on the way to Siberia. Not only the ailing Ivan but even the law-abiding Alyosha urges his brother to take advantage of this opportunity, for Alyosha knows that Dmitry is too weak to be able to bear his punishment and would rebel against it. Dmitry is not "ready," and such a cross is not for him, Alyosha tells his brother; and Mitya himself concurs. "Could Mitya Karamazov do anything but run away?" he asks as he promises to accept his guilt. "I shall condemn myself for it and I shall always pray that my sin should be forgiven."

With the aid of bribery, Dmitry will escape with Grushenka to America, a land he already hates and where he is determined to put down no roots. As soon as ever he can he will return to Russia, even if in disguise, to die in the native land he loves. Before he leaves, Katerina appears to seek his pardon, and the two women rivals for the prisoner's love are at least superficially reconciled.

Alyosha, meanwhile, hurries off to the funeral of little Ilyusha Snegiryov, whose short life has been ended by a virulent disease. To the dead boy's comrades, Alyosha delivers a rapturous homily on the theme of brotherhood and love. "Everyone," he says, must find a place in his/her heart for "everyone," for it is "really true that, as our religion tells us, we shall all rise from the dead and come to life and see one another again."

This lengthy summary will have given the reader some indication of the scope and variety of the themes developed in *The Brothers Karamazov*. Interwoven with the narrative are countless elements that are rooted in the folklore of the Russian people. The little tales, hints, anecdotes, and superstitions sprinkled throughout the novel belong to the rich heritage of Russian ethnology and religion, transmuted by Dostoevsky's literary art and subsequently analyzed at length by specialized scholars.

It goes without saying that *The Brothers Karamazov* has been the subject of innumerable literary, psychological, and philosophical commentaries by critics of various faiths and convictions, writing in an assortment of languages. In the few pages remaining, there is room for little more than a brief reference to the "timelessly" archetypal quality of the main characters and a look at the Karamazov family group as a social organism of inherently self-destructive character. Additional illumination may flow from a preliminary examination of certain mythological parallels that throw into high relief the universal bearing of Dostoevsky's towering creation.

Although the Karamazov family, which gained "such a sad notoriety throughout Russia," is at least nominally Europeanized in its culture and in many ways reflects Dostoevsky's own milieu, the parricide motif that underlies the novel is older than any written history. Its origins go back at least as far as the mythological concept of the Erinyes, those retributive beings one finds, for instance, in the Greek legend of Orestes, the slayer of his mother and her paramour.

The Erinyes, in Greek mythology, were supernatural creatures who served as instruments of vengeance and justice, residing in the netherworld but ascending to earth to pursue the wicked, especially parricides, fratricides, and murderers of friends and relatives. Often they provoked madness in their victims, a trait that explains their Greek appellation of *maniai* (senders of madness) and perhaps accounts for their Latin name of the "Furies," derived from the word *furor*. Similarly, in Dostoevsky's treatment of the theme, one of the Karamazov brothers, Smerdyakov, is driven to the madness that provokes suicide, while another, Ivan, falls prey to a mental disturbance culminating in traumatic neurasthenia.

As upholders of the established moral order, the Erinyes were just but implacable toward their victims, refusing to consider any circumstances that might warrant mitigation of their punishment. Similarly, Dmitry, the third Karamazov victim, is declared guilty with no extenuating circumstances or grounds for leniency.

Even Alyosha, the least reprehensible of the brothers, experiences one of the Furies' torments early in the narrative when he is attacked by the young Snegiryov: "[Ilyusha] grew vicious like a little wild beast: he dashed forward and flew at Alyosha...lowered his head, and seizing his left hand with both of his, bit his middle finger painfully, he dug his teeth into it and did not let go" (II, 4, III). This scene, too, evokes the legend of Orestes, who, driven to frenzy by the Erinyes, bit off his own finger at Megalopolis, where a temple to his healing was later erected.

The poet Hesiod tells us that the Erinyes were daughters of the goddess Earth and her spouse Uranus, who was castrated by their son Kronos in revenge for his father's misdeeds. It was from the blood that fell upon the Earth on that occasion that the Erinyes sprang — a myth that finds a double analogy in the parricide Smerdyakov, who was born in slime mixed with placental blood in Grigory's bathhouse and grew up to become the paradigmatic son who sheds his father's blood.

Virgil assigns names to three of the Erinyes — Tisiphone, Megaera, and Alecto; and it is not too fanciful to match them with the Karamazov brothers. Smerdyakov, it may be suggested, is the victim of Tisiphone ("avenger of murder"), who pursues the parricide until he hangs himself from a sturdy nail he has driven into the wall. To Dmitry may be assigned Megaera ("the jealous one"), since he willed the parricide out of jealousy of his father's bestial love for Grushenka. Similarly, Alecto ("unceasing in anger") may be coupled with Ivan, the rebellious brother who refused to admit the existence of God's world and is described by his visiting devil as "angry again...always angry...spoiling for a fight" (IV, 11, IX).

Unrelentingly tracked by these avenging furies, their victims in Greek mythology sought desperately to flee to new lands and escape their implacable pursuers. Similarly, each of the Karamazov brothers seems driven by an efferent force impelling him to try to escape his normal surroundings. Alyosha is told to leave the monastery and go out into the world; Smerdyakov dreams of beginning a new life abroad; and Ivan seeks refuge from his torments in Moscow or in Europe.

Dmitry's projected escape to America, and his determination to return to Russia, recall the familiar version of the Orestes legend in which the mythical hero, after having sought refuge from the Erinyes at Delphi, returns to Athens to plead his case before the Areopagus. Even after Orestes was acquitted by that body, the Erinyes did not cease tormenting him until he offered sacrifices — analogous to Dmitry's repentance and suffering — at one of their temples associated with the *Charites* (spirits of pardon). Only then were the avengers appeased and only then did he receive their blessing.

One reason for the universal fascination exerted by the Karamazov story may lie in the agelessness of these flawed characters, who, relentlessly pursued by the avenging fury of their own consciences, must come to terms with their feelings of guilt and make expiation for the sin of parricide — identified both in antiquity and in modern times as humanity's (and the individual's) principal and primal crime.[4]

The fractured family unit at the center of *The Brothers Karamazov* is one torn asunder by terrible forces of egoism, hatred, jealousy, and thirst for destruction. The depraved, licentious head of the family, Feodor Pavlovich Karamazov, whose house "stinks of [crime]," is a libertine and a monster of lust and debauchery. To his sons, the reader is told, he has transmitted a bestial sensuality, a certain shrewdness in business matters, and a "propensity to drunkenness." Insensitive to the social and spiritual duties of a father, this grotesque paterfamilias "brought up his children in the backyard and he was glad to be rid of them. Indeed, he forgot all about them." His son Ivan, at the age of ten, became "aware that their father was a man of whom one ought to be ashamed to talk."

"Many of our fathers today are like him," Dostoevsky's public prosecutor admits in his lengthy speech (IV, 12, VI); while the counsel for the defense asks rhetorically, "What is a father, a real father?" Pleading with the jury not to attach "mystical prejudices" to the mere fact that a man begets a child, his counsel asks that Dmitry not be judged as an insensitive, egoistic monster but rather as a boy who had "grown up like a wild animal," receiving neither a proper education nor any expressions of love.

Perhaps, the defense counsel suggests, Dmitry longed to embrace his father but was met only by cynical sneers, suspicions, and attempts to cheat him out of the money rightfully due him. Though Karamazov complained of his son's disrespect and cruelty, it was actually the father who had given Dmitry a bad name in society, denouncing and slandering him and even buying up his IOUs in order to get him imprisoned. "Such a father as the murdered old Karamazov cannot and does not deserve to be called a father," the defense counsel asserts. "The love for a father who does not deserve such love is an absurdity, an impossibility."

Summoning the murdered man to an imaginary confrontation with his son, the spokesman for the latter invites Dmitry to stand before his father and ask him, "Why should I love you? Father, prove to me that I must love you!" "And if his father is able to," the lawyer continues, "then we are dealing with a real, normal family, based not merely on mystical prejudices, but on rational, responsible, and strictly humane foundations. If, on the other hand, the father cannot prove it, there is at once an end to the family relationship: he is not a father to him, and the son is free and entitled to look upon his father as a stranger, and even as his enemy" (IV, 12, XIII).

Can there in fact be such "an end to the family relationship," and can old Feodor Pavlovich indeed be considered an enemy of Dmitry and his other sons? Born a nobleman, endowed with good mental faculties and an innate capacity to see into the deeper motives of human behavior, Karamazov, instead of developing his mind, had chosen to lead a parasitic life as a hanger-on in rich families. Inwardly tormented by the feelings of humiliation he experienced in this wealthy milieu, he, like so many of Dostoevsky's acrobatic characters, had played the role of a a poor rogue and smooth-tongued clown until his wife's dowry unexpectedly put him in control of a small fortune.

His new trade of moneylender had enabled him to divest himself of his former servile obsequiousness, yet the lackey in him had never died. The reader's final impression of this "Europeanized" Russian father is that of a malicious, cynical voluptuary, totally abandoned to the brutality of his carnal instincts and egoistic promptings.

There is in the "broad Karamazov nature" a noticeable duality shared in some degree by Feodor Pavlovich with each of his sons. Natural intelligence goes hand in hand with base pride, unrestrained wickedness with tearful sentimentality. Each of the Karamazovs seems precariously balanced between "two abysses," one inviting to "the most uncontrollable . . . dissipation," the other to "love [that blazes] up like gunpowder" (IV, 12, XI). A Karamazov, Dostoevsky tells the reader, might "suddenly give up everything and go on a pilgrimage to Jerusalem in search of salvation, or . . . suddenly set fire to his village, and . . . perhaps . . . do both the one and the other" (I, 3, VI).

Even Alyosha does not escape this devastating Karamazov dualism. "Three sensualists," the seminarist Rakitin tells him, "are now constantly watching each other — with a knife stuck in the leg of their boots. They're knocking their heads together, the three of them, and, for all I know, you may be the fourth. . . . The Karamazov problem boils down to . . . sensualists, money-grubbers, and saintly fools!" (I, 2, VII). Alyosha, immersed in a fearful struggle with this " 'earthbound Karamazov force' . . . earthbound, unrestrained, and crude," utters this desperate cry: "I don't know whether the spirit of God moves over that force. All I know is that I, too, am a Karamazov. I a monk, a monk? . . . And yet I don't think I even believe in God" (II, 5, I).

Old Karamazov's first wife, Dmitry's mother, had been an indomitable and fearless lady who deserted her husband in order to run away with an impoverished schoolteacher, leaving the three-year-old Mitya to be looked after by his dissolute father. In contrast to Makar Dolgoruky of A Raw Youth, Karamazov had chosen to play the ridiculous part of the injured husband, but at the same time had turned his household into "a regular harem . . . giving disorderly drinking parties." After the death of Mitya's mother — and while still wearing a mourning crape on his hat — he had seen fit to rape the "Stinking Lizaveta" and beget the child who would grow up to be his murderer.

That child, Smerdyakov, may be seen as a composite symbol of all that is repellent and loathsome in the disintegrated Karamazov family — a "stinking" blot on the Karamazov scutcheon. In this furtive, unsocial, and taciturn product of rape lay dormant the seeds of parricide and suicide. Denied equality with his legitimate brothers, his relegation to the position of cook and valet in his father's household had furthered his descent into baseness and servility. Toward his surrogate father, Grigory, Smerdyakov showed himself incapable of even a spark of gratitude.

But neither was Grigory altogether guiltless toward Smerdyakov. Outraged by the skeptical bent the lad had inherited from his real father — for the boy had precociously questioned the source of light during the first three days of Creation, before God had created the sun, moon, and stars — Grigory had struck him a violent blow across the cheek that precipitated his first epileptic fit. (This act of violence may be compared with Zossima's unjustified slapping of his servant Afanasy.) Smerdyakov's impertinent yet reasonable question seems, moreover, to echo Dostoevsky's own religious difficulties. It reinforces the feeling that the four-sided figure constituted by the Karamazov brothers — including the parricide Smerdyakov — in some way embodies attributes of the author's own personality.

Smerdyakov, though aware of his own baseness, seems to have sincerely believed he could reform and escape to a better life. Having acquired from Ivan the notion that "all is permitted," he cleverly involved his half brother as a tacit accomplice in the crime he was about to commit. But Ivan's subsequent reproaches disillusioned Smerdyakov about this "teacher" who was too weak-kneed to practice the principles he himself preached. Renouncing any hope of reaping the benefits the parricide might have brought him, Smerdyakov, disenchanted and despairing yet never without malice, can find no better solution than to end his own life, taking with him the key to the unraveling of the crime.

Karamazov's second wife, the meek and inoffensive Sophia Ivanovna, had led an existence of tragic indignity as spouse to a man who brutishly trampled on the ordinary decencies of married life. In their home and in her very presence, he entertained women of the streets at wild parties. His scandalous behavior precipitated her contraction of "one of those women's nervous diseases . . . accompanied by terrible fits of hysteria." Vestiges of this disorder, which "at times deprived her of her reason," appeared also in her sons, especially in Ivan, who suffered innumerable nervous crises even before his celebrated "encounter" with the devil.

Sophia Ivanovna had died when her son Alyosha was in his fourth year — a "pure cherub" of serene disposition and even temper, loved by everyone. "His gift of arousing a special kind of love in people," Dostoevsky tells the reader, "was inherent in his very nature, artless and spontaneous" — not unlike that of the "idiot" Prince Myshkin. The thoughtful and apparently self-composed boy had grown up attaching no importance to the money that so obsessed the other members of the family; while those traits of lust and sensuality he had inherited from his father had been introverted or transmuted into what is described as "absurd modesty and chastity." He had even stopped his ears against his schoolmates' obscenities, and had been especially pained by "certain conversations about women," perhaps because he continued to feel the presence of his mother "standing alive before [him]."

As the only one of the Karamazov brothers who bears no grudge against their father, Alyosha is in no way guilty of complicity in his murder. Yet, he too admits, to Rakitin's probing (I, 2, VII), that he "couldn't help feeling that I'd thought about [a crime] myself." He thus acknowledges his own vague sense of a guilt that seems rooted in his very membership in the Karamazov community.

Resentment against the father, in contrast, is piled high in the heart of Mitya, Alyosha's eldest brother. From his dissolute parent, Mitya has inherited an unbounded love of life, unrestrained sensuality, and a crippling lack of willpower — traits mitigated, however, by a certain warmth of heart and even a sensitivity to beauty, exemplified in his half-intoxicated recitation, interspersed with sobs, of Schiller's "Ode to Joy."

"Beauty is not only a terrible, but also a mysterious, thing," Dmitry declares. In it, he claims, "God and the devil are fighting for mastery, and the battlefield is the heart of man" (I, 3, III). Though Dmitry's debauchery has not destroyed his sensitivity to the beauty of poetic expression, the deeper meaning of life seems constantly to elude and baffle him. In his blood, "lust raises storms"; in his paroxysms of extreme enthusiasm and optimism, he stands ready to kill himself — because, as he says, "life exists and death doesn't."

The negative elements in Dmitry's makeup are constantly on view as the novel proceeds. He is violently jealous of his father, and quite prepared to kill him if he should find him in Grushenka's company.

He brutalizes Captain Snegiryov and bullies the latter's young son. He viciously strikes the defenseless old servant, Grigory, with his brass pestle on the fatal night, though this may be more the effect of nerves than the expression of a violent temperament. It is, however, only "the hand of God" that deflects the weapon and tempers the blow sufficiently to preserve Grigory's life.

Yet Dmitry is by no means irreclaimable. When he pauses to wipe the servant's bleeding face and forehead, he is in effect performing a ritual that will set him on the path of moral rebirth and eventual redemption. In a telling account of his figurative "Journey through Hell" (III, 9, III), Dmitry reveals his awareness of the change he is undergoing:

> What has made me unhappy all my life is that I longed to be an honorable man, to be ... a martyr to honor and to seek for it with a lantern, with the lantern of Diogenes, and yet all my life I've been playing dirty tricks on people.... You see, gentlemen [of the jury], I didn't like the way he looked. There was something dishonorable about him, boastful and trampling on everything sacred, jeering and lack of faith — horrible, horrible! But now that he's dead, I think differently.... I'm sorry I hated him so much.

Insisting to the end that he did not strike the blow that actually killed Karamazov, Dmitry nevertheless admits to having desired his father's death. Thus, though technically not guilty, he is not altogether innocent either, a status he shares with larger segments of humanity ensnared in life's ambiguities.

Ivan, the intellectual of the family and the only son to have completed his university studies, has likewise inherited his father's love of life, though his conception of the world is pessimistic and anarchistic. To the public prosecutor, he is "one of our modern young men, a man of brilliant education and a fairly powerful intellect who, however, no longer believes in anything. Like his father, he has rejected and expunged too much already from life" (IV, 12, VI). Dostoevsky himself sees Ivan as an incarnation of his father's rationalism — and, in so far as he is a freethinker and nonbeliever, a representative of evil. At the same time, Ivan seems disposed to believe, and in a strange way actually does believe, in God, even though he never achieves real faith. He seems to thirst for redemption, yet always to stop short of slaking his thirst, preferring instead his spasmodic desire for revolt. Good and evil are as inseparable in Ivan as they were in Dostoevsky himself.

Rather than a purely rational product of European ideas, Ivan is thus a despairing, divided soul, profoundly at odds with himself.

His basically insubordinate nature refuses balance, prefers rebellion, and oscillates between a real love of life and an illusory search for God's reasons for his unjust world. Beneath inherited feelings of inferiority, Ivan conceals intense pride and an aspiration to super-human amorality. "All is permitted" is the principle he taught to Smerdyakov, who naively put the weakling-superman's ideas into practice.

But the realization of Smerdyakov's guilt dashes Ivan's belief that Dmitry was the parricide, and with it his hope that Katerina would leave the parricide and turn to him. He is guilty, therefore, on three counts: he is himself a would-be parricide ("who doesn't wish his father dead?"); he desires his innocent brother's guilt because of his own jealousy; and he is directly responsible for Smerdyakov's suicide.

Katerina Verkhovtsev is the beautiful, imperious, and haughty member of a trio of female characters, each one of whom acts directly on one or more of the ill-fated Karamazovs. Katerina, Grushenka, and Lise Kokhlakov, the little cripple, are in a sense complementary to the three brothers, feminine counterparts to their pride, their evil, their search for both love and destruction. Although the townsfolk look on Katerina as a lady of character and elevated moral principles, one feels that in reality she would stoop to any baseness to rob Grushenka of Dmitry's attachment, even while she herself is holding Ivan, whom she loves, on a string.

Obsessed by the idea that Dmitry had inwardly despised and sneered at her when she bowed down to him, Katerina has per-suaded herself that in order to obliterate her act of self-abasement she must transmute their relationship into one of real love. As Aly-osha realizes in one of his "illuminations," she is a woman who feels the need of exerting her power and might in fact be able to bring the malleable Mitya under her sway, whereas a man as proud as Ivan would never submit to her control. Alyosha perfectly understands, therefore, that Katerina would not be a suitable match for either of his brothers (II, 4, V).

Having convinced herself that she would remain faithful to Mitya all her life, Katerina let it be understood that she intended to appeal to the government for permission to accompany him to Siberia. Such a role, however, would never have suited this hysterical, power-hungry female. It is to the more genuine, generous, and earthy Grushenka that Dostoevsky accords the responsibility of becoming the instrument of Dmitry's redemption.

Grushenka is a sensual and supple creature, "a rosy-cheeked, plump Russian beauty, a woman of bold and determined character, proud and brazen, who knew the value of money." To the towns-people, indeed, she is merely the very ordinary, far from beautiful low-class girl who has driven Feodor Karamazov and his unhappy son, Dmitry, to total ruin. But Dmitry, for Alyosha's edification, of-fers this vision of her satanic appeal: "That she-devil Grushenka has a kind of curve of the body which can be detected even on her foot. You can see it even in the little toe of her left foot.... If she wants me to, I shall marry her at once. If not, I shall stay with her just the same. I shall be the caretaker in her yard!" And yet this small-town courte-san is destined to play a positive role in both Dmitry's and Alyosha's life. As an authentic child of Mother Russia, she emerges as one who, "after ... years of agony, as soon as someone ... said a sincere word to her, forgave everything, forgot everything" (III, 7, III).

Lise Khokhlakov, the fourteen-year-old "woman-child" who "sometimes dream[s] of devils," seems, on the other hand, to be a real she-devil in the eyes of her creator. A decided streak of evil courses in the blood of this girl who has grown up without a father and is utterly spoiled by her widowed, wealthy, and weak mother. Though Lise has had every advantage in life, she refuses happiness in a manner reminiscent of Stavrogin in *The Devils,* with whom she has been compared in their common attraction to the "beauty" of acts that shame, embarrass, or degrade others.

So loathsome does Lise find her own life that she desires to destroy herself or to have someone "marry me and then tear me to pieces, deceive me and leave me. I don't want to be happy." Her will to self-destruction finds expression in the gratuitous act of slamming a door on her own finger in order to relish the pain and gloat on the blood that oozes from under the nail. Full of inner perversions and ambiguity, Lise has in her makeup "something spiteful and at the same time innocent." Alyosha is the only person whose company she seeks — perhaps, it has been suggested, because she hopes his benign influence will free her from her own inner chaos.

The workings of Lise's sick mind are aimed at bringing into the Khokhlakov household the very forms of disorder, disintegration, and destruction against which Dostoevsky so often inveighs. To Alyosha she confesses a tormenting desire to set the house on fire. Although Alyosha naively assumes that such nefarious urges stem from her very affluence, Lise disabuses him. Her evil inclinations go beyond wealth or poverty. "If I were poor, I'd kill someone, and if I'm rich, I shall probably kill someone too," she says.

To Alyosha's thoughtful reflection that "there are moments when people love crime," Lise offers a frightening correction. "They always love it, and not only at 'moments,' " she insists. "...It's as though everyone had agreed to lie about it, and they have been lying about it ever since. They all say that they hate evil, but in their heart of hearts they all love it.... Your brother is being tried now for murdering his father, but in their hearts they love it," she says, anticipating the "bread and circuses" theme of Ivan's later testimony in court. Sadly, Alyosha acknowledges that "there's a grain of truth in what [Lise says] about everyone" (IV, 11, III).

Alyosha's use of the word *everyone* strikes the note of universality, of the responsibility of all to all, that serves as the moral foundation of this great novel. As a concept that embraces all humanity, it offers Dostoevsky's readers a hope that rationalism, negativism, anarchy, and atheism can at long last be overcome. To the Karamazov egoism — "Let the whole world perish in flames so long as I'm all right" (IV, 12, VI) — Dostoevsky opposes the persistent theme of "everyone and everything," a doctrine of universal guilt and all-encompassing brotherhood that will, he hopes, lure evil to its destruction and assure the triumph of right.

Speaking in part through his own voice and in part through that of Father Zossima, Dostoevsky repeatedly affirms that "each one is guilty of everything, towards everyone," that "until you have actually become everyone's brother, the brotherhood of man will not come to pass." Once this truth is grasped and acted upon, he hopes, "an end will...come to this dreadful isolation of man.... Everyone will realize...how unnaturally they have separated themselves from one another.... A man has to set an example at least once and draw his soul out of its isolation and work for some great act of human intercourse based on brotherly love.... He has to do so that the great idea may not die" (II, 6, II).

The one means of salvation is specified in Father Zossima's "Discourses and Sermons": "Take hold of yourself and make yourself responsible for all men's sins...for the moment you make yourself responsible...for everyone and everything, you will see...that you are, in fact, responsible for everyone and everything" (II, 6, III). Zossima, too, had said that "if you love, you are of God.... Everything can be atoned for, everything can be saved by love.... Love is such a priceless treasure that you can redeem everything in the world by it, and expiate not only your own but other people's sins" (I, 2, III). Alyosha is echoing his elder's doctrine when he tells Ivan that Christ "can forgive everything, everyone and everything *for everything*."

Love, for Dostoevsky, is a power even stronger than faith —

which, like hope and knowledge, is an imperfect, human virtue, appropriate to a world like Ivan's, in which humans see God not clearly but "darkly, as in a mirror." Love, for Dostoevsky, is the only superior, perfect, complete, and absolute virtue; it alone can afford to humans a glimpse of God, the object of their desire. Love, as absolute present and absolute future, allows them to receive God's light here and now, without waiting and postponing indefinitely as faith and hope counsel one to do. If humans can learn to love each other, Dostoevsky maintains, God will immediately fill their hearts to overflowing.

In illustration of the power of universal love, two dreams are narrated in *The Brothers Karamazov,* both hinging on the idea of universal responsibility and guilt and on the collective need to help and love "everybody" and "everything." Dmitry's and Alyosha's awakenings from their respective dreams — which will be recounted in a moment — are accompanied in each case by a spiritual transformation that deepens the sense of universal involvement. One wonders why Dostoevsky once again has chosen the vehicle of the dream to emphasize what is to all intents and purposes the ruling idea of all his work. Was it because he felt that the idea itself was made of the stuff of dreams — elusive, illusory, evasive, and intangible? Was he indulging in whim and fantasy in positing the solidarity of all in the common error of sin and in a general declaration of love? Is it fated that there must always be people who exclude themselves from moral obligations to others and consider themselves above and outside the human herd? Or was Dostoevsky giving expression, in the visionary creations of his imagination, to an ideal of a better humanity that he not only desired but conceived as possible through the very fact that man can dream of it?

Dmitry's strange dream comes to him as he sleeps in a corner during the preliminary interrogation of witnesses before his trial. Near a burnt-out village, a row of thin, haggard peasant women line the roadside. One of them, whose "breasts were probably so dried up that there was not a drop of milk in them," holds a crying baby in her arms. "And the baby cried and cried, holding out its little bare arms with its little fists quite blue from cold." In his dream, the driver of his cart explains to Dmitry that "they're poor, sir. Burnt out. Ain't got no bread, sir."

Dmitry begins to ask wild, senseless questions: "Why are the people poor? Why's the [baby] poor? Why's the steppe so bare? Why don't they embrace and kiss one another? Why don't they sing joyous songs? Why are they so black with misfortune?" Never-before-experienced emotions surge in Dmitry's heart. He wants to weep, to do "something for everyone so that the [baby] should cry no more, that no one should shed tears from that moment, and that he ought to do it now, now, without delay and regardless of everything, with all the Karamazov impetuosity" (III, 9, VIII).

Having once experienced pity and a sense of shared responsibility for the frozen baby and the burnt-out peasant mothers, Dmitry awakens, transformed. He is now able to accept his personal guilt for the parricide. Turning to the witnesses, he shouts, "We are all cruel, we are all monsters, we all make people weep, mothers and babies at the breast, but of all...I am the most vile and despicable wretch!" In this extraordinary declaration, Dmitry echoes words already uttered by Zossima's brother, Markel: "Every one of us is responsible for everyone else in every way, and I most of all." The doors to Dostoevsky's world of universal, paradisiac love will open when everyone has found like courage to acknowledge personal guilt, when everyone will forgive and be forgiven reciprocally: "I may have sinned against everyone, but that is why they will all forgive me, and that is paradise" (II, 6, II).

In Alyosha's dream of the biblical marriage at Cana, one sees how Christ, in comradely concern for the host who has run short of wine for his guests, is willing to lower himself to the performance of a mere "household" miracle. Alyosha, on awakening from his dream, goes out into the night to experience an all-encompassing love and rapturous vision of a world infinitely larger than Cana, infinitely larger than the entire living planet. "All those innumerable worlds of God met all at once in [Alyosha's] soul, and it was trembling all over 'as it came in contact with other worlds.' He wanted to forgive everyone and for everything, and to beg forgiveness — oh! not for himself, but for all men, for all and for everything" (III, 7, IV).

The words "for all and for everything" express the essence of Christian love as Dostoevsky conceives it, in what amounts to a reaffirmation of the concept of *agape* (love, or "charity") expounded by the apostle Paul in I Corinthians 13. *Agape,* as Dostoevsky, like Paul, understands it, does not refer to specific acts of charity enjoined by divine command, not even to such sacrifices as the giving of all one possesses to the poor or the suffering of martyrdom in the name of Christ. It is a constant, unselfish concern for others, an affection, tenderness, and compassion for all others at all times, the assumption of continuing responsibility for others, and the loving of "everyone" and "everything" — an ethic of equalization, a fitting foundation for a stable society of dignified human beings freely engaged in reciprocal exchanges of benefits and requitals.

Such a quality is the very opposite of the amour propre so elegantly and bitterly described by the seventeenth-century French moralist, La Rochefoucauld, in his well-known *Maximes*. No less decisively does it repudiate the doctrinaire, materialistic egalitarianism that Dostoevsky saw as the pernicious outcome of the European intellectual tradition. Our own age, too, is the arena of an unending contest between the promptings of self-preservation and self-aggrandizement and those of human solidarity, compassion, and love for one's neighbor. A summons to exercise one's freedom to love "everyone and everything" — from the steppes of Russia to the seedbeds of the great religions, from the America to which Dmitry escaped to the Europe from which Dostoevsky recoiled — is, perhaps, the best note on which to end this book about the towering genius who sought

> ... tongues in trees, books in the running brooks,
> Sermons in stones, and good in every thing.

> — *As You Like It*, II, i, 1. 16.

Conclusion

Two passages in *House of the Dead,* Dostoevsky's unique reminiscences of prison life, are sure to strike the observer of developments in the former Soviet Union and Eastern Europe in the closing years of the twentieth century. One of them has to do with the devastating psychological consequences of a lack of personal freedom. Any organizational setup that stifles the unquenchable human demand for freedom, Dostoevsky insists, is doomed to failure as a social framework. Profoundly aware as he was of the interdependence of social structure with the moral and psychological condition of the individual, Dostoevsky knew from experience how suffocating, even lethal, is the atmosphere in any human community where the basic human aspiration toward freedom and self-expression has been crushed.

The second observation, also arising from Dostoevsky's experience in the Siberian labor camp, is concerned with the psychological benefits of work — work, that is, which is undertaken as a "private," voluntary, self-assigned activity — and of its corollary, private property. "Without work, without lawful normal property, man cannot live; he becomes depraved and is transformed into a beast.... Work saved [the convicts] from crime; without [private] work the[y] would have devoured one another like spiders in a glass jar." A task autonomously set, work freely performed, Dostoevsky emphasizes, offers a mind-saving escape from the inhumanity and never-ending futility of labor imposed by an outside authority.

Still a third element in Dostoevsky's outlook, his strongly felt, expansionary Russian nationalism, is equally pertinent to contemporary affairs though less likely to command widespread assent. On this point there is the startling testimony of a fellow prisoner, the Polish exile, Szymon Tokarzewski:

How painful it was to listen to this conspirator [Dostoevsky], this man sentenced to prison for the cause of freedom and progress, when he confessed that he would be happy only when all the nations would fall under Russian rule. He never admitted that the Ukraine, Volynia, Podolia, Lithuania, and finally the whole of Poland were countries seized by Russia, but affirmed that all these regions ... had forever been the property of Russia, that the divine hand of justice had put these provinces and countries under the scepter of the Russian Tsar because they never would have been able to exist independently and that for a long time they would have remained in a state of dark illiteracy, barbarism, and abject poverty. The Baltic provinces, in Dostoevsky's opinion, belong to Russia proper; Siberia and the Caucasus he put in the same category. Listening to these arguments we acquired the conviction that Feodor Mikhailovich Dostoevsky was affected by insanity.[1]

Holding such views, and out of sympathy with any strain of nationalism except the Russian, the Pan-Slavist Dostoevsky believed as implicitly in Russia's mission as the leader of humankind as he did in the necessity of individual freedom and the benefits of spontaneous labor.

It is of interest, in the light of subsequent developments, that two of the questions addressed by Dostoevsky in the last pages of *The Diary of a Writer* had to do with "the Russian mission in Asia" (II, 3) and "the ruble as a European currency" (I, 1). Students of Dostoevsky's writings are constantly discovering passages so relevant to the contemporary scene that they might have been written yesterday. Whether one agrees with him or not, Russia's greatest psychological novelist possessed an uncanny knack of highlighting issues as central to our period as to his own.

"Is it not strange," asked a critic in the year of the Bolshevik Revolution, "how Dostoevsky seems to revive every time our way of life dissolves in a fiery ferment?"[2] During the fiery ferment in the then Soviet Union at the beginning of the 1990s, a parliamentarian[3] of the Russian republic, in calling for a condemnation of the Communist party's criminal acts of the past, exhorted his hearers to remember Dostoevsky's admonition that happiness cannot be constructed if its foundation is flawed by the tears of a single child.

Appendix

Russian Periodicals in Dostoevsky's Time

A journal is a terribly important thing; it is the sort of activity with which one must not take risks, because no matter what happens, journals, as the expression of all shades of contemporary opinion, must remain. (*Letters*, II, 37)

Newspapers, literary magazines, and other periodicals were a prominent feature of the Russian literary scene in the middle and later years of the nineteenth century. Their relatively late development may be attributed to three main factors: the very slow emergence in Russia of an educated middle-class readership; the prevalent use of French and German, rather than Russian, as the favored languages of the aristocracy; and the suspicion and hostility toward new ideas that at most periods characterized Russia's despotic government.

A significant change, particularly in this last respect, occurred with the death of the reactionary Tsar Nicholas I (1825–55) and the accession of his more liberal son, Alexander II (1855–81). Whereas only six newspapers and nineteen monthlies, mostly of a specialized character and all heavily censored, had been authorized to appear during the last decade of Nicholas's reign,[1] the first ten years of his successor's regime saw a tenfold increase in the combined number of newspapers and periodicals. Encouraging and promoting the spirit of reform that accompanied the new reign, culminating in the emancipation of the serfs in 1861, no fewer than 66 newspapers and 156 monthly periodicals helped shape new ideas and mold the public mind.

1

A handful of publications initiated at earlier periods of Russian history survived into the era of Dostoevsky and his contemporaries. Most venerable among them was the *Moskovskie vedomosti*

(Moscow news, also known as Moscow gazette), a conservative newspaper that had been founded as far back as 1756 and continued publication until 1918. Dostoevsky, who came to share many of this state-owned journal's conservative views, referred to it in *The Diary of a Writer* during the 1870s as "unquestionably our best political newspaper."

Two other publications that achieved early celebrity were founded by the historian Nikolay Mikhailovich Karamzin (1766–1826), one of them in the reign of the Empress Catherine, the other in that of her grandson Alexander I. The monthly *Moskovski zhurnal* (Moscow journal, 1791–92) was the vehicle for the publication of Karamzin's well-known "Letters of a Russian Traveler," which described his eighteen months' experience in western Europe in 1789–90 and helped to introduce into Russia the cult of literary sensibility associated with Jean-Jacques Rousseau and other Western writers. A decade later, Karamzin founded and became the first editor of the periodical *Vestnik Evropy* (Messenger of Europe), which was published from 1802 to 1830, although Karamzin himself left it in 1803 to devote himself entirely to historical research. As will be noted below, this periodical was revived in the 1860s and continued until after the Bolshevik Revolution.

Still another early periodical that displayed remarkable staying power and played an important part in Dostoevsky's career was *Otechestvenniye zapiski* (Notes of the fatherland, also known as Fatherland annals or Country notes).[2] Beginning publication in 1820, *Notes of the Fatherland* went through several transformations before its final suppression in 1884. Under Andrey Alexandrovich Kraevsky, who took over its direction in 1839,[3] it became the leading organ of the Russian liberalism of the time, publishing the major articles of Vissarion Grigorievich Belinsky, the well-known critic, as well as most of Dostoevsky's early works (except *Poor Folk*) and Mikhail Dostoevsky's 1848 translation of Goethe's "Reineke Fuchs," one of the classic Russian renderings of that satirical poem. Although the very talented young writer Valerian Maikov became chief critic of *Notes of the Fatherland* when Belinsky broke with Kraevsky in 1847, the magazine declined and temporarily took on an antiradical coloration, only to reemerge in the 1860s as a leading radical organ (see below).

Less political in character was *Biblioteka dlya chteniya* (The library for reading, 1834–65), a review of "literature, science, arts, industry, news, and fashion" that was edited in St. Petersburg by the Polish émigré-scholar Osip I. Senkovsky. This most widely read journal of the late 1830s, which aimed largely at a provincial readership and was the first to obtain any commercial success, owed its auspicious beginnings to the publication of a number of Pushkin's works, including *The Queen of Spades* in 1834. Other collaborators included Tolstoy, Goncharov, the dramatist Alexander Ostrovsky, the poet Mikhail Lermontov, the realist writer Alexey Pisemsky, and Mikhail Dostoevsky, whose translation of Schiller's *Don Carlos* was accepted for publication in 1848. The magazine also allotted much space to translations of such Western writers as Hugo, Balzac, Dumas, George Sand, Eugène Sue, and Thackeray.

Scurrilous criticism and feuding among periodicals and their editors were commonplace features of the time. Particularly noteworthy were the barbed exchanges between Alexander Pushkin and the editor of *Severnaja ptseda* (The northern bee), Faddey Benediktovich Bulgarin, who was an agent of the secret police and one of the most distasteful figures in nineteenth-century Russian literature. Bulgarin had founded the *Northern Bee* not only as an aid to the tsarist police but also as a weapon against the major exponents of progressive Russian literature and criticism. Its denunciation of Pushkin's works continued sporadically up to the time in 1836 when Pushkin, always in need of money, obtained permission to start his own St. Petersburg periodical in the hope of strengthening his economic position and his polemical armory.

Featured in the first issue of Pushkin's *Sovremennik* (The contemporary, 1836–66) was a major contribution by Nikolay Gogol — a review of the leading periodicals of the day, entitled "On the Trend of Journal Literature." Gogol, however, left for western Europe immediately afterward, and Pushkin during the brief remainder of his life made unsuccessful efforts to obtain the services of the young Belinsky, who was then in Moscow writing for *Telescop* (The telescope), the periodical to which Pushkin had contributed two articles in 1831. Belinsky did not join the staff of *The Contemporary* until 1847, a decade after Pushkin's death and a year before his own.

The standing of *The Contemporary* declined after Pushkin's death, and the magazine was purchased in 1846 by Nikolay Alexeevich Nekrasov, a radical poet[4] and journalist whose pleas for sympathy for Russia's downtrodden peasantry were a constant irritant to the tsarist regime. Nekrasov, an able businessman as well as a writer, had previously edited and published various literary collections, among them an almanac entitled, *Petersburgskij sbornik* (Petersburg miscellany, also known as Petersburg almanac) that published works representative of Belinsky's "Natural School" of socially conscious literature and, in 1846, Dostoevsky's *Poor Folk*. Under the editorial control of Nekrasov and Ivan Ivanovich Panaev, *The Contemporary* became a major literary journal and featured the early work of Turgenev and Tolstoy, although its increasingly radical tone after 1856 led to its eventual suppression a decade later (see below).

2

As already indicated, the death of the reactionary Nicholas I and the accession of his son Alexander II in 1855 marked a turning point in Russian intellectual and literary affairs, all the more fundamental because it coincided with the ending of the Crimean War and a refocusing of Russian foreign policy as well. New problems and goals — the abolition of serfdom, judicial reform, the emancipation of women — engaged the interest of many Russians who now turned from card playing, dancing, drinking, and gossiping to serious reading of periodicals and books, at home, in sweetshops, in city reading rooms, or at Sunday school sessions where free instruction for the illiterate masses was offered by members of the educated class.

"Our young but still timid press," Dostoevsky wrote with some irony in *The Brothers Karamazov,* "has done some good service to society, for without it we should never have learnt so fully about those horrors of unbridled license and moral degradation which it is continually reporting in its pages to everyone and not only to those who attend our new public courts, granted to us in this present reign" (IV, 12, VI).

The craft of writing gained new respectability at this period, and publishers of periodicals competed for the output of such prominent writers as Turgenev, Tolstoy, Goncharov, and Nekrasov. Dostoevsky, in 1857, lamented that the novelist Ivan Goncharov was paid seven hundred rubles per signature and that Turgenev was paid four hundred, whereas he himself could ask only fifty or one hundred rubles for the same amount of copy. "Tendentious" writing was much sought after at this time — the very word *tendentious* acquired a favorable connotation for Russian critics and readers — as journals and periodicals armed themselves for battle on political, ideological, and personal fronts.

The position of the press, however, was still far from one of complete freedom, and the growing currency of radical ideas — together with some acts of outright terrorism — led to the imposition of new repressive measures and even the closing of some publications. Particularly obnoxious to the tsarist regime were the ideas of such "nihilistic" writers as Nikolay Gavrilovich Chernyshevsky, Nikolay Alexandrovich Dobrolyubov, Dmitri Ivanovich Pisarev, and, later, Nikolay Konstantinovich Mikhailovsky. Temporary measures against some radical periodicals as early as 1862 were codified in 1865 in a set of rules inspired by the authoritarian regime of Napoleon III in France. Books of more than ten sheets (160 pages) were nominally exempt from preliminary censorship, but censors nevertheless continued to seize printed books before publication, while periodicals were subjected to regular, ongoing censorship.

One means of circumventing such restrictions was publication outside of Russia. This was the method adopted by Alexander Ivanovich Herzen, the well-known radical and socialist writer, who, in London, established the first Free Russian Press in exile. Herzen was editor of *Kolokol* (The bell, 1857–67), a revolutionary politico-literary review, and an almanac, *Polyarnaya Zvezda* (Polar star, 1855–62). Smuggled into Russia, these "underground" periodicals exerted considerable influence, especially in promoting Alexander II's program of emancipation of the serfs. Among *The Bell*'s collaborators was the celebrated anarchist, Mikhail Alexandrovich Bakunin, who made his way to London after escaping from a Siberian penal settlement.

In 1866, the first of several unsuccessful attempts on the life of the Emperor Alexander II resulted in a crackdown on the radical press and the disappearance of Nekrasov's well-known magazine, *The Contemporary*, which, as already noted, had been founded by Alexander Pushkin three decades earlier. *The Contemporary*, in recent years, had developed into an organ of militant radicalism under the influence of its subeditor, Nikolay Chernyshevsky, leader of the so-called Utilitarians, and the brilliant young nihilist critic, Nikolay Dobrolyubov. As a rallying point for so-called Westernizers and revolutionaries, the magazine became a logical target for the repression that followed the 1866 assassination attempt.

Also suppressed in 1866 was a newer left-wing publication, *Russkoe slovo* (The Russian word, 1859–66), a monthly review founded in St. Petersburg by Count Grigory Alexandrovich Kushelev-Bezborodko. The original editors of this journal, which published Dostoevsky's story *Uncle's Dream* in its first year, were Apollon Grigoryev, a friend of Dostoevsky, and the poet Yakov Petrovich Polonsky. Both left in the course of 1859, however, and the magazine took on an increasingly nihilist coloration under the influence of D. I. Pisarev, an advocate of extreme individualism who joined the staff in 1860 and became its leading critic. Suppressed by the government in 1866 (though revived in the twentieth century), the *Russian Word* was replaced by *Delo* (Fact), a monthly cultural review with democratic tendencies that retained its liberal coloring even amid the still more repressive conditions that followed the assassination of Alexander II and the enthronement of his son Alexander III in 1881.

Conservative journalism was not lacking in the Russia of the 1850s and 1860s. Its most celebrated exponent was Mikhail Nikiforovich Katkov, a well-known publicist, Russian Orthodox nationalist and Pan-Slavist who was appointed editor of *Moscow News* in 1851. In 1856, Katkov founded *Russky vestnik* (Russian messenger, also known as Russian herald, 1856–1906), an ultimately highly conservative monthly that would endure for half a century and was praised by Dostoevsky in 1857 as "indisputably the premier Russian journal at present" (*Letters*, I, 320).

Though initially quite progressive in tendency, the *Russian Messenger* soon lost its liberal tone and, from the time of the Polish uprising against Russian rule in 1863, stood out as the leading champion of nationalism and reactionary causes in all fields. Dostoevsky, though engaged in open controversy with Katkov as late as 1863, had himself become a collaborator of the *Russian Messenger* by 1866, when *Crime and Punishment* (at 150 rubles per signature) became the first of a series of works published in its pages. But he never was intimate with Katkov, who became Russia's most influential journalist after 1866. Other contributors to the *Russian Messenger* included Tolstoy, Turgenev, and Goncharov.

A reconciliation of the antithetic philosophies of Slavophilism and Westernism was the stated aim of the St. Petersburg journal *Svetoch* (The torch, 1860–62), published by D. I. Kalinovsky and edited by Alexander Milyukov. Although short-lived, *The Torch* is remembered for its publication of Mikhail Dostoevsky's translation of Schiller's "The Gods of Greece" — as well as of Victor Hugo's novel protesting the death penalty, *Le dernier jour d'un condamné,* which exerted a profound influence on Feodor Dostoevsky's life and writings.

Dostoevsky's own debut in the field of periodical journalism was likewise inspired by the idea of striking a balance between the Slavophiles and conservatives on one side and the Westernizing, revolutionary group around *The Contemporary* on the other. *Vremya* (Time), the Dostoevsky brothers' own magazine, was authorized July 8, 1860, and began monthly publication in 1861, with Mikhail Dostoevsky as titular director and Nikolay N. Strakhov (idealist philosopher and friend of Tolstoy) as literary critic, but with Feodor Dostoevsky as its chief editor and guiding genius.

Originally, Feodor had conceived the publication as "a purely literary newspaper . . . a literary feuilleton, a critical review of journals, a critical review of what's good and what's mistaken, enmity toward the *mutual back scratching* now so widespread, more energy, fire, sharpness of mind, firmness."[5] He and his main collaborators had also hoped that *Time* would become a "big review" on the scale of *The Contemporary*, the *Russian Messenger*, or *Notes of the Fatherland*.

The number of subscribers to *Time* did reach the four thousand mark — thus equaling the circulation of *Notes of the Fatherland* — but the magazine had meanwhile taken on a strongly Russian nationalist tone and become embroiled in polemics both with the intransigently radical *The Contemporary* and the "Utilitarians," and, on aesthetic questions, with the *Russian Messenger* and *Notes of the Fatherland*. *Time* did, however, publish the first complete Russian translation of Victor Hugo's *Notre Dame de Paris* (1831), which had been banned in Russia for several decades, and offered Feodor's perceptive comments on translated works by such foreign writers as Elizabeth Gaskell, Edgar Allan Poe, and Giovanni Jacopo Casanova.

Because of misinterpretation by the censors of an article by Strakhov on the Polish question, *Time* was suspended in 1863 and replaced the following year by *Epokha* (Epoch), which was founded in Mikhail Dostoevsky's name and continued, after Mikhail's death in July 1864, by Feodor Dostoevsky with the collaboration of Strakhov and a minor writer named Alexander Poretsky. (Feodor's later editorship of *The Citizen* and *The Diary of a Writer* will be considered below.)

3

The later 1860s brought further developments in the field of Russian periodical journalism. The year 1866 witnessed not only the demise of *The Contemporary* and the *Russian Word* but also the revival. of the old *Messenger of Europe,* dormant since 1830, as a typical liberal review with contributors that included such prominent figures as Turgenev, Goncharov, Ostrovsky, and Russia's greatest satirist, Shchedrin, the pseudonym of Mikhail Evgrafovich Saltykov (1826–89).

Shchedrin, who had been bitterly opposed to Dostoevsky in 1863, was closely associated with N. A. Nekrasov, previously editor of the defunct *The Contemporary,* who took control of *Notes of the Fatherland* in 1868 and remained as its editor and publisher until his death in 1877. Although its contributors represented various political trends, this publication once again took on a distinctly radical tone, and Shchedrin, who became editor after Nekrasov's death, further accentuated its "populist" tendency. *Notes of the Fatherland* was finally suppressed in 1884 after the secret police discovered that some of its collaborators were connected with the clandestine revolutionary movement.

Leaning first left, then right, the St. Petersburg review *Novoe vremya* (New time, 1868–1917) maintained a progressive stance throughout the early 1870s but turned reactionary in 1876 under the editorial hand of Alexey Sergeevich Suvorin, at one time a democratic journalist. (Suvorin, who was commended by Dostoevsky in *The Diary of a Writer,* late in life became interested in the theater and was a friend of Chekhov.)

Among *New Time*'s collaborators was the critic and poet Viktor Petrovich Burenin, who translated Byron, Hugo, Heine, and others into Russian and who — like Suvorin, Dostoevsky, and so many others — had begun as a liberal but subsequently joined the reactionary camp. Burenin was also the author of a personal attack on Dostoevsky — whom he called a "great novelist" but one subject to nervous seizures — which was published in the newspaper *Sankt Peterburgskie vedomosti* (St. Petersburg gazette, also known as St. Petersburg news).[6]

The occasion for this attack was another Dostoevsky venture into periodical journalism in the early 1870s. This was the editorship of *Grazhdanin* (The citizen), a conservative weekly politico-literary review that was founded in 1871 and directed by Prince Vladimir Petrovich Meshchersky, a somewhat reactionary journalist whose Wednesday "at homes" Dostoevsky frequented during 1871–72. To this periodical, Dostoevsky contributed a series of articles on current affairs that appeared regularly as an appendix entitled *The Diary of a Writer.* This feature should not, however, be confused with the separate monthly periodical, likewise entitled *Dnevnik pisatelya* (The diary of a writer), which was begun in 1876 under Dostoevsky's editorship and published several of his lesser works as well as many of his articles on current political and literary affairs.

No periodical was without some special antagonist. Contemporaneous with *The Citizen* was *Russky mir* (The Russian world, 1871–80),[7] a daily newspaper, founded in St. Petersburg in 1871, which at first displayed a conservative coloration but rapidly evolved into a moderate liberal organ and engaged in frequent polemics with *The Citizen*. Dostoevsky in *The Diary of a Writer* often criticized the contributions of historian and critic S. A. Vengerov to the paper's literary supplement.

4

It remains to touch upon some aspects of Dostoevsky's experience as the author of works of fiction that were published serially in some of these periodicals and reviews. Though economically dependent on the modest payments vouchsafed him by journal editors, he found the relationship both humiliating and frustrating from an artistic standpoint. The ongoing advances received from Kraevsky and *Notes of the Fatherland,* he complained, put him in a position of sustained indebtedness that made for "slavery and literary vassalage." Lacking time to crystallize more than the main idea of a work, or resorting to cumbersome subplots to fill up space, he feared lest writing against a deadline should "profane" his best work. At times, four days before a publication date, he would force himself to think up and complete a story in spite of nagging worry about attaching his name to "something bad."

Related concerns were the "mutilations" of editors who "corrected" or "improved" the pages of their contributors, and the difficulty of adjusting the flow of a story to the requirements of periodical publication. "I'm tearing my hair out over the fact that the episode [in *Netochka Nezvanova*] hasn't been presented in its entirety," he wrote to Kraevsky in 1849; "...only curiosity has been aroused. But curiosity aroused at the beginning of the month is not the same thing as at the end of the month; it cools down, and even the best words suffer.... Where is the impression? It will disappear" (*Letters*, I, 167).

Dostoevsky did what he could to assist his readers by repeating or summarizing previous events at the beginning of each new installment. His main reliance, however, lay in the opportunity to review and reedit his writings prior to publication in book form — which, in addition, was more remunerative than magazine publication. Bound books, he observes in *The Devils*, reflect a higher stage of cultural development: "Russia hasn't yet reached that second stage, but in Europe they've been binding books for a long time" (III, 5, II). Thus readers are doubly fortunate that Dostoevsky's masterpieces survived their initial publication and remain in their definitive form.

Notes

Chapter 1: The Story of His Life

1. Dostoevsky to Catherine Feodorovna Junge, 1880, quoted by Louis Allain, *Dostoïevski et l'Autre* (Villeneuve d'Ascq: Presses Universitaires de Lille, 1984), 107. The same writer quotes a contemporary of Dostoevsky who described him as belonging to that category of individuals who are strongly male yet have much of the female nature in them (ibid., 99–100).

2. Marc Slonim, *Three Loves of Dostoevsky* (New York: Rinehart and Co., 1955), 278.

3. This recollection, which aided Dostoevsky's inward acceptance of his brutal, quarrelsome fellow convicts, is treated by Joseph Frank, *Dostoevsky: The Years of Ordeal, 1850–1859* (Princeton, N.J.: Princeton University Press, 1983), 123, as the key to Dostoevsky's so-called conversion.

4. Cf. *Letters*, I, 54 n. 1; Joseph Frank, *Dostoevsky: The Seeds of Revolt, 1821–1849* (Princeton, N.J.: Princeton University Press, 1976), 86–87.

5. Pierre Pascal, *Dostoïevski. L'Homme et l'oeuvre* (Lausanne: Editions de l'Age d'Homme, 1970), 30.

6. Frank, *Seeds of Revolt*, 172–98, provides an excellent analysis of the influence of Belinsky's thought on Dostoevsky.

7. For a full analysis of these groups see Frank, *Seeds of Revolt*, 239–91.

8. The bloody repression of the Decembrist revolt in 1825 set the tone of Russian public life for decades thereafter. A group of aristocratic officers, influenced by Western political ideas, attempted to take advantage of the confusion following the death of Tsar Alexander I (1801–25) in order to install their own candidate — Alexander's brother Constantine — as a means of enforcing their demands for a liberal constitution and the abolition of serfdom. Their move was promptly quelled by Alexander's younger brother, Nicholas I (1825–55), whom Alexander had designated as his heir and who repressed the revolt with great severity, thus inaugurating a reign of thirty years whose reactionary rigor was visited upon Dostoevsky himself as well as legions of his fellow countrymen.

9. Quoted in Frank, *Years of Ordeal,* 72, italics added.

10. Recent scholarship has stressed the ambivalence of Dostoevsky's attitudes during his prison experience and has questioned the spontaneity of his "conversion," which can be plausibly ascribed at least in part to consid-

erations of practical expediency. After his release, it is argued, Dostoevsky needed to present himself as a convert to Russia's ruling ideology in order to safeguard himself against further political difficulties, impress the authorities with his loyalty, and encourage a revocation of the imperial order barring him from the literary scene. Cf. Nicolas Milochevitch, *Dostoïevski penseur* (Lausanne: Editions l'Age d'Homme, 1988), 42–72. See *The Diary of a Writer*, below.

11. For analysis of the role of Dostoevsky's epilepsy in his life, his "conversion," and his creativity, see inter alia James L. Rice, *Dostoevsky and the Healing Art* (Ann Arbor: Ardis Publishers, 1985); Jacques Catteau, *La création littéraire chez Dostoïevski* (Paris: Institut d'études slaves, 1978), 141–80; Frank, *Seeds of Revolt*, 25–28, 379–91.

12. Quoted in Frank, *Years of Ordeal*, 198.

13. Quoted by Frank, ibid., 201.

14. *Letters*, I, 263, but Frank's translation, ibid., 210.

15. *Winter Notes on Summer Impressions*. Translated by David Patterson (Evanston, IL: Northwestern University Press, 1988), 36–37.

16. For Dostoevsky's editorial comments on her stories, "Mikhail" and "A Dream," see *Letters*, II, 140.

17. Slonim, *Three Loves*, 200.

18. Frank, *Seeds of Revolt*, 62.

19. Quoted by Laurence Irving, introduction to *Crime and Punishment* (London: J. M. Dent & Sons, Ltd., 1911), x.

Chapter 2: *Crime and Punishment*

1. Irving, ibid., vii, xi.

2. Romano Guardini elaborates a portrait of Sonia as a child of God in *L'Univers religieux de Dostoïevski* (Paris: Editions du Seuil, 1963), 50–63.

3. Cf. "The Case Against Porfiry," in Leslie A. Johnson, *The Experience of Time in "Crime and Punishment"* (Columbus, OH: Slavica Publishers, Inc., 1985), 76–95.

4. Cf. Jacques Rolland, *Dostoïevski. La question de l'Autre* (Lagrasse: Editions Verdier, 1983), 131–39.

Chapter 4: *Netochka Nezvanova*

1. Cf. Ugo Persi, "Le musicien et la musique dans l'oeuvre de Dostoevskij et de Wackenroder," *Revue de Littérature Comparée* 219–20 (1981): 308.

2. Slonim, *Three Loves*, 103.

Chapter 6: *The Idiot*

1. Gary Cox, *Tyrant and Victim in Dostoevsky* (Columbus, OH: Slavica Publishers, Inc., 1983), 52–59.
2. Guardini, *L'Univers religieux,* 223.
3. Ernest J. Simmons. Introduction to *A Raw Youth* (New York: Dell Publishing Co., 1959), 16.

Chapter 7: *The Devils*

1. Cf. Linda J. Ivanits, "Folk Beliefs About the 'Unclean Force' in Dostoevskij's *The Brothers Karamazov,*" in *New Perspectives on Nineteenth-Century Russian Prose,* George J. Gutsche and Lauren G. Leighton, eds. (Columbus, OH: Slavica Publishers, Inc., 1982), 143.

Chapter 8: *A Raw Youth*

1. Cox, *Tyrant and Victim,* 94.

Chapter 9: *The Double*

1. Ibid., 46–51.
2. There are many well-known archetypal figures of the double in world literature. Less familiar than the creations of E. T. A. Hoffmann, Gogol, and Poe, but closer to Dostoevsky's ambiance is the contribution of the Polish writer, Jan Potocki (1761–1815), who had held a diplomatic position in St. Petersburg. The theme of the double permeates the pages of his fantastic novel, *Manuscript Found at Saragossa* (written from ca. 1797–1815). Cf. *Manoscritto trovato a Saragozza* (Parma: Guanda, 1990).
3. Jessie Coulson, introduction to *Notes from Underground/The Double* (Harmondsworth: Penguin Books, 1972), 8.

Chapter 10: *Uncle's Dream* and *The Village of Stepanchikovo and Its Inhabitants*

1. Thomas Mann, preface to *The Short Novels of Dostoevsky* (New York: Dial Press, 1945), xvii. There are two misdatings in Mann's preface. He mistakenly believes that *The Eternal Husband* was written in 1848 and *Crime and Punishment* in 1867. Actually the former was first published in 1870 and the latter in 1866.
2. Cf. Ignat Avsey, introduction to *The Village of Stepanchikovo and Its Inhabitants* (Ithaca, NY: Cornell University Press, 1987), 20.
3. Avsey, ibid., 19.

Chapter 11: Notes from Underground

1. Mann, *Short Novels*, xix.
2. Cf. Franco Quadri, "Iperrealismo in scena: Rileggendo Bulgakov e Dostoevskij," *La Repubblica*, September 23, 1989, 29.
3. André Gide, *Dostoïevski* (Paris: Gallimard, 1981 [Librairie Plon, 1923]), 133, 157, 159.
4. Joseph Frank, *Dostoevsky: The Stir of Liberation, 1860–1865* (Princeton, NJ: Princeton University Press, 1986), 333.

Chapter 12: The Gambler

1. Cf. Nikolay Andreyev, introduction to *Fyodor Dostoevsky: Poor Folk, the Gambler* (London and Melbourne: J. M. Dent, 1962), x.
2. Stefan Zweig's *Vingt-quatre heures de la vie d'une femme* (Paris: Editions Stock, 1981) may be recommended as an absorbing tale on a similar theme.

Chapter 13: The Eternal Husband

1. Cf. Cox, *Tyrant and Victim*, 58.
2. Gide, *Dostoïevski*, 143.

Chapter 14: Pre-Siberian Stories

1. Quoted in Frank, *Seeds of Revolt*, 178.
2. Quoted ibid., 179, 181.
3. Cf. Marina T. Naumann, "Dostoevsky's 'The Boy at Christ's Christmas-Tree Party': A Paraphrase of Andersen's 'The Little Match Girl,'" *Revue de Littérature Comparée*, 219–20 (1981): 319. For a full analysis and mythopoetic interpretation of the 1848 story, see Robert L. Jackson, "The Garden of Eden in Dostoevsky's 'A Christmas Party and a Wedding' and Chekhov's 'Because of Little Apples,'" ibid., 331–41.
4. Cf. Slonim, *Three Loves*, 25.
5. For a study of notions relating to the age of chivalry in *A Little Hero*, see Pierre R. Hart, "The Passionate Page: 'First Love' and 'The Little Hero,'" in *New Perspectives*, Gutsche and Leighton, eds., 111–20.
6. Frank, *Seeds of Revolt*, 283.

Chapter 15: Post-Siberian Stories

1. Frank, *Stir of Liberation*, 364–65.
2. Mikhail M. Bakhtine considers *Bobok*, despite its apparently narrow structural frame, to be a key work, indeed almost a microcosm of all Dos-

toevsky's works. Cf. *Problèmes de la poétique de Dostoïevski* (Lausanne: Editions l'Age d'Homme, 1970), 169–72.

3. Cf. Naumann, "Dostoevsky's 'The Boy,' " 317–30.

4. For a study of Dostoevsky's pessimistic world vision as revealed in *A Gentle Creature* — including further analogies with *Notes from Underground* — see Milochevitch, *Dostoïevski penseur,* 240–43, 251–54.

5. Cox, *Tyrant and Victim,* 74–75. Modern readers may note a parallel with Albert Camus's "Stranger," another solipsist who falls victim to the irrational nature of the world, accepts his guilt, and allows himself to be executed amidst a jeering crowd.

6. Andrew R. MacAndrew, *Notes from Underground. White Nights. The Dream of a Ridiculous Man. Selections from the House of the Dead* (New York: New American Library, 1961), 234, 239.

Chapter 16: Theater, Memoirs, and Journalism

1. Cf. *Letters,* I, 82 n. 4.

2. Avsey *Stepanchikovo,* 13, 22.

3. Dostoevsky personally had this fear of being buried alive and asked his friends and acquaintances, if they should happen to find him unconscious and think him dead, to wait three days before burying him.

4. *The House of the Dead.* Introduction by David McDuff (New York and London: Penguin Books Ltd., 1985), 18.

5. Frank, *Stir of Liberation,* 233.

6. *Winter Notes on Summer Impressions.* Translated by David Patterson (Evanston, IL: Northwestern University Press, 1988), vii.

7. *Diario di un scrittore.* Traduzione e introduzione di Ettore Lo Gatto (Firenze: Sansoni, 1981), xiv, l–li, passim.

8. Milochevitch, *Dostoïevski penseur,* 42–72.

9. Gide, *Dostoïevski,* 108, 110.

10. Lo Gatto, *Diario,* lviii.

Chapter 17: *The Brothers Karamazov*

1. Letter to Katkov, quoted in *The Brothers Karamazov.* Translated with an introduction by David Magarshack (London: Penguin Books, 1958), xix–xx.

2. Magarshack, ibid., xxiii.

3. This tradition may have originated in a natural phenomenon evidenced at Pecherskaya Lavra (Monastery of the Caves) in Kiev, where bodies of dead monks (especially thin ones) buried in the hollowed-out logs of certain trees indigenous to the area were protected from decomposition by the peculiar qualities of the wood.

4. Sigmund Freud, "Dostoevsky and Parricide," in *Stavrogin's Confession.* Translated by Virginia Woolf and S. S. Koteliansky. With a

psychoanalytic study of the author by Sigmund Freud (New York: Lear Publishers, 1947), 96. René Girard sees as the primordial crime in Dostoevsky's writings not patricide but infanticide ("The Underground Critic," in *To Double Business Bound: Essays in Literature, Mimesis, and Anthropology* [Baltimore: Johns Hopkins University Press, 1978], 56, quoted in Cox, *Tyrant and Victim,* 100.)

Conclusion

1. Quoted in Frank, *Years of Ordeal,* 112.
2. Quoted by Avsey, *Stepanchikovo,* 23.
3. The Russian Orthodox priest, Gleb Yakunin, in a harangue addressed to the Twenty-eighth Congress of the Communist party of the Soviet Union in July 1990.

Appendix

1. Dostoevsky condemned the ravages of censorship in his "explanation" to the Commission of Inquiry after his arrest in 1849. See Frank, *Years of Ordeal,* 39–41.
2. Both this publication and *The Contemporary* (below) are described in part 2, chapter 3 of Dostoevsky's *The Village of Stepanchikovo and Its Inhabitants.*
3. Kraevsky was also director of the progressive newspaper *Golos* (The voice, 1863–84), which supported government economic reforms in the 1860s and 1870s, much to Dostoevsky's gratification (cf. *Letters,* II, 300). But Dostoevsky frequently crossed swords with *The Voice* in the pages of *The Diary of a Writer* because of ideological or personal differences.
4. A sample of Nekrasov's poetry is the lengthy extract from his poem, "When from the darkness of depravity...," published in *Notes of the Fatherland* in 1846, which serves as epigraph to part 2 of Dostoevsky's *Notes from Underground.*
5. *Letters,* I, 351, but Frank's translation, in *Years of Ordeal,* 300.
6. Professor Frank gives considerable deserved attention to the four feuilletons Dostoevsky wrote in 1847 for this newspaper. See Frank, *Seeds of Revolt,* 217–38.
7. Not to be confused with the earlier *Russky mir* (St. Petersburg, 1859–62), a politico-literary weekly that probably would have been completely forgotten had it not published in 1860 the first four chapters of Dostoevsky's *House of the Dead.*

Bibliography

Dostoevsky's Works

The Brothers Karamazov. Translated with an introduction by David Magarshack. London: Penguin Books, 1958.

Complete Letters. Volume one, 1832–1859. Edited and Translated by David Lowe and Ronald Meyer. Ann Arbor: Ardis Publishers, 1988.

Complete Letters. Volume two, 1860–1867. Edited and Translated by David A. Lowe. Ibid., 1989.

Crime and Punishment. With an introduction by Laurence Irving. London: J. M. Dent & Sons Ltd., 1911.

Crime and Punishment. Translated with an introduction by David Magarshack. London: Penguin Books, 1951.

The Crocodile. Translated by Samuel D. Cioran. Ann Arbor: Ardis Publishers, 1985.

The Devils. Translated with an introduction by David Magarshack. New York: Viking Penguin Inc., 1971.

Diario di uno scrittore. Traduzione e introduzione di Ettore Lo Gatto. Firenze: Sansoni, 1981.

The Gambler/Bobok/A Nasty Story. Translated with an introduction by Jessie Coulson. Harmondsworth: Penguin Books Ltd., 1966.

The House of the Dead. Translated with an introduction by David McDuff. New York: Penguin Books Ltd., 1985.

The Idiot. Translated with an introduction by David Magarshack. Harmondsworth: Penguin Books Ltd., 1955.

The Insulted and Injured. Translated from the Russian by Constance Garnett. London: Grafton Books, 1987.

Netochka Nezvanova. Translated with an introduction by Jane Kentish. Harmondsworth: Penguin Books Ltd., 1985.

Notes d'hiver sur des impressions d'été. Traduit du russe par J. W. Bienstock. Présentation et notes de Catherine Meyer. Paris: Editions Entente, 1988.

Notes from Underground. The Double. Translated with an introduction by Jessie Coulson. Harmondsworth: Penguin Books Ltd., 1972.

Notes from Underground. White Nights. The Dream of a Ridiculous Man. Selections from The House of the Dead. A new translation with an afterword by Andrew R. MacAndrew. Revised and updated bibliography. New York: New American Library, 1961.

Poor Folk. The Gambler. Translated by C. L. Hogarth. Introduction by Nikolay Andreyev. London and Melbourne: J. M. Dent & Sons Ltd., 1962.

The Possessed. Translated by Andrew R. MacAndrew, with an afterword by Marc Slonim. New York and Scarborough, Ontario: American Library, 1962.

A Raw Youth. Translated by Constance Garnett. Introduction by Ernest J. Simmons. New York: Dell Publishing Co., Inc., 1959.

The Short Novels of Dostoevsky. With an introduction by Thomas Mann. New York: Dial Press, 1945.

The Short Novels of Dostoevsky. Edited with an introduction by William Phillips. New York: Dial Press, 1946.

Stavrogin's Confession. Translated by Virginia Woolf and S. S Koteliansky. With a psychoanalytic study of the author by Sigmund Freud. New York: Lear Publishers, 1947.

Tutte le opere di Fjodor Dostojevskij. A cura di Eridano Bazzarelli. 8 volumes. Milano: Ugo Mursia Editore, 1960.

The Village of Stepanchikovo and Its Inhabitants. Translated with an introduction by Ignat Avsey. Ithaca, New York: Cornell University Press, 1983.

Winter Notes on Summer Impressions. Translated by David Patterson. Evanston, IL: Northwestern University Press, 1988.

Secondary Works

Allain, Louis. *Dostoïevski et l'Autre.* Villeneuve d'Ascq: Presses Universitaires de Lille, 1984.

———. *Dostoïevski et Dieu.* Lille: Presses Universitaires de Lille, 1981.

Arban, Dominique. *Dostoievski.* Paris: Editions du Seuil, 1962.

Bakhtine, Mikhail M. *Problèmes de la poétique de Dostoïevski.* Lausanne: Editions de l'Age d'Homme, 1970.

Berdiaeff, Nicolas. *L'esprit de Dostoievski.* Paris: Stock, 1974.

Bouson, J. Brooks. *The Empathetic Reader.* Amherst: The University of Massachusetts Press, 1989.

Busch, R. L. *Humor in the Major Novels of F. M. Dostoevsky.* Columbus, OH: Slavica Publishers, 1987.

Catteau, Jacques. *La création littéraire chez Dostoïevski.* Paris: Institut d'études slaves, 1978.

Cox, Gary. *Tyrant and Victim in Dostoevsky.* Columbus, OH: Slavica Publishers, Inc., 1984.

Evdokimov, Paul. *Dostoievsky et le problème du mal.* Paris: Desclée De Brouwer, 1978.

Frank, Joseph. *Dostoevsky. The Seeds of Revolt, 1821–1849*. Princeton, NJ: Princeton University Press, 1976.

——. *Dostoevsky. The Years of Ordeal, 1850–1859*. Ibid., 1983.

——. *Dostoevsky. The Stir of Liberation, 1860–1865*. Ibid., 1986.

Gide, André. *Dostoïevski*. Paris: Gallimard, 1981. (Librairie Plon, 1923).

Gifford, Henry. "Radicals," in *New York Review of Books*, January 17, 1991, 36–38.

Girard, René. *Dostoïevski: du double à l'unité*. Paris: Plon, 1963.

Guardini, Romano. *L'Univers religieux de Dostoïevski*. Paris: Editions du Seuil, 1963.

Gutsche, George J., and Leighton, Lauren G., eds. *New Perspectives on Nineteenth-Century Russian Prose*. Columbus, OH: Slavica Publishers, Inc., 1982.

Icone russe in Vaticano. Cento capolavori dai musei della Russia. Roma: Fratelli Palombi Editori, 1989.

Johnson, Leslie A. *The Experience of Time in "Crime and Punishment."* Columbus, OH: Slavica Publishers, Inc., 1985.

Knapp, Bettina L. *A Jungian Approach to Literature*. Carbondale and Edwardsville: Southern Illinois University Press, 1984.

La Mettrie, Julien Offroy de. *L'homme machine*. Utrecht: Jean-Jacques Pauvert, 1966.

Milochevitch, Nicolas. *Dostoïevski penseur*. Traduit du serbo-croate par Laurence Koltirine et Zorica Hadji-Vidoïkovitch. Lausanne: Editions l'Age d'Homme, 1988.

Pascal, Pierre. *Dostoïevski. L'homme et l'oeuvre*. Lausanne: Editions l'Age d'Homme, 1970.

Revue de Littérature Comparée 219–20 (1981): *Dostoevskij européen*.

Rice, James L. *Dostoevsky and the Healing Art: An Essay in Literary and Medical History*. Ann Arbor: Ardis Publishers, 1985.

Rolland, Jacques. *Dostoïevski. La question de l'Autre*. Lagrasse: Editions Verdier, 1983.

Slonim, Marc. *Three Loves of Dostoevsky*. New York: Rinehart and Co., 1955.

Steiner, George. *Tolstoy or Dostoevsky*. New York: Alfred A. Knopf, Inc., 1959.

Suares, André. *Trois hommes. Pascal — Ibsen — Dostoievski*. Paris: Gallimard, 1935.

Index